Philosophy Made Slightly Less Difficult

A Beginner's Guide To Life's Big Questions

Garrett J. DeWeese
J.P. Moreland

16pt

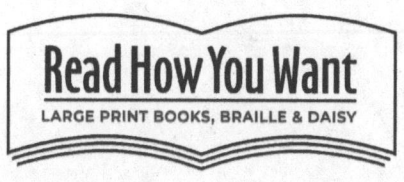

Copyright Page from the Original Book

InterVarsity Press
P.O. Box 1400, Downers Grove, IL 60515-1426
ivpress.com
email@ivpress.com

Second edition ©2021 by Garrett J. DeWeese and J. P. Moreland
First edition ©2005 by Garrett J. DeWeese and J. P. Moreland

All rights reserved. No part of this book may be reproduced in any form without written permission from InterVarsity Press.

InterVarsity Press® is the book-publishing division of InterVarsity Christian Fellowship/USA®, a movement of students and faculty active on campus at hundreds of universities, colleges, and schools of nursing in the United States of America, and a member movement of the International Fellowship of Evangelical Students. For information about local and regional activities, visit intervarsity.org.

All Scripture quotations, unless otherwise indicated, are taken from The Holy Bible, New International Version®, NIV®. Copyright © 1973, 1978, 1984, 2011 by Biblica, Inc.™ Used by permission of Zondervan. All rights reserved worldwide. www.zondervan.com. The "NIV" and "New International Version" are trademarks registered in the United States Patent and Trademark Office by Biblica, Inc.™

The publisher can't verify the accuracy of website hyperlinks beyond the date of print publication.

Cover design and image composite: David Fassett

Images: triangle pattern: © CSA Images / Getty Images
  abstract pattern: © CSA Images / Getty Images
  grey halftone pattern: © Ben Stevens / iStock / Getty Images Plus
  abstract background design: © Nadiinko / iStock / Getty Images Plus
  white background texture: © R. Tsubin / Moment Collection / Getty Images
  fiber texture: © Katsumi Murouchi / Moment Collection / Getty Images

TABLE OF CONTENTS

PREFACE TO THE SECOND EDITION	i
ACKNOWLEDGMENTS	iii
1: WHERE DO I START?	1
2: WHAT IS REAL?	43
3: HOW DO I KNOW?	106
4: HOW SHOULD I LIVE?	181
5: WHAT AM I?	242
6: HOW SHOULD CHRISTIANS THINK ABOUT SCIENCE?	325
7: WHAT IS BEAUTY? WHAT ABOUT ART?	385
8: WHAT SHOULD WE WORSHIP?	408
9: WHERE DO I GO FROM HERE?	456
FOR FURTHER READING	471
PRAISE FOR PHILOSOPHY MADE SLIGHTLY LESS DIFFICULT	481
ABOUT THE AUTHORS	486
Discover more titles from InterVarsity Press	488
Index	493

PREFACE TO THE SECOND EDITION

We are delighted and honored that InterVarsity Press asked us to develop a revised and expanded edition of our book *Philosophy Made Slightly Less Difficult.* Since the publication of the first edition in 2005, we have received encouraging feedback about how useful the book has been at the college and seminary level. But just as or even more exciting has been how God has used the book to introduce a general audience to important concepts and distinctions in philosophy. We have both walked with the Lord for over fifty years, and during those decades, our hearts have been directed toward evangelism, discipleship, church planting, and the growth and maturation of the body of Christ. We have focused our energies on equipping, training, empowering, and emboldening believers toward these ends. And we have long recognized that developing a biblically based and philosophically informed Christian worldview is absolutely critical for the church, especially in our chaotic and secularized culture. Philosophy has always been of supreme help in developing a Christian worldview and teaching believers why they believe what they believe.

In addition to minor corrections, we have added material to several chapters and have included two new chapters: one on aesthetics, another on philosophy of religion. And we add our thanks to our editors at IVP, Dr. David McNutt and Ms. Rebecca Carhart. Thus, we offer this exciting updated and revised edition in the hopes that it will increase the impact for Christ that began with our first edition.

ACKNOWLEDGMENTS

We have attempted to write a readable book that provides a useful discussion of basic philosophical distinctions relevant for doing theology and for constructing and defending a Christian worldview. Many have helped us in this undertaking. We wish to thank our dear colleagues in the Talbot philosophy department—William Lane Craig, David Horner, and Scott Rae—for the deep friendship, vibrant Christian testimonies, and philosophical stimulation they regularly provide. We are grateful to our graduate assistants Brian Pinkston, Scott Sevier, and Gary Osmundsen for serving us so cheerfully and skillfully in preparing this book. We are grateful to Biola University for providing a faculty development grant to help fund our research and writing. J.P. Moreland is thankful to the Eidos Christian Center for providing him similar resources. As always, Jim Hoover has done an excellent job as editor for InterVarsity Press, and we are grateful to him for his hard work. Our wives,

Barbara DeWeese and Hope Moreland, simply give us what we need to carry on. It is hard to conceive of this book's coming into being without their love and commitment to the cause of Christ. Finally, we are grateful to each other. We have been friends for thirty years now, and it is a joy to write a book together. Of course, any mistakes in the book are due to my coauthor (a vicious circle indeed).

1

WHERE DO I START?

> Ought not a Minister to have, first, a good understanding, a clear apprehension, a sound judgment, and a capacity of reasoning with some closeness?
> **JOHN WESLEY**

> We live in what may be the most anti-intellectual period in the history of Western civilization. We must have passion—indeed hearts on fire for the things of God. But that passion must resist with intensity the anti-intellectual spirit of the world.
> **R.C. SPROUL**

"I just don't understand you. How can anyone with your education, who reads as much as you, believe the things you believe? How can you possibly believe in God, a kindly 'grandfather in the sky,' when you see the suffering in the world caused by AIDS and tsunamis and famines and wars? You understand a lot about modern science—how can you deny evolution and believe there is anything more to the 'real you' than your body and your brain? You must know that miracles—*violations* of the laws of nature—are impossible. How can you believe that 'spooky' things like angels and demons are real? And your claims to know absolute truth—don't get me started! Given everything we know about all the different religions and cultures in the world, how can you be so arrogant to believe that any one religion or morality is true and not merely a useful, culturally constructed fiction?"

Versions of these challenges to Christian faith are replayed repeatedly, day after day; doubtless, you have encountered them in some form. And if you have thought about the challenges much, you have thought philosophically. For the nature of the challenges is not really scientific or theological or anthropological, but philosophical.

Indeed, your philosophical thinking probably started long ago. At some time you asked yourself whether something was real or what was real. You asked what you know or how you know something. And you asked what was the right thing to do in some situation or how you should live your life. These questions lie at the heart of philosophy.

So what is philosophy? *Philosophy is thinking critically about questions that matter.* Conceived this way, philosophy is something everyone does. Everyone has beliefs about what is real, what is valuable, and how we come to know such things. For most people, such fundamental beliefs are largely unexamined and perhaps even mutually inconsistent, but in forming such beliefs and acting on them, everyone is doing philosophy. At a more developed level, philosophy refers to a body of knowledge, often the subject matter of college courses, which organizes and presents the thinking of major thinkers throughout the ages about such things as reality, values, and knowledge.

At a still more refined level, philosophy is the specialized activity engaged in by certain "professional thinkers" who build on the thought of those who have gone before, utilizing certain tools and methods, with the goal of developing, presenting, and defending carefully examined conclusions about reality, values, and knowledge. Since philosophy is above all concerned with discerning the truth about these things, it is natural that philosophy has influenced every corner of life—both inside and outside academia—and that philosophical terms, tools, arguments, and conclusions can be found in almost any book pulled from the library shelf.

Unfortunately the terms and tools are sometimes misused, and the arguments and conclusions often misrepresented. As with any discipline, the professional can quickly spot the errors, but to the untrained eye, all appears as it should.

We are deeply concerned about the impact of philosophy on theology. The medieval theologians believed that theology was the queen of the sciences (that is, of domains of knowledge) and philosophy was her handmaid. The development of theology in both the Eastern and the Western churches has been deeply affected by philosophy, and theology in turn has affected Western philosophy. But since the Enlightenment, roughly, the flow has been one way, from philosophy to theology, and for the most part it has been corrosive to orthodox theology.

In our day, theology has largely been banished from the university (even many Christian colleges have reduced the required credits in Bible and theology), and philosophy has been largely ignored (liberal arts curricula in general have been weakened to make room for more "practical" courses). Couple this with a trendy anti-intellectualism in many evangelical churches, and the result is that most young women and men who desire to enter seminary or join the staff of a parachurch ministry are ill prepared to understand and engage the philosophical aspects of biblical studies, in particular, and the culture in which they minister, in general. And most pastors have neither the time nor the background to keep up with trends in contemporary philosophy, even where it has a direct bearing on theology and ministry.[1]

Our goal in this "philosophical toolkit" is to redress this problem by providing you with a brief, nontechnical, practical guide to selected philosophical terms and concepts and to illustrate their importance and usefulness in teaching the Bible and doing theology in light of contemporary issues.[2] We are not aiming at making you a professional philosopher. But we do want you to be able to recognize and understand the philosophy that you come across every day so that you can be more philosophically discriminating, whatever

---

[1] For more on the dangers and remedies for the church's anti-intellectualism, see J.P. Moreland, Love Your God with All Your Mind: The Role of Reason in the Life of the Soul, rev. ed. (Colorado Springs, CO: NavPress, 2012).

[2] For a much more detailed and thorough introduction to philosophy, see J.P. Moreland and William Lane Craig, Philosophical Foundations for a Christian Worldview, 2nd ed. (Downers Grove, IL: InterVarsity Press, 2017).

your particular path of service to our Lord.

LOGIC

We have often (too often!) heard someone say, "Why is logic so important in theology? You make it sound as if logic is even over God!" We believe the question reflects a common misunderstanding of logic.

If God did not exist, then logic would not exist (nor would anything else, for that matter). But if God does exist, then a whole lot of other things also exist, including the laws of logic.[3] For example, consider the law of identity: God is who he is, and not another God. Consider, too, the law of

---

[3] Arguably, numbers, sets, universals, propositions, relations, and so on also exist. Another way to say this is that if anything exists, then everything that is logically necessary must exist. But nothing can exist at all unless something that is metaphysically necessary exists. And God necessarily exists in this latter sense, so all logical necessities depend on his existence.

noncontradiction: God cannot be both good and not good. These laws (and other things that exist timelessly) would not exist if God did not exist, so they depend on God for their existence. But they were not created by God in the sense that he could have made them otherwise. So to say that the laws of logic apply to God is not to make logic sovereign over God. It is simply to recognize that once something exists, then many other things also exist that cannot be any other way.

Another objection we hear often is this: "Well, there are many different logics. How can we tell which one is the right one? Isn't that pretty arbitrary?" Again, we believe, this rests on a misunderstanding.

The short answer is yes, there are many different logics. But we should keep two points in mind. First, there are also many different algebras and many different geometries. (Mathematicians and logicians are quite creative!) Some of these different systems were devised for dealing with specific problems and do not claim universal validity (e.g., "fuzzy" logic, versions of multivalent logic, and many systems of abstract algebra). Second, none of these systems could have been "built" apart from certain fundamental "laws of thought." (If the law of noncontradiction did not hold universally, we could not even claim that there were different systems!)

A final objection goes this way: "Your logic is a relic of the male-dominated West, and it ignores Eastern logic and feminist logic, for example." Again, we believe this reflects a deep misunderstanding.

With regard to "Eastern logic," there really is no such thing. It is true that certain strands of Hinduism and Buddhism teach that contradiction lies at the heart of reality, that on the path to enlightenment one must learn to embrace contradiction. But as Mortimer Adler pointed out, as long as Hindus and Buddhists accept the results of modern science and technology, they are tacitly affirming the law of noncontradiction, which lies at the very foundation of science.[4]

As for "feminist logic," this is almost certainly a matter of emphasis and values, not different logics. We may grant, for the sake of argument, that women are in general more relational and more emotionally connected, while men are more objective and linear in their thought. But of course women can use objective logic when required, and men can learn to value relationships and emotional connections. Difference in emphasis is not difference in kind.

The laws of thought. Three logical laws are so fundamental that they are sometimes called *laws of thought.* We've already mentioned two of them, the law of identity and the law of noncontradiction. The third is the law of the excluded middle.

THE THREE LAWS OF THOUGHT

---

[4] Mortimer Adler, Truth in Religion: The Plurality of Religions and the Unity of Truth (New York: Macmillan, 1990), 69-76.

> ***The law of identity:*** Something is what it is and not anything else.
>
> ***The law of noncontradiction:*** For any property F, nothing can be both F and not-F at the same time and in the same way.
>
> ***The law of the excluded middle:*** Any proposition is either true or false and not something in between.

These laws are sometimes called *axioms* or *fundamental principles.* They cannot be proved, but their truth is inescapable, for as soon as you try to disprove any one of them, you find you must assume it. Suppose, for example, you were to try to disprove the law of identity. Then you assume you are trying to disprove the law of identity and not the law of gravity; the law of identity is what it is, and it is not the law of gravity. Or suppose you were trying to disprove the law of noncontradiction. That is, you'd be trying to prove that it was false that something could not be both true and false at the same time and in the same way. But that, of course, assumes the very law you're trying to disprove. (There's a famous story about the great Princeton logician Saul Kripke. In a meeting of faculty from other departments, several were trying to argue that the law of noncontradiction should be done away with, as it was a relic of male-dominated, Western, polarizing thinking. Kripke replied, "Good, let's get rid of it. Then we can keep it too.")

Do these laws have anything to do with theology? Most certainly! In Isaiah 45:5, for instance, God makes a strong claim: "I am the Lord, and there is no other; apart from me there is no God." Now, according to the law of identity, it is Yahweh (the Lord) who speaks, and Yahweh is not Krishna or Brahmin or Baal. According to the law of noncontradiction, the Lord cannot be the only God and also just one of many gods. And according to the law of the excluded middle, either it is true that the Lord is the only God or it is false; it cannot be the case that "the Lord is the only God" is true for Christians but false for Buddhists. (For more on the law of identity, see chapter two.)

VALIDITY, SOUNDNESS, COGENCY

Validity: An argument is formally valid if its form is such that the conclusion follows from the premises according to the laws of logic. An argument whose form violates the laws of logic is invalid, even if the conclusion is true. An argument is informally valid if it contains no informal fallacies.

Soundness: An argument that is valid (that is, has the proper form) and has true premises is sound. An argument that has false premises is unsound, whether or not the form is valid and even if the conclusion is true.

Cogency: An argument is cogent for a person if that person believes that it is valid and that the premises are more likely than their denial. Cogency is person-relative, and a sound argument may seem to a person not to be cogent (thus

> explaining why not everyone accepts the conclusion of a sound argument).

Arguments. A philosophical argument is not a heated quarrel, nor is it a rhetorical contest. Philosophical arguments are not decided on the basis of majority vote or how someone feels about an argument. Arguments in philosophy consist in a set of premises that lead to a conclusion. There is a fundamental difference between *deductive* and *inductive* arguments. Below, we'll examine inductive arguments, but here we'll deal with deductive arguments specifically. In a deductive argument, the relation between the premises and the conclusion is a logical matter. The truth of the premises guarantees the truth of the conclusion; or, put differently, if the premises are true, the conclusion must be true. Still, not just any old set of premises together with a conclusion form a good argument. A successful argument—one that persuades someone of a true conclusion—must be valid, sound, and cogent.

Validity. An argument is valid if its *form* is correct—that is, if the conclusion follows from the premises according to the laws of logic. An argument that does not have a correct form is invalid, even if the conclusion is true. Here's an example of an invalid argument:

1. Some politicians are liars.
2. Jessica is a not a politician.
3. Therefore, Jessica is not a liar.

Even assuming that Jessica is not a politician, (3) doesn't follow from (1) and (2). Here's another example:

1. If Jupiter is the fifth planet from the sun, then it is the largest planet.
2. Jupiter is the largest planet.
3. Therefore, Jupiter is the fifth planet from the sun.

Even though each of the premises and the conclusion is true, this is an invalid argument because its form is incorrect. We say that the argument commits a *formal fallacy.* Shortly we'll explain what is wrong with the form of these two arguments (if it isn't apparent to you already). The point is that the validity of an argument depends on the form of the premises and the conclusion, not their truth.

Soundness. Why worry about validity? Simple. The conclusion of a valid argument is guaranteed to be true if the premises are true. An argument that has a valid form together with true premises is called *sound.* The conclusion of a sound argument is guaranteed to be true. So in evaluating arguments, it is very important to ensure the argument has the proper form (validity) and the premises are true (soundness).

Of course, it is not always apparent whether a premise is true, and often it may be very difficult to tell. So philosophical arguments generally spend most of the time trying to show in some way that the premises are indeed true (or, at the very least, are more probable than their denials), and that leads to the issue of cogency.

Cogency. A cogent argument is one for which the validity and soundness are apparent to the reader, and so she accepts the conclusion of the argument. Unfortunately, this complicates things. No conclusion can be stronger than the strength of the weakest premise, and it frequently happens that we think we have stronger reasons to reject a conclusion than to accept at least one of the premises. In that case, even if we cannot demonstrate the falsity of a premise, and even if the argument is valid, it will not be cogent for us. It will not demand acceptance or compel belief. Cogency, then, is person-relative. Many factors—psychological, personal, volitional, prejudicial, or theological (think of original sin or the work of the Holy Spirit)—enter into the mix when a person evaluates an argument. Especially in the case where the premises are not clearly and undeniably true, a perfectly valid argument may lack cogency for someone. Some arguments are so complicated, the logic so sophisticated, that only specialists are able to grasp them. Such arguments may lack cogency even for the average philosopher. In part this explains why two people can look at the same argument and disagree completely about whether it is a good argument.*

[* Here's an example of a valid argument that lacks cogency for many philosophers: Alvin Plantinga's modal version of the "ontological argument." (Don't worry if you don't get it; that's the point.)

1. There is a possible world in which maximal greatness is instantiated.
2. Necessarily, a being is maximally great only if it has maximal excellence in every world.
3. Necessarily, a being has maximal greatness in every world only if it has omniscience, omnipotence, and moral perfection in every world.
4. Maximal greatness in possibly exemplified.
5. So there is a possible being x and a world W' such that x is exemplified in W' and x entails "has maximal greatness in W."
6. But if x has maximal greatness in W', then x has maximal greatness in all possible worlds.
7. If W' had been actual, it would have been impossible for x not to have been exemplified.
8. What is impossible is invariant across possible worlds.

9. Therefore, there exists a being that has maximal greatness in every possible world.
10. Therefore, there exists a being that has maximal greatness in the actual world.]

This is important for a couple of reasons. First, you may be deeply convinced that a particular argument for, say, the existence of God is sound, but you find that someone—a very smart friend, perhaps—rejects it. That doesn't automatically mean the argument is a bad argument and you should give it up. Rather, other factors may be at work in your friend's life that make it more plausible to him to deny the conclusion that God exists than to accept the validity of the argument or the truth of the premises, even if he can't say just where the argument went wrong.

Second, you may encounter an argument in your study that leads to a conclusion you find dead wrong. It just isn't cogent for you. If you have stronger reasons to reject the conclusion of the argument than you do to accept its soundness, you are within your intellectual rights not to accept the conclusion. But—and this should go without saying—the fact that we don't like a particular conclusion is not in itself a sufficient reason to reject it. We must be honest with the argument and with ourselves, and sometimes that means doing some hard thinking and research to discover just where the argument went wrong. Or we may discover that we were wrong and accept the conclusion after all.

One final matter before moving on has to do with the notion of *certainty*. Sometimes authors use the term *certain* to refer to a proposition that is infallible (such as the proposition "Anything that is red is colored"). But more often, and in the general population, certainty is a psychological predicate, indicating that someone believes a proposition and entertains no doubt about it. We have all been certain about some false propositions (and in all likelihood we are right now as well). "Certain" often serves a rhetorical purpose in an argument, and just because an author labels a premise as certain does not mean it is beyond question. In short, certainty belongs to persons, truth to propositions.

Valid forms of deductive arguments (and associated fallacies). We begin this section with a caveat: this is not nearly a complete survey of valid argument forms.[5] Nevertheless, a few merit attention. In what follows, the letters *p, q,* and *r* represent propositions (for now, think of a proposition as a declarative sentence). Several of the forms use an *if, then* form: If *p,* then *q.* This is called a *conditional statement;p* is called the *antecedent,* and *q* is called the *consequent.* In addition, we'll use the standard symbol ~ (the tilde) to stand for *not.* For each form below we'll use both symbolic notation and provide an example. For the sake of illustration we've used simple examples, but most arguments you encounter will not be so simple. See if you can think of other more complicated sentences to

---

[5] For more a thorough introduction to the material of this section, see Moreland and Craig, Philosophical Foundations, chap.2.

substitute for *p, q,* and *r* and reflect carefully about the resulting argument.

Modus ponens:

If p, then q	If Mary has a sister, then Mary is a sibling.
p	Mary has a sister.
Therefore q	Therefore Mary is a sibling.

Modus ponens is perhaps the most intuitively obvious inference pattern; anyone who thinks about it will see that it is clearly valid.

The associated fallacy is that of *affirming the consequent.* One states a conditional, claims that the consequent is true, and concludes that the antecedent must be true. But this is clearly invalid:

If p, then q	If Mary has a sister, then Mary is a sibling.
q	Mary is a sibling.
Therefore p	Therefore Mary has a sister.

(Of course, Mary could be a sibling who has only brothers.)

Modus tollens:

If p, then q	If Mary has a sister, then Mary is a sibling.
~q	Mary is not a sibling.

Therefore ~p   Therefore Mary does not have a sister.

The associated fallacy here is *denying the antecedent.* Again, the fallacy should be clear:

If p, then q   If Mary has a sister, then Mary is a sibling.

~p   Mary does not have a sister.

Therefore ~q   Therefore Mary is not a sibling.

Hypothetical syllogism:

If p, then q   If it's snowing, then it's below 32°.

If q, then r   If it's below 32°, then it's cold.

Therefore if p, then r   Therefore if it's snowing, then it's cold.

Disjunctive syllogism:

p or q   Either Bill is in his apartment or he is out.

~p   Bill is not in his apartment.

Therefore q   Therefore Bill is out.

Here the *or* statement (called a *disjunction*) is assumed to be true. So if one of the terms ("disjuncts") is false, the other must be true. There's an associated fallacy here also, but it is not a formal fallacy—that is, it is not a matter of an incorrect form. It's the informal fallacy of *false dilemma:*

p or q	Either Bill is in his apartment or he is in the library.
~p	Bill is not in the library.
Therefore q	Therefore Bill is in his apartment.

Remember that the truth of the conclusion depends on the truth of the premises. A disjunctive syllogism relies on an exclusive sense of *or* such that the two alternatives are the only ones possible. The disjunction "*p* or *q*" is true if and only if *p* is true, or *q* is true, or both are true. If, in our example, it is possible that Bill is en route, then the conclusion will not follow. In such a case, where the disjunction "*p* or *q*" does not express mutually exclusive possibilities, the premise presents a false dilemma.

We have pointed out only four of nine rules of inference that determine valid deductive argument forms, but these are perhaps the four most common. (As an exercise, see how many you can identify in comments on social media.) We've also noted two associated formal fallacies and one informal fallacy. As might be expected, it turns out that an argument can go wrong in many ways even if it is in the correct form. These ways are called *informal fallacies.* There is no complete list of informal fallacies, perhaps because there is no end to the creativity of illogical people! But the following survey should be helpful in recognizing common informal fallacies (in addition to false dilemma, discussed above).

Informal fallacies. Perhaps the most frequent informal fallacy, and therefore the one to be most wary of, is the one with which we begin.

Begging the question (petitio principii). It has become somewhat common for people to use the phrase *and that begs the question* in the sense of "that invites the question" or "that makes me wonder." The fallacy of begging the question is quite different: it is circular reasoning. An argument begs the question if the conclusion is somehow smuggled into or assumed by one of the premises. Note how in this example the conclusion is incorporated into a premise:

> "I'm all for women having equal rights," said pro wrestler Mad Mountain, "but I repeat: a woman shouldn't be a pro wrestler, since wrestlers are men!"

Equivocation. Another very common informal fallacy is equivocation. Equivocation happens when a term is used in a different sense in two premises.

> "Officer, I didn't rob the bank [of America]. I swear, I wasn't anywhere near the bank [of the river] yesterday!"

Equivocations are sometimes hard to spot. By carefully defining the terms of the argument, we can avoid equivocation in our own arguments.

Appeal to pity (argumentum ad misericordiam). Appeal to pity is another common mistake.

> "Ladies and gentlemen of the jury, you must find it in your hearts to acquit my client of killing his parents. Remember, he is a poor orphan!"

(Note how often you find this fallacy in arguments favoring abortion, embryonic stem cell research, physician-assisted suicide, and many other issues in bioethics.)

Ad hominem. Ad hominem (against the person) arguments frequently find their place in political debate.

> "It's too bad that Senator Bullmoose cannot see that his bill will steal from the poor and pay the rich. His holier-than-thou attitude toward labor unions smacks of bigotry and condescension."

We should watch ourselves closely on this one. The fact that someone is an evil person does not in itself invalidate anything he says. (Even Hitler probably said that 2+2=4. In German, of course.)

Appeal to the people (argumentum ad populam). This can take several forms, but a very common form is the use of opinion polls:

> "Eighty-two percent of voters surveyed believe that Senator Bullmoose is a bigoted thief."

Whether he is or isn't, such premises have a bandwagon effect—people think they should believe what the majority believes.

Argument from ignorance (argumentum ad ignorantium). This fallacy involves citing the absence of evidence for a proposition as evidence against it. But of course absence of evidence is not evidence of absence.

> "In spite of 150 years of searching, no 'missing link' fossil has been found. Therefore Darwinism is false."

Straw man. A straw man is the distortion of an opponent's position so that it can more easily be attacked. By destroying the straw man, the impression is given that the real argument has been defeated.

> "Jones claims that the war in Iraq does not meet the criteria for a just war. Does Jones want us to believe that the terrorists care about just war theory? Does he expect us to stop checking for weapons at airports, to bring home all our military forces and to wait, cringing, for the next attack?"

There are a number of other informal fallacies that we'll name but not illustrate. They include *hasty generalization, false cause, slippery slope, weak analogy,* and *complex question.* (Details can be found in most books on logic or critical thinking.)

In summary, a good argument must have a logically correct form, have true premises, be cogent to the reader, and avoid informal fallacies. You might be surprised just how much effort philosophers devote to crafting good arguments for their position and to finding the flaws in arguments they oppose. But the effort is worth it—for philosophers and for you as well.

Remember, the truth of God is not well served by bad arguments or sloppy thinking!

Inductive arguments. To this point we have been considering deductive arguments, those which, if the form is valid and the premises are sound, guarantee a true conclusion. Inductive arguments form a second and important class of logical arguments. In an inductive argument, the truth of the premises together with the absence of fallacies does not guarantee the truth of the conclusion. The conclusion of an inductive argument is probable, given the truth of the premises.

It is important to point out a common misunderstanding at this point. There is a difference between the truth of a proposition (be it a premise or a conclusion) and the degree of probability we attach to the proposition. Since the conclusion of an argument can be no more certain than the premises, we may find ourselves having more confidence in the conclusion of an inductive argument than in the conclusion of a valid deductive argument.

Inductive arguments do not fit into neat patterns the way deductive arguments do. Rather, induction is the term applied to various sorts of arguments, such as arguments by *analogy* (used, e.g., in legal and moral reasoning), *causal* arguments, *statistical* and *probabilistic* arguments, and *hypothetical* arguments (used, e.g., in scientific reasoning). We will comment briefly on only two of these sorts of arguments: probability and hypothetical reasoning.

Probability. Inductive arguments are often formulated in terms of the *probability calculus.* Theorists have discovered specific rules for determining the probability of a statement's truth (or an event's occurrence) based on the probability of other statements being true (or other events occurring). While the details are beyond the scope of this book, something called *Bayes' theorem* is often used, a formula that evaluates the conditional probability of two or more mutually exclusive and jointly exhaustive statements or events.[6] What we need to determine in instances of probabilistic inductive reasoning (whether using Bayes' theorem or not) is the nature of the probabilities assigned. If the probabilities are objective (e.g., the probability of drawing a club from a full deck of cards) and if the sample size is sufficiently large (e.g., the number of smokers who contracted lung cancer out of a study group of 100,000 people), then the probability calculus yields a strong inductive argument. On the other hand, the probabilities may represent *epistemic probability,* a subjective assignment of the degree of belief or

---

[6] For details, see Moreland and Craig, Philosophical Foundations, 60-61.

confidence placed in the premise (e.g., the probability that the amount and kinds of evil observed in the world would exist given the existence of a good, omniscient, omnipotent God). In many such cases the epistemic probabilities depend more on the arguer's worldview than on anything objectively quantifiable, and in other cases the probabilities are downright inscrutable. Probabilities of this sort yield weaker inductive arguments.

Hypothetical reasoning. A different sort of inductive reasoning is *hypothetical,* often used in scientific (and criminal) investigation but also widely used in daily life. Here we are confronted with a problem of some sort, certain observations or data that need explanation. We form a hypothesis based on the observations, then draw out implications of the hypothesis and devise tests of the implications. If things come out as expected, the hypothesis is confirmed; if not, it is disconfirmed. (Note that because this is an inductive form of argument, the hypothesis is not proved or disproved.) A closely related form of argument is *inference to the best explanation.*

In many (perhaps most) cases, when confronted by a problem to be solved, a number of live hypotheses could explain the data, not just one. It is often impractical or even impossible to construct independent tests to confirm or disconfirm the various live hypotheses, so from the pool of hypotheses that explain the data, we infer which one is the best explanation. Several different criteria enter into an inference to the best explanation, including the following:

- explanatory power—the best hypothesis will explain the observed data better, making the data more probable (epistemically) than its rivals
- scope—the best hypothesis explains a wider range of data (e.g., observations from other experiments or other crimes) than its rivals
- fertility—the best hypothesis will generate more possibilities for new research than its rivals
- less ad hoc—the best hypothesis will involve fewer new assumptions

not implied by other theories than will its rivals
- coherence with accepted theory—the best hypothesis will agree with a wider variety of accepted theories than its rivals
- simplicity—other things being equal, the best hypothesis will be simpler than its rivals

Clearly it will be rare if one explanation comes out ahead on all of these criteria; knowing how to judge and rank the different criteria is more a matter of art, gained through experience working in a particular field.

METHOD

As we indicated above, careful definition of terms is essential for good arguments. How many times have you heard someone say (or you've said yourself), "We're just arguing over semantics"? Too often the statement is meant dismissively, as if there were nothing really at stake in the argument. But semantics has to do with *meaning,* and so an argument about semantics is important, one that cries out for careful definitions. The histories of both theology and philosophy are filled with arguments about meanings and with attempts by different thinkers to state carefully what they mean. So we need to pay attention to definitions in this section.

We will also need to pay attention to what has been called *conceptual analysis,* which amounts to a fancy way to get at the meaning of a concept. Together with argument and definition, conceptual analysis is one of the most useful tools in the philosopher's toolbox.

Definitions. The primary interest of philosophers is not in the definitions of words in general, but in *terms*—a word or group of words that may serve as the subject of a statement. Proper nouns, common nouns, and descriptive phrases are all terms.

Lexical definition. It would be natural to look in a dictionary to see how a term is defined. But—and this point may be so obvious that it is often overlooked—a lexical definition is a definition of a word, not of a thing. This will become clearer as we consider other types of definitions. Another way of looking at the matter is by way of distinguishing *intensional* (with an *s*) from *extensional* meanings. The intension of a term is what it connotes, while the extension of a term is what it denotes. The intension is the concept, while the extension consists in the class of things that fall under the concept.

Intensional definition. An intensional definition of a term specifies the *essence* of the object the term refers to. Often this is done, following Aristotle, by specifying a genus and a species—that is, by specifying a general class and then the difference that sets the specific term off from other things that are also part of the genus. Aristotle's classic example was that "man" connoted a "rational animal," where "animal" was the genus and "rational" was what differentiated man from all other animals.

Extensional definition. An extensional definition specifies the *class of things* in the world that the term picks out. Sometimes this is done *ostensively,* by pointing ("This, that, and that one over there are my children"), and sometimes it is done by giving the requirements for membership in the extension class, the conditions that are *individually necessary and jointly sufficient* for an object to fall under the concept. This is the common method since it is usually impractical or impossible to point to all the members of the extension class. (Note that some terms have a clear, intensional definition—e.g., a unicorn is "a white horse-like creature with one horn"—but no extension. We say the extension of such terms is empty.)

One more word about *necessary and sufficient conditions.* A necessary condition is a property without which an object will not fall under a concept, while a sufficient condition is a property the presence of which locates the object under the concept.

Stipulative definitions. Sometimes an author will specify the precise sense in which she is using a term that is capable of several meanings, or she may give a particular technical sense to a term that generally does not bear that sense. Such stipulations are a legitimate practice, especially when done for the purpose of avoiding equivocations.

Conceptual analysis. Philosophers generally see a large part of their work to be that of conceptual analysis. When doing conceptual analysis, most philosophers are not so much interested in how a term is used in the language as they are in discovering the essence of that to which the concept applies. So, for example, if we ask the question, "What is justice?" the answer will be found in an analysis of the concept of justice—seeking what justice consists in, what its essence is—and not simply in an analysis of the ways in which the word is used or in an examination of the things to which the term is applied (for some of them, it might turn out, are misapplications of the term). The process of conceptual analysis is often carried on through progressively refining the analysis, seeking out possible counterexamples and then re-refining. It may seem tedious, perhaps, but remember that the goal is clarity and precision.

PHILOSOPHY AND THEOLOGY

If you are reading this book, the chances are that you already sense something of what philosophy has to do with theology. We want to mention three ways in which the two disciplines interact that we think are especially important for pastors, seminarians, Christian workers, and, indeed, all thinking Christians to consider.

Understanding worldviews. In the words of James W. Sire,

> A worldview is a commitment, a fundamental commitment of the heart, that can be expressed as a story or in a set of presuppositions (assumptions which may be true, partially true or entirely false) which we hold (consciously or subconsciously, consistently or inconsistently) about the basic constitution of reality, and that provides the foundation on which

we live and move and have our being.[7]

Critical thinking about worldviews is a philosophical matter, and worldviews likewise influence how philosophy is done. As we noted above, the cogency of an argument for a particular person is often more a matter of that person's worldview than of the philosophical strength of the argument. We believe that as Christians, we should examine our own worldview, ferreting out the implications of our Christian faith for all aspects of our lives. And since worldviews largely determine a person's "plausibility structure" (the background against which proposed beliefs or ideas are evaluated), we believe that it is crucial for evangelism that Christians should become familiar with the basic

---

[7] James W. Sire, Naming the Elephant: Worldview as a Concept (Downers Grove, IL: InterVarsity Press, 2004), 122. For more on worldviews, we recommend this as well as Sire's The Universe Next Door: A Basic Worldview Catalog, 6th ed. (Downers Grove, IL: InterVarsity Press, 2020).

tenets of the worldviews of those around us.

Setting the agenda. The philosophical problems and solutions on offer at any given time go far to determine the agenda for theology at that time. This is not to say that theology does not in part set its own agenda. But it is clear from the history of theology that philosophical questions have strongly influenced its trajectory. For example, when the Council of Nicaea declared in 325 that the Son was "of the same substance" with the Father, or when in 451 the Council of Chalcedon explained how Jesus can be both God and man in terms of "one person, two natures," the language reflected philosophical concerns with terms such as *essence, substance, nature,* and *attribute.* And the contemporary debate over open theism reflects philosophical concerns with the nature of free will, the meaning of omniscience, the nature of time, and the epistemic or metaphysical status of propositions about future free actions—concerns that have shaped theological discussion. Because theology must always keep one eye on apologetic issues of the time, philosophical awareness will always be a requirement for doing theology.

Sharing methodology. A final area where philosophy and theology overlap is in method. The careful definition and conceptual analysis characteristic of philosophy also characterize the best theology. Common theological terms such as *substance, essence, hypostatic union, person, soul, omniscience, omnipotence, foreknowledge, eternity, infallibility, inerrancy,* and so on need to be defined precisely, used unequivocally, and defended carefully. In addition to having the knowledge and skills required for biblical exegesis and for historical and theological reflection, a good theologian must also have some skill in philosophical methodology.

Both of us believe we are better philosophers because of our theological study, and we believe equally that our theological abilities have been sharpened by our philosophical work. Our goal, our hope, our prayer is that this book will help you as well.

2

WHAT IS REAL?

Metaphysics

What is seen is temporary, but what is unseen is eternal.
2 CORINTHIANS 4:18

That all depends on what the meaning of *is* is.
WILLIAM JEFFERSON CLINTON

Metaphysics has a public relations problem. When some people hear the word *metaphysics,* they are likely to think of a certain area of the bookstore at the mall where you get books on the New Age movement and crystals and psychic phenomena. With an image like that, it's easy to see why many would dismiss metaphysics as weird and irrelevant. Others may think of metaphysics as a totally impractical, dry endeavor fit only for those stuck in the ivory tower!

Neither of these opinions is accurate. Metaphysics is really exciting and very practical. Metaphysics has had a long, distinguished history, boasting some of the greatest thinkers of all time: Plato, Aristotle, Augustine, Thomas Aquinas, René Descartes, Gottfried Wilhelm Leibniz. And metaphysics has been the long-standing friend of theology. Many of the greatest metaphysicians have been and are Christians. And many of the great Christian pastors and thinkers throughout church history have studied metaphysics. For example, in his advice to pastors, John Wesley said,

> Do I understand metaphysics; if not the depths of the Schoolmen, the subtleties of Scotus or Aquinas, yet the first rudiments, the general principles, of that useful science? Have I conquered so much of it, as to clear my apprehension and range my ideas under proper heads?[8]

---

[8] John Wesley, "An Address to the Clergy," delivered February 6, 1756. Reprinted in The Works of John Wesley, 3rd ed. (Grand Rapids, MI: Baker Books, 1996), 6:217-31.

In this chapter, we want to help you get the "first rudiments, the general principles, of that useful science."

GETTING STARTED

What is metaphysics? The term *metaphysics* was first used as a title for a group of works by Aristotle (384–322BC). One set of his writings was about "the things of nature" and came to be called the *Physics.* Another set of works (which Aristotle himself never named) was called "the books after the *Physics*" (*ta meta ta physika*) by some ancient editors who collected and edited his writings in the first century BC. Thus, metaphysics originally meant "after the *Physics,*" and although metaphysical reflection existed before Aristotle, the term has continued to refer to a certain branch of philosophy ever since.

It is difficult, if not impossible, to come up with an adequate definition of metaphysics. Usually it is characterized as the philosophical study of reality. But the best way to understand metaphysics is not through a definition but by investigating examples of metaphysical reflection.

Examples of metaphysical reflection. Ever had a conversation like this?

>Believer: Have you heard of the Four Spiritual Laws?
>
>Unbeliever: I'm not interested.
>
>Believer: How come?
>
>Unbeliever: 'Cause you Christians are crazy. You believe some pretty weird things.
>
>Believer: Like what?
>
>Unbeliever: You say that moral values are real. But if something is real, you've got to be able to see it, to locate it somewhere. Cleveland is real. You can see it, and I can tell you where it is. But who's ever seen a moral value, and where are these things anyway?
>
>Believer: Love's real, isn't it?
>
>Unbeliever: It's just a word, an idea in people's heads, but while we're on the subject of love, it brings up another crazy thing you Christians believe.
>
>Believer: Sounds like I walked into a trap.

Unbeliever: Trap or no trap, here's the problem. You say that God is love, but how can that be true? Love's just an idea, or maybe it's an attitude or action, but love isn't alive. You can't pray to it. If your God is real, then he would be alive, but he sure isn't the same thing as an attitude or action. So it's nuts to say that God is love.

Believer: Well, Jesus still died for your sins and you have to decide what you are going to do with that fact.

Unbeliever: The topic of Jesus raises another problem. If the 2005 US president is the same thing as George W. Bush and if Laura Bush's husband is the same thing as George W. Bush, then the 2005 US president is the same thing as Laura Bush's husband.

Believer: So what?

Unbeliever: Well, if Jesus is the same thing as God, and the Holy Ghost is the same thing as God, then Jesus is the same thing as the Holy Spirit. But you Christians believe that they're different. How can that be?

This dialogue brings to the surface a number of issues and exhibits several confusions. In this chapter, we'll try to clear up some of them. As a start, let's look at the following four sentences:

1. Moses is human.
2. Moses is 5'7".
3. Moses is the teacher of Joshua.
4. Moses is skin and bone.

Each of these sentences uses a different sense of the word *is*. Part of metaphysical investigation is the task of distinguishing these different senses and saying something helpful about each one of them. The dialogue above included certain statements that fit into sentences (1) through (4) in some way or another: Moral values are real. God is love. Jesus is God. What's going on with these statements? How can we help our believing friend do better next time he is greeted with these questions?

THE PROBLEM OF UNIVERSALS

What's the problem? The first two sentences—Moses is human and Moses is 5'7"—ascribe properties to Moses and use what philosophers call an *is of predication.* The best way to understand this is to look at one of the great issues in the history of philosophy: *the problem of universals.* The problem of universals is actually a set of related issues involving the existence and nature of properties (where a property is just a quality of some sort that a thing can have). It certainly seems that properties exist. Indeed, one of the most obvious facts about the world is that it consists of individual things like dogs and cars that have properties. A dog could have the property of being brown, or a car, red. It seems that several objects can have the same property; for example, several cars can possess the same shade of red. But both the existence and nature of properties have long been a matter of dispute, and the problem of universals is the name for the issues central to this debate.

Historically the problem of universals has been closely connected to what is called *the problem of the "one and the many"* (a.k.a. "one over many" or "one in many"), which involves giving an account of the unity of natural classes. To illustrate, consider the following words: *red, red, blue.* How many words are in the sequence? Two answers seem possible, either two or three words. There seem to be two word types and three word tokens, where a type is something that can "show up" or be instanced in different places, and a token is a specific instance of a type. If we form a set containing the first two tokens *{red, red}*, the unity of the set would seem to be grounded in the fact that both tokens have the same word type (both are examples of *red* and not *blue*) in common.[9]

Similarly, if we had seven red and three blue balls, there would be a sense

---

[9] See J.P. Moreland, Universals (Montreal: McGill-Queen's University Press, 2001), 1-2.

in which we would have two different colors and another sense in which we would have ten different colors. There would be two kinds of colors—red and blue—and ten instances of color. A set containing the seven red balls seems to exhibit a natural unity in that each ball has something in common that is not possessed by any of the blue balls—namely, the color red.

Contrast the set of red balls with the set containing these members: the 1969 New York Mets, the square root of −1, the planet Mars. This isn't a real natural set. What distinguishes a class of members that marks off a real natural set from a contrived set? What grounds set membership in natural sets? The obvious answer is that the members of a natural set literally have something in common—all seven balls are red—but this isn't true of the members of a contrived set. So the problem of the "one and the many" is this: How is it possible to group together a number of individual things that all share something in common, thereby forming one natural set of those things? The problem of universals includes the issues and options surrounding the "one and the many." However, since the problem of universals is about the existence and nature of properties, it goes beyond the "one and the many" and includes these questions:

1. Do properties exist?
2. If properties exist, are they universals or particulars?

Who cares? Life's short and we're all busy, so you might be thinking, *Who cares if properties exist and are universals? What difference does any of this make to my life? Isn't this far too abstract to have any real practical importance? Does all this really matter?* These are fair questions, and the short answer to them is, "Yes, it does!" The following are three examples of how important the debate about properties and universals really is.

Several years ago the Christian theologian Bernard Ramm argued that one reason for the breakdown of the family was the rise of extreme and moderate nominalism. We will look at these views shortly, but for now, they amount to the denial that there are universals. Why think that one cause for the breakdown of the family was a rejection of universals? According to Ramm, a realist says that the class of all families literally has certain properties in common, certain universals—having a father, a mother, which in turn have certain important properties in common (being nurturing)—such that a group is not a family just because we say it is but, rather, because it exemplifies the same properties at all times and in all places. Nominalists of either form claim that there is no such universal attribute to a family and, thus, feel free to define a family in relativist terms. Advocates of same-sex marriage claim that being a good father is whatever one believes sincerely that it is, and they deny that there are true, universal moral values. All involve a rejection of certain universals relevant to the topics in question.

As a second example, consider love. This is a property—being loving—that people and their actions may or may not exemplify. It is a real property, not just a word, and it is a universal that is present in all individual acts of love or loving people. In fact, since being loving is a real universal, being loving itself has further properties that we could discover. What are these second-order properties that the first-order property being loving has? Paul describes some of them in 1 Corinthians 13: patience, kindness, and so on. Since love and its properties are real universals, passages like 1 Corinthians 13 are describing reality as it is in all cultures in their descriptions of love. These descriptions give us true knowledge of reality—in this case, of properties understood as universals.

Finally, debates about postmodernism involve the acceptance or rejection of universals. As a philosophical standpoint, postmodernism is primarily a reinterpretation of what knowledge is and what counts as knowledge. More broadly it represents a form of cultural relativism about such things as reality, truth, reason, value, linguistic meaning, the self, and other notions. All such notions are social constructions—arbitrary creations of language that are relative to different cultures.

Postmodernists deny the existence of universals. Remember, a universal is an entity that can be in more than one place at the same time or in the same place at different, interrupted time intervals. Redness, justice, being even, and humanness are examples of universals. If redness is a universal, then if one sees (the same shade of) redness on Monday and again on Tuesday, the redness seen on Tuesday is identical to, is the very same thing as, the redness seen on Monday. Postmodernists deny such identities and claim that nothing is repeatable, nothing is literally the same from one moment to the next, nothing can be present at one time or place and literally be present at another time or place. Thus, postmodernists hold to some form of nominalism.

Because postmodernists reject universal properties, they also reject essentialism. According to essentialism, some things have *essential* and *accidental* properties. A thing's essential properties are those such that if the thing in question loses them, it ceases to exist. A thing's essential properties answer the most fundamental question: What sort of thing is this? For example, being even is an essential property of the number two, being human is essential to Socrates, being omnipotent is essential to God, being H_2O is essential to water. An accidental property is one such that a thing can lose it and still exist. For example, being five feet tall is accidental to Socrates.

According to postmodernists, there is no distinction in reality between essential and accidental properties. Rather, this division is relative to our interests, values, and classificatory purposes, and, as such, the division is itself a social construction that will not be uniform throughout social groups. For example, if a group's definition of birds includes having a beak, then, assuming for the purpose of illustration that everything that has a beak has feathers, having a feather is an essential property of birds. If the group defines birds so as to include bats, having a feather is an accidental property. Thus, what is essential to birds is not a reflection of reality; it is a construction relative to a group's linguistic practices. It should be clear that postmodern nominalism, if widely accepted, would have a disastrous impact on the objective existence of important universals relating to truth, values, and Christian teaching.

What are the different solutions to the problem of universals? Suppose we have before us two red, round spots named Socrates and Plato. Socrates and Plato are exactly alike in all their properties. Since they have the same size, shape, color, and so on, Socrates and Plato are a case of what is called *property agreement.* Socrates and Plato are concrete particulars—that is, particular individual things that seem to have properties (in this case, spots that seem to have the property of being red and of being round).

How are we to account for property agreement? Three broad answers to this question have been offered. First, there is *extreme nominalism:* properties do not exist, and concrete particulars and groups of concrete particulars are the only things that are real. An extreme nominalist would explain the property agreement between Socrates and Plato as follows:

> Socrates (or Plato) has the property redness if and only if_____.

Different versions of extreme nominalism would fill in the blank in different ways. Here are two:

> 3. The word *red* is true of Socrates.
>
> 4. Socrates is a member of the set of red, concrete particulars.

For the extreme nominalist, properties (e.g., redness) do not exist at all; only concrete particulars (individual red things) and the property words (e.g., the word *red*) true of them or the sets to which they belong (the set of all and only red things) exist.

A second view of property agreement is called *moderate nominalism*. Advocates accept the existence of properties but hold that they are particular, individualized qualities called *abstract particulars* that cannot be possessed by more than one concrete particular. Here the term *abstract* means "something that is brought before the mind by disregarding other things in its environment." For example, if one disregards the shape, smell, or size of a tomato and focuses only on its surface color, the tomato's redness is abstract in this sense. Returning to Socrates, it has its own particular redness, and Plato has its own particular redness that we can call the redness of Socrates and the redness of Plato, respectively. Redness in general is a set of individual, abstract particulars—that is, the redness of Socrates, the redness of Plato, the redness of a particular apple, and so on—that are in all the concrete particulars (individual apples, spots, cars). Socrates is a whole composed of all its abstract particulars (the particular redness of Socrates, the particular roundness of Socrates, etc.) as parts.

A third school of thought is *realism*. On this view, Socrates and Plato have the very same property, redness, in each of them. Properties are ones-in-many; they can be possessed by many concrete particulars at the same time. The relationship between a property like redness and concrete particulars like Socrates and Plato is called *exemplification.* Socrates and Plato exemplify redness. Properties are *universals*—multiple exemplifiable entities that can be had by many things at the same time. The redness exemplified by Socrates is identical to the redness exemplified by Plato.

In sum, extreme nominalism, moderate nominalism, and realism are different positions about the existence and nature of properties. Extreme nominalists accept only the existence of concrete particulars (and sets of such particulars along with words true of them), nominalists embrace concrete and abstract particulars (along with sets of abstract particulars), and realists assert the reality of concrete particulars and properties understood as universals—that is, as entities that can be exemplified by many concrete particulars at once.

What are the arguments for deciding who's right? Three main types of evidence have been center stage in this dispute: *predication, exact resemblance,* and the fact that *properties themselves have properties* (e.g., redness is a color). Let us briefly look at these in order, beginning with predication. Consider these sentences:

5. Socrates is red.
6. Plato is red.

The realist has a powerful, straightforward way of explaining the truth of these sentences: (5) and (6) express the fact that Socrates and Plato exemplify the same property, redness, which grounds the unity of the class of red things. Thus, redness is a universal predicated of each. This can be made explicit in this way:

5'. Socrates has redness.
6'. Plato has redness.

The realist has a clear way of explaining predication and accounting for the "one and the many," for example, for the unity of the set of red things. The realist challenges the extreme nominalist and the nominalist to offer a better account of predication.

How would an extreme nominalist treat (5)? He would claim that (5) really asserts the same thing as

5". Socrates is a red thing.

(5") says that Socrates is a red, concrete particular. Note that (5") avoids any reference to properties.

Now the realist wants to know what accounts for the fact that Socrates and Plato are members of the set of red things and that Aristotle (a round, blue spot) is not. The realist has an answer: Socrates and Plato have the property of redness and Aristotle does not. The unity of the set is grounded in a property shared by all members of the set. However, the extreme nominalist cannot make this move because of his denial of properties. Thus, he can give no answer as to what grounds the unity of the set of red things, even though an obvious answer is staring us in the face. If the extreme nominalist tries to solve the problem of how red things can all be red by saying that the word *red* is true of each thing, he would seem to imply that it is the *very same word (red* in this case) that is used of each red thing, and this treats the word *red* as a type (a universal). The extreme nominalist gets rid of the universal property redness by reducing it to the word *red* being true of all red things. But this only replaces one universal (redness itself) with another one (the word type *red*).

How might a moderate nominalist solve the problem of predication? She could do so in this way:

5'''. Socrates has its own redness, and the redness of Socrates is a member of the class of red abstract particulars.

Similarly, Plato has its own redness, and the redness of Socrates and the redness of Plato are individual members of the class of reds (individualized properties), not of red things. Remember the class mentioned in (5''') is not the class of red concrete particulars but of red abstract particulars.

Unfortunately the moderate nominalist view of predication suffers from the same problem that was raised against extreme nominalism. What grounds the class of red abstract particulars such that the redness of Socrates and the redness of Plato are members of that class but the blueness of Aristotle (a particular instance of blue in Aristotle, a round, blue spot) is not? Again, the realist would say that the redness of Socrates and the redness of Plato have the same property (redness) in them and the blueness of Aristotle does not. But the moderate nominalist ultimately has no such answer to give.

In sum, predication is a problem for extreme and moderate nominalism because these views do not have an adequate account of what it is that places something in its class, that unifies the class, and that excludes other things from class membership. The realist can explain this, however, by appealing to the possession of the same property or the failure to possess that property.

The second piece of evidence to consider in this debate about universals is exact resemblance. Things in the world resemble or fail to resemble each other in various ways. Socrates, Plato, and Aristotle are exactly alike in being round, but Socrates and Plato resemble each other in respect to being red, while Aristotle does not. In general, when two things, *a* and *b,* are exactly alike, there will be a respect *F* in which they resemble each other. This respect will be the property *F*-ness, possessed by *a* and *b.* For the realist, therefore, the exact similarity of color between

Socrates and Plato is explained by the fact that each exemplifies the very same property, redness, and this is precisely the respect in which they are alike. The realist challenges the extreme and moderate nominalist to come up with an adequate account of exact similarity.

The extreme nominalist will respond to this challenge by claiming that all red things simply stand in the exact similarity relation with each other and that this is just a basic fact that cannot be explained. As a matter of simple, brute fact, Socrates and Plato resemble each other and not Aristotle. However, there are two problems with this approach. First, there does, in fact, seem to be a respect of resemblance between Socrates and Plato; namely, they resemble each other in being red. Socrates, Plato, and Aristotle all resemble each other in a different respect—being round. Despite what the extreme nominalist claims, these different respects of resemblance are not brute facts but, rather, metaphysical phenomena that can be explained by citing a property (redness, roundness) held in common among the resembling entities that constitutes their respect of resemblance. The extreme nominalist simply has no adequate reply to this. Second, the extreme nominalist view of resemblance either collapses into realism or involves a vicious infinite regress. To see this, note that when Socrates, Plato, and a red brick all resemble each other, the extreme nominalist will explain this by saying that they all stand in *the* relation of exact similarity. But if this is so, then the relation of exact similarity will itself become a universal that is repeated in every case where two things exactly resemble each other. Socrates will stand in the same exact similarity relationship to Plato that Plato stands in to the red brick. But this collapses into realism by treating the exact similarity relation as a universal.

To avoid this problem, the extreme nominalist will have to say that each pair of red things stands in its own, individual exact similarity relation. Here, Socrates and Plato stand in their own exact similarity relation to each other (ES1) and so on with Plato and the red brick (ES2) and Socrates and the red brick (ES3). But now a problem arises.

Each of these exact similarity relations itself will exactly resemble each of the other exact similarity relations. How is this to be explained? The extreme nominalist will have to postulate higher exact similarity relations between each pair of lower exact similarity relations. This extreme nominalist strategy can be repeated to infinity, and it generates a vicious regress.

The moderate nominalist has the very same problem. The only difference between the moderate and extreme nominalist is that the moderate nominalist will replace Socrates, Plato, and the red brick with the redness of Socrates, the redness of Plato, and the redness of the brick. But then the redness of Socrates and the redness of Plato will stand in an exact similarity relation (ES1), as will the redness of Socrates and the redness of the brick (ES2) and the redness of the brick and the redness of Plato (ES3), and the problem begins all over again.

In sum, even if the extreme and moderate nominalists leave the exact resemblance among concrete or abstract particulars as basic, unexplainable phenomena, there will still be respects of resemblance that can be specified by citing the property held in common by the resembling entities. Moreover, either the exact similarity relation itself will be a repeatable, relational universal or else there will be a vicious infinite regress of such relations. The exact resemblance among things, therefore, would seem to count in favor of realism.

The third piece of evidence in this debate is the fact that properties themselves have properties:

7. Red is a color.

This says that the first-order property, being red, has a second-order property, being a color. First-order properties are those directly predicated of individuals like Socrates or Plato. Second-order properties are properties of first-order properties. For example, redness and blueness have the second-order property of being a color, but sweetness does not have that second-order property. Properties come in hierarchies. The realist has a straightforward way of explaining sentences like (7):

7'. Redness has coloredness.

The realist challenges the extreme and moderate nominalist to explain sentences like (7).

Many extreme nominalists claim that (7) says the very same thing and therefore can be replaced by (7"):

7". Red things are colored things.

Note that (7") only refers to concrete particulars and makes no reference to properties. But does (7") really say the same thing as (7) and, in general, do reductions of this sort really work? If we can find an example of this type of strategy that fails, the extreme nominalist view will be refuted. Is there such an example? Yes.

8. Red things are spatially extended things.

8'. Red is spatial extension.

The extreme nominalist would be committed to this reductive pattern because, in his view, (8) and (8') say the same thing; (8) makes mention of properties and therefore should be replaced by (8'), which does not. Sentence (8) is true since red things like bricks are extended throughout a region of space. However, (8') is clearly false. Red is a color, not a spatial extension. Being six inches long is an example of the property of extension; being red is not. Thus, the extreme nominalist reduction strategy leads to falsehoods and therefore fails.

The same things can be said of the nominalist reduction strategy. He will handle (7) as follows:

7'''. Reds are colors.

Here the reference is not to concrete but to abstract particulars. However, every red abstract particular is also extended in space (e.g., the particular redness of Socrates is extended throughout Socrates' surface). Thus, the following sentence will be true:

9. Reds are extensions.

The moderate nominalist reductive strategy will then enable us to derive (9') from (9):

9'. Redness is extendedness.

But (9') is clearly false; redness is a color, not an extendedness. It would seem, then, that sentences like (7) in which properties are possessed by other properties cannot be adequately handled by extreme or moderate nominalism, but they can be explained by the realist.

Here's how this helps us when applied to our dialogue above. When the Bible says that God is love, it isn't using "love" as a mere word, nor is it saying that God is the same thing as love. Rather, it is saying that love is a real property, an attribute that God has. And it is a universal property that we can have too, though to a lesser degree. And in different ways to be investigated below, the sentences (1) Moses is human and (2) Moses is 5'7" predicate the properties of the humanness of Moses and of being 5'7" tall. But consider the next sentence: (3) Moses is the teacher of Joshua. How are we to understand *is* in this sentence? To answer this question, we need to look at a new area of metaphysical reflection, the nature of identity.

IDENTITY

How to avoid an identity crisis. Sentence (3) uses *is* in a sense called "the 'is' of identity." Sentence (3) says that Moses is identical to—that is, Moses is the very same thing as—the person who actually was the teacher of Joshua. What exactly is identity? Suppose you wanted to know whether J.P. Moreland is identical to (is the same thing as) Eileen Spiek's youngest son. If "they" are identical, then, in reality, there is only one person: J.P. Moreland who *is* (identical to) Eileen Spiek's youngest son. If they are not identical, then there are two people, not one. Everything is identical to itself and thus shares all properties in common with itself. That's not too heavy, is it? This implies a test for nonidentity: if we can find one thing true of x that is not true of y or vice versa, then x is not identical to y.

Now something may happen to be white or 5'8", but nothing just happens to be the same as itself. Things are stuck with themselves! For all x and y, if x is identical to y, then necessarily, x is identical to y. On the assumption that x and y are the same thing, there is no possible world where that thing which is x is not identical to that thing which is y. For example, a cat may happen to be yellow and twenty pounds, but it does not just happen to be identical to itself. It is necessarily identical to itself. The fact that something is identical to itself is a necessary feature of everything. Suppose that person who is J.P. Moreland and that person who is Eileen Spiek's youngest son are different but both are 5'8". Then, in the actual world, they do not differ in height. However, if it is just possible for them to differ in height—if there is a possible world where one is 5'8" and the other is 6'—then they are not identical. Of course, an individual could grow in size from age five to twenty, or weigh a certain amount on earth and a different amount on the moon. But it would be the identical person who *was* 4' tall and now *is* 5'8", or who *weighed* a certain amount on earth and *now* weighs a different amount on the moon.

The identity relation is a relation that everything has to itself and to nothing else. This relation should be kept distinct from three other notions with which it is sometimes confused: *cause-effect, coextensionality,* and *inseparability*. If A causes B, then A is not identical to *B.* Fire causes smoke as its effect, but smoke is not identical to fire. Further, two things can be coextensional; that is, like Siamese twins they always show up together. But just because two things are coextensional, that doesn't prove they are identical. For example, the property of being triangular is coextensive with the property of being trilateral. One obtains if and only if the other obtains; no object has one without the other. If the two properties were identical, then whatever is true of being triangular would be true of being trilateral, and conversely. But the two properties are not identical, because the property of triangularity has something true of it—namely, being an angle—that is not true of the property of being trilateral.

Finally, two entities can be parts of some whole and be inseparable either from each other or that whole and yet still not be identical. For example, the individual white instance of color in a sugar cube cannot be separated from the individual square instance of shape in that cube and still exist, like the leg and back of a chair can be separated from each other or from the chair taken as a whole. But the instance of whiteness in the cube is an instance of color, and its instance of shape is not; thus, they are not identical. Again, a person's emotions cannot be separated from the person or from the person's beliefs and placed in different locations of the room like the hand and leg of his body can. But one's various emotions and beliefs are all distinct and not identical to other emotions or beliefs.

Speaking of identity. The identity relation itself is independent of language users. The sun would be identical to itself if no language user existed. Nevertheless, we use identity statements to express claims of identity (e.g., "George Bush is identical to the president of the United States"), so it is important briefly to mention them. Here are two different kinds of identity statements:

Meaning identity statements. These occur when the two referring expressions are synonyms: "A bachelor is an unmarried male" and "A motor car is an automobile" are examples.

These can be found in dictionaries. These are examples of analytic truths, those truths in which either the predicate is already contained in the subject ("All red and round objects are red") or the predicate is a synonym for the subject.

Referential or name identity statements. These occur when two proper names (names of individuals like "Tom Jones") or two natural kind terms (terms that name naturally occurring kinds of things like "H_2O" or "the lion") each function merely to tag or refer to its object of reference in every circumstance in which it could exist: "Mt. Everest is Chomolungma" or "water is H_2O" are examples. "Water is H_2O" amounts to the statement, "The stuff out there which is actually water is identical to the stuff out there which is actually H_2O." Referential identity statements are not found in dictionaries. Instead they express necessary truths about the world (see following).

SUBSTANCES, ESSENCES, AND NATURES

The English term *substance* has many different meanings associated with it. Likewise, there have been different uses of the term in the history of philosophy. However, the most central idea of substance in the history of metaphysics, the idea that may be called the *classical view* of substance, is that substances are particulars—individuals—which can have properties (a dog can be brown) and stand in relations (a dog can be larger than a cat) but which themselves are not "had" by anything. Most of the substances, thus understood, which we encounter in day-to-day life are material things, to the point that the common view held by most people takes substance as "stuff," the material *out of which* something is made, rather than as a thing—especially an immaterial or spiritual thing. On the common view, chemical elements are the paradigm cases (the standard, clearest examples) of substances. It is important to realize, however, that the classical view took living organisms—individual human beings, butterflies, dogs, oak trees—as the paradigm of substances. In fact, for centuries, most theologians have held that all persons—human, angelic, and divine—were spiritual substances. As Boethius (ca. AD480–524) said, "A person is an individual substance with a rational nature."[10]

In recent years, belief in substances in general and spiritual substances in particular has fallen on hard times, even among many Christian thinkers. The current rejection of the reality of substances, especially as applied to persons, is usually the result of a significant error about the nature of a substance. Often today a substance is mistakenly taken to be a static, inert entity, incapable of entering into significant relationships. For example, Francis L.K. Hsu opines that the Western, substantial concept of the person is problematic because it pictures personality "as a separate entity distinct

---

[10] Boethius, Against Eutyches and Nestorius 3.

from society and culture. Since personality is seen as a distinct entity, there is an inevitable failure to come to terms with the reality of man."[11] Similarly, several theologians reject the view, long embraced in church history, that God is a substance. But there is nothing in the classical conception of substance that prevents persons (whether human or divine) from being substances even while strongly emphasizing the importance of relationships in our understanding of persons.

In our study of substance, we will have space only to describe different features of the classical view. But since this view has been so important throughout the history of philosophy, getting clear on what it entails is a most worthwhile endeavor, especially since confusions like the one just listed

---

[11] Francis L.K. Hsu, "The Self in Cross-Cultural Perspective," in Culture and Self: Asian and Western Perspectives, ed. A.J. Marsella, G. DeVos, and Francis L.K. Hsu (New York: Tavistock, 1985), 25.

rest on a misunderstanding of the traditional position.

The traditional view of substance. The traditional view of substance is the one held by Aristotle and St. Thomas Aquinas. Consider a particular dog Fido. There are five things apparently true of Fido that form the core of the traditional position.

Ownership of properties. Properties do not show up in the world all by themselves. One does not, for example, find brownness sitting on a bookshelf all by itself. Properties have owners, and a substance is an owner of properties. Substances have properties that are "in" them; properties are had by the substances that possess them. Fido has brownness, a certain shape, the property of weighing twenty-five pounds, and so on. These properties are present in Fido. In this sense substances are more basic than properties. It makes sense to ask of a property, "What has that property?" but it does not make sense to ask of a substance, for example, Fido, "What has that substance?" Properties are in substances, but substances are basic in that they are not in or had by things more basic than they. Substances do the having; properties are had. The etymology of the word *substance* (*sub* means "under," *stance* means "stand," *substance* means "to stand under") brings out this aspect of substance as that which stands under properties as their owner.

Unity and wholeness at a time. A substance like Fido is a whole and, as such, is a unity of properties, parts, and capacities. First, a substance is a unity of properties. Properties come together in groups, not individually; for example, brownness, being twenty-five pounds, and having a certain shape are three different properties that form a unity in Fido. Moreover, the brownness is united to the shape of Fido in a way that the redness of a nearby apple is not. This would be true even if the apple was inside Fido's mouth and, thus, the redness of the apple was spatially closer to parts of Fido (e.g., his nose) than the brownness of his tail. Finally, Fido is a deeper unity of properties than, say, a heap of salt. Such a heap would be a unity of whiteness and the heap's shape. But such a whole, though a true unity of these properties, is not as deep a unity as is Fido. Fido's properties are much more intimately related to each other than are the properties in lesser unities like heaps of parts. All of Fido's properties are united because they all are owned by (or inhere in) the same substance that stands under them.

A substance is also a unity of parts. Fido's nose, eyes, heart, and legs are parts that form a unified whole. The difference between a property and a part is this: a property is a universal that would still exist even if a substance having it were extinguished from being. A different dog could have brownness even if Fido ceased to be. A part is a particular that would not survive if a substance having it were extinguished. If Fido and everything composing him were to "pop out of existence," all of his parts (e.g., his nose) would cease to be.

There are two kinds of parts—*separable* and *inseparable.* Separable parts are parts of a whole that could exist and still be identical to themselves when taken out of that whole. A grain of salt in a saltshaker and a light bulb in a lamp are examples of separable parts. Inseparable parts are those that get their identity from the wholes that contain them and that cannot be separated from those wholes and still exist. The mind, will, and emotional parts of the human soul are different from one another and, in fact, are parts of the human being having them. But they cannot be taken out of the person's soul and placed in different locations like the separable parts (e.g., the four legs) of a table can.

Many of the parts of a living substance seem to be inseparable parts. They are united in such a way that the whole is prior to its parts in this sense: the parts of a substance are what they are in virtue of the role they play in the substance as a whole. Thus, the identity of a substance's parts presupposes the substance as a whole. The chamber of a heart is what it is in virtue of the role it plays in the heart as a whole; a heart is what it is in virtue of the role it plays in the circulatory system; the circulatory system is what it is in virtue of the role it plays in the organism as a whole. Moreover, when the parts of a substance are removed, they change. As Aristotle said, a severed human hand is no longer human because it is no longer a part of the substance that gave it its identity. The severed hand is merely a heap of atoms and other parts that will become evident in a few weeks! It has lost its unity.

Finally, a substance is a unity of capacities (potentialities, dispositions, tendencies). In philosophy we distinguish between some x that is F but can be G from some x that is F but cannot be G. For example, salt is solid but can be dissolved in water, and a diamond is solid but cannot be dissolved in water. *Counterfactual statements* are true of substances. A counterfactual statement is a claim that says what would be the case if, contrary to fact, such and such were to happen. For example, if an acorn were to be put in the soil (even though it is in a jar), then it would sprout. Such counterfactuals are explained by saying that a substance has a set of capacities that are true of it even though they are not actualized.

The salt has the capacity of solubility while in the saltshaker; the acorn has the capacity to sprout while in a jar. A substance is a deep unity of its capacities. Fido has the capacity to bark even while silent, to run, to wag his tail, and so on, and he is a deep unity of his capacities.

Capacities come in natural groupings and in hierarchies. For example, a human has various capacities to believe and think certain things, various capacities to feel certain things, and various capacities to choose certain things. These different capacities form natural groupings in an individual substance (e.g., a particular human being) that can be called intellectual, emotional, and volitional capacities. Psychologists, doctors, biologists, and others study the groupings and interconnections among the capacities of various types of substances (e.g., of birds, of plants).

Capacities also come in hierarchies. There are first-order capacities, second-order capacities to have these first-order capacities, and so on, until ultimate capacities are reached. For example, if Jill can speak English but not Russian, then she has the first-order capacity for English as well as the second-order capacity to have this first-order capacity (which she has already developed). She also has the second-order capacity to have the capacity to speak Russian, but she may lack the first-order capacity to do so.

A substance's capacities culminate in a set of its ultimate capacities that are possessed by it solely in virtue of the substance belonging to its natural kind: for example, Smith's ultimate capacities are his because he has a specific nature—humanness—that explains why he is a member of the *natural kind* "being human." A substance's *nature* includes its ordered structural unity of ultimate capacities. A substance cannot change in its ultimate capacities; that is, it cannot lose its ultimate nature and continue to exist. Smith may change his skin color from exposure to the sun and still exist, but if he loses his humanness, his inner nature of ultimate capacities that constitutes being human, then Smith ceases to exist.[12]

Recall from the preceding section of the chapter that the unity of a natural set of things, say, the set of red objects, is explained by the realist by saying that each member of the set has the very same property in it—in this case, redness. This property explains the unity of the set, why certain objects (a fire truck) belong in the set, and why other objects (a banana) do not.

The same point can be made regarding substances. Substances fall into natural groupings called natural kinds: for example, the class of dogs, class of humans, and so forth. This can be explained by saying that each member of a natural kind has the very same nature in it. All humans have humanness, and that explains the unity of the set of humans, why certain

---

[12] Some content in this section is adapted from J.P. Moreland and Stan Wallace, "Aquinas Versus Locke and Descartes on the Human Person and End-of-Life Ethics," International Philosophical Quarterly 35, no.3 (1995): 319-30.

things (Smith) belong in that set, and why other things (Fido) do not. A nature is also called an *essence.* An essential property is a property such that if a thing loses it, the thing ceases to exist. Being human for Smith and being even for the number two are essential properties. An accidental property is a property such that a thing could lose it and still exist. Being 150 pounds is an accidental property of Smith, and being the number of moons of Mars is an accidental property of two. A thing's essence is the set of all its essential properties. A thing's essence also provides the deepest, most informative answer to the question "What kind of thing is it?" Smith's essence—being human—is the deepest answer to the question "What kind of thing is Smith?" which is deeper than saying that Smith is 150 pounds or an American.

These important points about first- and higher-order capacities and an inner nature have tremendous implications for end-of-life ethical deliberation. To see this, consider this claim by ethicist Robert Wennberg:

When an individual becomes permanently unconscious, the *person* has passed out of existence, even if biological life continues. There cannot be a person where there is neither the capacity for having mental states nor even the potentiality for developing that capacity.[13]

According to Wennberg, taking the life of a permanently unconscious individual with biological life may be permissible because there is no person made in the image of God that is present.

But Wennberg's claims rest on a confusion between first- and higher-order capacities. A fetus or a permanently unconscious individual may not have the first-order capacities of consciousness, but that does not mean they lack the second-order capacity to have this first-order capacity again if certain things happen (normal development for the fetus, medical or

---

[13] Robert Wennberg, Terminal Choices: Euthanasia, Suicide and the Right to Die (Grand Rapids, MI: Eerdmans, 1989), 159.

miraculous healing for the unconscious patient). Indeed, if one is a human person, then part of one's very essence is the possession of higher-order capacities for consciousness regardless of what may be said about how it is with respect to one's first-order capacities.

Identity and absolute sameness through change. A substance is a *continuant* that remains the same through change. Change presupposes sameness. If some *x* (a teenager) goes from being *F* (being blonde) to being *G* (being blue-haired), then the very same *x* (the teen herself) must be present at the beginning, during, and at the end of the change. She changes. In fact, a *change* can be understood as the gaining or losing of a property by a substance at or throughout a period of time. A substance regularly loses old parts, properties, and lower-order capacities and gains new ones. But the substance itself underlies this change and remains the same through it.

A long event like a baseball game has temporal parts and, in fact, is the sum of its temporal parts. A baseball game is a sum or totality of nine innings, and each inning is a temporal part of the game. By contrast, substances do not have temporal parts. Substances move *through* their histories: for example, Fido is fully present at every moment of his life. Fido is not a sum of individual "dog stages" like a baseball game is a sum of "game stages" (innings).

Law and lawlike change. As a substance like an acorn grows, it changes through time. These changes are lawlike. That is, each new stage of development and growth comes to be and replaces older stages in repeatable, nonrandom, lawlike ways. These lawlike changes are grounded in a substance's nature. The acorn changes in specific ways because of the dynamic inherent tendencies latent within its nature as an oak. Each natural kind of thing will have its own type of lawlike changes that are normal for members of that kind, and these changes are grounded in the nature of the substances of that kind.

Moreover, this nature sets limits to change. If a substance breaks these limits, the substance no longer exists. For example, as a caterpillar changes into an adult butterfly, the organism's inner nature specifies the precise sequence of stages the organism can undergo in the process of growth. If the organism goes beyond the boundaries of such a change, say, if the caterpillar turned into a fish, we would not say that the caterpillar still exists as a fish; rather, we would say that the caterpillar ceased to be and a fish came to be. Thus, the lawlike changes that make up a substance's nature (1) specify the ordered sequence of change that will occur in the process of maturation and (2) set limits to the kind of change a thing can undergo and still exist and be counted as an example of its kind.

Final causality. The traditional doctrine of substance contrasts *efficient, material, formal,* and *final causes.* An efficient cause is that *by means of which* an effect takes place. The efficient cause brings about the effect. For example, when one ball hits and moves another, the first ball is an efficient cause. A material cause is that *out of which* something is made, the matter or "stuff" of which something is made (e.g., the statue is made of clay). A formal cause is that *in accordance with which* something is made; it is the blueprint, the archetype, the essence, or whatness of a thing (the blueprint of a house, the humanness of Smith). A final cause is that *for the sake of which* an effect or change is produced (e.g., the water is boiling for the sake of having tea, the eye functions for the sake of aiding one to see). Many advocates of the traditional view hold that an individual substance has, within its nature (formal cause), an innate, immanent tendency (final cause) to realize fully the potentialities within its nature. An acorn changes "in order to" realize a mature oak nature; a fetus grows with the end in view of actualizing its potentialities grounded in human nature. Today the doctrine of final causality is viewed by many to be outdated and unscientific. Instead it is often thought that efficient and material causes are all that is needed to explain a substance's change; for example, explaining an acorn's growth only requires citing the chemical parts and processes in the acorn, together with whatever biological laws supervene on those parts and processes. We cannot evaluate this claim here, but it should be pointed out that the notions of formal and final causes are primarily philosophical, and arguments for and against them are beyond the scope of science.

SUBSTANCES, MEREOLOGICAL AGGREGATES, AND MEREOLOGICAL ESSENTIALISM

According to the standard scientific picture of ordinary objects (e.g., cars, rocks), our bodies and brains are not genuine substances.[14] Rather, they are mereological aggregates. We may define

---

[14] For more on this, see J.P. Moreland, The Soul: How We Know It's Real and Why It Matters (Chicago: Moody Publishers, 2014), 132-37.

a mereological aggregate as a particular whole that is composed by separable parts (a separable part like an electron or table leg is one that can be removed from the whole of which it is a part and still exist and retain its self-identity) and a structure composed of external relation-instances between and among those separable parts. An external relation (such as being-on-top-of that relates a pen and a desk) is such that the items (the pen, the desk) can cease standing in that relation to each other (the pen can move and stand in the to-the-left-of relation to the desk) and still exist. An external relation-instance is a particular example of a kind of relation. For example, two objects that are on top of two tables exhibit two examples of the kind of relation being-on-top-of.

Mereological aggregates are very different from genuine Aristotelian substances. Many philosophers believe that mereological essentialism applies to mereological aggregates. According to mereological essentialism, a whole could not have had other parts than those that compose it. Thus, if a mereological aggregate like the brain gains or loses a single part, it is no longer the same whole.

Why should we believe that ordinary material objects composed of parts do not remain the same through part replacement?[15] To see why this makes sense, let's start with some simple illustrations. Consider five scattered boards, *a–e,* each located in a different person's backyard. Commonsensically, the boards don't seem to form an object. They are just isolated boards. Now, suppose we collected those boards and put them in a pile with the boards touching each other. We would now have, let us suppose, an object called a pile or heap of boards. The heap is a weak object, indeed, and the only thing unifying it would be the spatial relationships between and among *a–e.*

---

[15] For more on problems of material composition, see Michael Rea, ed., Material Constitution: A Reader (Lanham, MD: Rowman & Littlefield, 1996); and Christopher M. Brown, Thomas Aquinas and the Ship of Theseus (London: Continuum, 2005).

They are in close proximity and are touching each other. Now, suppose we took board b away and replaced it with a new board f to form a new heap consisting of a, c–f. Would our new heap be the same as the original heap? Clearly not, because the heap is only the boards and their relationships to each other, and we have new boards and a new set of relationships. What if we increased the number of boards in the heap to one thousand? If we now took one board away and replaced it with a new board, we would still get a new heap. The number of boards does not matter.

Now imagine that we nailed our original boards a–e together into a makeshift raft. In this situation, the boards are rigidly connected such that they do not move relative to each other; instead, they all move together if we pick up our raft. If we now took board b away and replaced it with board f, we would still get a new object. It may seem odd, but if we took board b away and later put it back, we would still have a new raft because the raft is a collection of parts and bonding relationships to each other. Thus, even though the new raft would still have the same parts (*a–e*), there would be new instantiated bonding relationships between *b* and the board or boards to which it is attached, even if those relationships were of the same kind as before board *b* was removed.

Mereological essentialism is a problem for virtually all versions of physicalism because they identify us as mereological aggregates (e.g., brains, bodies), and mereological essentialism cannot be avoided for such wholes. But it seems pretty clear to our immediate awareness of acts like humming a tune that we remain literally the same substantial self throughout the time it takes to hum the tune. As I hum through a tune for, say, sixty seconds, I am simply aware at the thirty-second mark that I am the same self that is now humming as the self who was humming from the one to twenty-nine-second mark, and I correctly anticipate it will be I myself who finishes the tune. But during that sixty-second period, my body and brain are constantly in flux, gaining new and losing old parts.

Strictly speaking, my body or brain is not literally the same through part replacement while I hum the tune, but I am aware of being literally the same self. Thus, my self cannot be my body or brain.

MODALITY: THE NECESSARY, THE POSSIBLE, AND THE ACTUAL

In ordinary conversation we regularly use the terms *possible, impossible,* and *necessary* with no apparent confusion. We have at least a rough idea of what we mean. And in certain contexts we also use the terms *actual* and *contingent,* again with no apparent problem. We have even used them earlier in this chapter without calling attention to them, assuming you will have a fairly good grasp of our meaning. But the notions conveyed by these terms are very important ones in philosophy and deserve to be discussed in more detail. The notions captured by these terms are called *modalities:*

possibility, impossibility, necessity, actuality, and contingency are *modal* concepts.

Modal concepts were discussed as far back as Aristotle, and in the thirteenth century, William of Sherwood developed the concepts further. In the late nineteenth and early twentieth centuries, many philosophers questioned the validity of using modal concepts in doing metaphysics. Some objections were technical, but many stemmed from a general commitment to empiricism: if a thing cannot be observed with the senses, even in principle, then it was not a legitimate concept, at least not in serious philosophy. And the notions captured by modal concepts cannot be observed with the senses. By simply staring at a caterpillar, you cannot tell whether it is possible or impossible for it to become a butterfly. The last fifty years or so, however, have seen a widespread resurgence of interest in and defense of modal concepts. As presently understood, modalities offer a powerful tool to philosophers and theologians.

The usual way of understanding modal notions is in terms of *possible worlds.* Intuitively we all have a sense that the world *could have* gone differently, and if it had, certain things that are now true, or that exist now, might not have been true or might not exist. For example, the proposition "George W. Bush was elected the forty-third president of the United States" is true, but had the vote gone differently in Florida, that proposition would be false. Philosophers say, then, that there is a possible world in which Al Gore won the 2000 US presidential election. But in the *actual world*—that one possible world which is real—Bush was elected.

A possible world, then, is a complete way things could be. A possible world might be very close to the actual world (that world in which everything is the same as the actual world but in which you lost one more hair in the shower this morning) or vastly different from the actual world (that world in which both Richard Nixon and Leonid Brezhnev pushed the missile launch buttons, thereby initiating nuclear war). Possible worlds are not strange science-fiction entities; they are fictional, a heuristic device to assist in analysis and understanding of modal concepts. (However, we should mention that at least one prominent philosopher, David Lewis, takes possible worlds as actually existing, but the bloated ontology of Lewis's system has not proved popular.)

The modal notion of *necessity* can be understood in terms of possible worlds in this way: to say, "Necessarily, 2+3=5" is to say that the proposition "2+3=5" is true in all possible worlds. There is no possible world in which 2+3 ≠ 5. Similarly, *impossibility* applies to a proposition that is true in no possible world (e.g., "It is impossible that a bachelor is married"). *Possibility,* then, applies to a proposition that is true in at least one possible world. A proposition that is true (false) but might have been false (true) had a different possible world been actual (had things been different) is *contingent.* So, "George W. Bush is the forty-third president" is contingently true since there is a possible world in which Gore won the election.

So far we have been illustrating modal notions in terms of the truth or falsehood of propositions. Technically this is called *de dicto* ("of the saying") modality. Modality also applies to the existence or nonexistence of entities that have their properties in certain ways and is called *de re* ("of the thing") modality. *De re* necessity and impossibility apply to an entity in every possible world in which that entity exists. When we speak of essences or natures of something, we are speaking of those properties that the thing necessarily has. For example, assuming that it is essential to gold that it has seventy-nine protons in its nucleus, then "Gold is necessarily that element with atomic number 79" expresses *de re* necessity: in any world in which gold exists, it will have atomic number 79 (but there may be worlds in which gold does not exist). To take another example, think of George W. Bush. It is plausible to claim that he is essentially a person (he could not be a poached egg, for example). In any world in which George W. Bush exists, he necessarily (*de re* necessity) has the property of personhood. But since there are possible worlds in which Gore was elected president, Bush possesses the property of being the forty-third president only contingently.

De dicto and *de re* modalities are not equivalent. Think about the following example. Suppose that George W. Bush, at this minute, is thinking of the number of dwarves in *Snow White*. Since seven is essentially a prime number, the *de re* proposition "The thing George Bush is thinking of is necessarily prime" is true. But the *de dicto* version of the same proposition—"Necessarily, the thing George Bush is thinking of is prime"—is false since Bush could have been thinking of (there are possible worlds in which he is thinking of) the number of states in the union or of poached eggs. So the *de dicto* proposition is only contingently true.

Theologians often employ modal notions in speaking of God's attributes. For example, to say that God's nature is such that he is omniscient, omnipotent, morally good, and so forth is to claim that, of *de re* necessity, God possesses the properties (attributes) of omniscience, omnipotence, and goodness in all possible worlds in which God exists. And to say that God is a necessary being—"Necessarily, God exists"—is to say that the proposition "God exists" is necessarily true *de dicto* in all possible worlds.

In this chapter we have made a lot of claims about what we do and do not know, what is reasonable to believe, and what is unreasonable. But we haven't said anything about what these notions mean. The task of examining these notions falls to the discipline of epistemology, and it is this branch of philosophy that we probe in chapter three.

3

HOW DO I KNOW?

Epistemology

All men by nature desire to know.
ARISTOTLE

The man who tells you truth does not exist is asking you not to believe him. So don't.
ROGER SCRUTON

Once truth has been devoured, people swallow falsehoods whole. Without confidence in the concept of truth, listeners are disarmed against lies.
FELIPE FERNÁNDEZ-ARMESTO

Consider these common questions:
"How do you know?"
"How do you know that?"
"Who knows?"

Surely, if anything is crucial in our day-to-day lives, it is knowledge. We don't trust a plumber who diagnoses our stomachache as appendicitis just because he believes it is, no matter how sincere his belief; we go to a doctor who knows about the appendix. When wondering whether to take an umbrella, we don't rely on a friend's hunch, even if she has good taste in raincoats; we rely on a meteorologist who has good reasons for his prediction. When building a case in court, the prosecutor (ideally) doesn't try to get the jury to feel angry with the defendant; she wants to establish the truth of his guilt.

When it comes to our religious faith, it is no different. Or it should be no different. What should count in matters of faith is knowledge, not merely sincere belief; good reasons for faith, not mere hunches; truth, not feelings. We can rightly say that Christianity is a knowledge tradition, meaning it is more than ritual or emotions. Christianity claims certain things can be known. The issues involved here cluster in the branch of philosophy called *epistemology,* the theory of knowledge.

Our purpose in this chapter is to sort out several of these issues.

Specifically, we will distinguish several different senses of the term *knowledge;* we'll carefully examine the nature of truth; we'll ask what constitutes good reasons (or justification) for our beliefs; and we'll end by thinking about how to answer the skeptic, the person who says we can't know anything.

KINDS OF KNOWLEDGE

We use *knowledge* (and the verb *to know*) in at least three different senses. Briefly, they are (1) propositional knowledge (knowing about facts),[16] (2)

---

[16] We will frequently speak of propositions. A proposition, philosophers say, is an extralinguistic abstract structure representing a state of affairs (a way the world is or could be). A statement is a linguistic representation of a proposition (a type, to use the terminology introduced in chapter two), while a sentence is a particular utterance or inscription (a token) of a statement. Thus, the statements "Snow is white," "La neige est blanche," and "Schnee ist weiss" (or the equivalent sentences, when said or written on a particular occasion) can each convey the very same proposition, representing the

knowledge by acquaintance (knowing something or someone directly), and (3) skill knowledge (know-how).

KINDS OF KNOWLEDGE

Propositional knowledge: Knowing about facts

Knowledge by acquaintance: Knowing something or someone directly

Skill knowledge: Know-how

To illustrate the difference, imagine you are planning a trip to Paris. You might study books and maps, look at pictures, talk to friends who have been there. You might know a lot about Paris. You'd have *propositional knowledge* of Paris. Propositional knowledge can be described as "knowledge that" something is the case, that some facts obtain.

Now let's say you stay in Paris for several months. You explore the city

---

state of affairs of snow's being white. The contents of certain kinds of mental states (beliefs, desires, fears, hopes, etc.) are generally taken to be propositions.

thoroughly, getting a feel for its sights and sounds and rhythms. You discover the best galleries and best markets and learn which restaurants to avoid. Now you know Paris; you don't simply know about the city. This direct sort of knowledge is *knowledge by acquaintance.*

But suppose you have done all this only by walking. You've never taken the Metro. You have propositional knowledge that the Metro exists and know which lines go where. Perhaps you even have some knowledge by acquaintance—you've seen the Metro from time to time. But you've never actually used the Metro. (Say you have an irrational fear of getting on the wrong train.) You don't know how to buy a ticket, how to insert the ticket in the turnstile, or how to operate the lever opening the doors of the cars. Your propositional knowledge and knowledge by acquaintance of the Metro are insufficient. You lack the *skill knowledge,* the know-how, to use the Metro.

Here are some other examples. A history buff may know all about

Abraham Lincoln, and a sports fan may know many facts about last year's batting champion, yet neither person's propositional knowledge constitutes the direct knowledge, knowledge by acquaintance, which Lincoln's wife or the hitter's teammates possessed. And pretty clearly, someone may have the know-how to ride a bike or play pool without having any propositional knowledge about force, inertia, or angular momentum. It is pretty clear that both knowledge by acquaintance and skill knowledge involve some propositional knowledge, which may or may not be consciously held. (If you truly know Paris, then you could easily give directions from the Gare du Nord to the Louvre, if asked, and that would constitute propositional knowledge.) You may know Jane well enough to know she would never do something like *that* (cheat on an exam, say), and only when pressed would you be able to describe what you know about her past behavior patterns, her character, her ethical commitments. But it is just as clear that propositional knowledge is quite different from the other two types.

You may know all about Chopin's piano works and not know how to play the piano. Or you may know just about all there is to know about your favorite film star but go through life disappointed, with no knowledge by acquaintance of her, never having met her in person.

Religious faith arguably involves all three types of knowledge. Eternal life, Jesus said, is knowing God (Jn 17:3). This knowledge by acquaintance is far different from knowledge of facts about the Bible or the details of systematic theology; indeed, it is very possible for someone to know a lot about the Bible and a lot about theology and not know God. But Jesus goes on to say that eternal life is knowing "Jesus Christ, whom you have sent" (Jn 17:3). This certainly involves knowing certain facts about Jesus of Nazareth, about his mission as Savior. Both knowledge by acquaintance and propositional knowledge are involved.

What about skill knowledge? Christianity holds that salvation is not by works, so no skill is involved in becoming a Christian. But to grow in faith would involve learning certain skills: how to study the Bible, how to think Christianly about decision-making, how to share one's faith, how to pray, how to practice spiritual disciplines, and so on.

As we prepare to move deeper into the theory of knowledge, we need to make it clear that philosophers are primarily concerned with the analysis of propositional knowledge. For it is obvious that the vast bulk of what we know, we know by means of propositions and not direct acquaintance or skill. So in what follows, when we refer to *knowledge,* you should understand us to be speaking of propositional knowledge.

WHAT IS KNOWLEDGE?

Most philosophers, today and historically, understand knowledge to be (approximately) *justified true belief.* Or as it is often expressed, K = JTB. We'll look at these elements in reverse order. (And we'll end with the need for the qualification "approximately" when we discuss the so-called Gettier problem below.)

Belief. First, a person can't be said to know something if she doesn't believe it. You ask a friend what time it is. She says, "Well, according to my watch, it's 10:15, but I don't believe it. That can't be right." Now suppose it is 10:15. Does your friend know what time it is? Of course not. Even though her watch is correct, she doesn't believe it. Belief is a condition of knowledge, a necessary (but not sufficient) condition.

What is belief? Two views predominate the literature. The first says a belief is a disposition to behave in a certain way, while the second says a belief is a mental state of a certain sort.

The dispositional view says that to believe p (where p stands for some proposition) means that a person is disposed to behave in a certain way in the relevant circumstances. Thus, to believe that "water quenches my thirst" is to be disposed to drink water when thirsty, or to believe that "the Battle of Hastings was fought in 1066" is to be disposed to answer 1066 when asked when the Battle of Hastings was fought.

But there seem to be good reasons to regard the dispositional analysis of belief as inadequate. For one thing, we all apparently have many beliefs that cannot be analyzed in behavioral terms. To see this, it is important to realize that one of the primary motivations behind the dispositional analysis of belief is the desire to avoid a commitment to minds or mental states and to give such apparently mentalistic terms as *belief* a purely physical analysis. Thus, the behavior in view in the dispositional view must be overt, bodily behavior. But it is easy to imagine asking yourself (while balancing your checkbook, say), *How much is eighty-seven minus thirty-nine?* and answering, *Forty-eight,* all the while never exhibiting the slightest change in bodily behavior. (It should be clear that doing the subtraction mentally involves beliefs.)

For another thing, we frequently invoke beliefs to explain behaviors, but if beliefs were nothing but dispositions to behave, this would be no explanation at all. Your friend, very hot after a tennis game, grabs your water bottle and takes a swig, only to spit it out and exclaim, "Yuck!" She didn't know that (for some strange reason) you had filled your water bottle with clear pickle juice. When another friend asks why she did that, it is not at all interesting to reply, "Because she is disposed to spit out pickle juice," because a meaningful answer would need to explain why she drank pickle juice in the first place. (Was she disposed to drink it?) The real explanation invokes belief: "She was thirsty, and she believed that my bottle held water."

The other view holds that beliefs are a certain sort of mental state. Commonly called the *state-object view,* this theory claims that a belief is an affirming or accepting mental state directed at an object—a proposition.[17]

---

[17] Mental states that are "of" or "about" something else are called intentional states. Intentionality is the "of-ness" or "about-ness" or "directedness" of the mental state. Intentional in this context is different from—but related to—the common use of intention to indicate

So according to this view, when you believe something, you have an affirming or accepting attitude about a particular proposition that represents the way the world could be. If you believe that George W. Bush was elected president in 2000, you accept that the world is such that it contains the fact of Bush's having been elected president in 2000. On this view, beliefs may, but need not, produce a disposition to behave in a certain way.

We should also distinguish between *standing* and *occurrent* beliefs. An occurrent belief is one that is currently before your conscious mind, while a standing belief is one that is necessary to explaining certain behavior but need not be consciously held at the time of the behavior. When driving, you see the traffic light turn yellow and you put your foot on the brake. The occurrent belief that explains the behavior might be something like, "The light will turn red before I get there." But a number of standing beliefs also enter into the

purpose. (Can you see how they are related?)

explanation, such as "Depressing the brake pedal will stop the car," "My brakes are in good working order," "I have a legal and moral obligation to stop for red lights," and so forth. All in all, it is a good thing that we can operate rather well without needing to hold all relevant beliefs as occurrent beliefs; who would have the time or intellectual capacity for all that?

In sum, it is necessary but not sufficient for knowledge of p that we believe p—that we have an affirming or accepting mental attitude toward the proposition p.

Truth. The second requirement for knowledge is that the proposition believed be true. For knowledge cannot be dependent on sincerity, psychological certainty, cultural agreement, or anything other than the truth of the proposition. I once had an argument with a friend that went something like this:

> Joe: Hey, would you like to get tickets for the Yo-Yo Ma concert?
> Garry: Sure, I'd love to hear her play!
> Joe: Her?

Garry: Sure, Yo-Yo Ma, that seventeen-year-old Japanese girl who's the violin prodigy.

Joe: No, Yo-Yo Ma is a guy—a Chinese American cellist.

Garry: No, she's a girl from Japan who plays violin.

And so the debate went until I won. I was very sincere, very certain, and (since we both *thought* I knew more about classical music than Joe), I won. Joe accepted the belief that Yo-Yo Ma was a Japanese girl. He did, that is, until the next day, when he showed me a CD with a picture of Yo-Yo Ma on it—a Chinese American cellist and very clearly a guy. No one would say that I knew. I was sincere, certain, but dead wrong. My belief was false.[18]

So granted that a belief must be true to be known, we must ask, as Pontius Pilate did long ago, "What is

---

[18] I was thinking of Midori, who was indeed a young Japanese female violin prodigy.

truth?"[19] While the concept of truth is, strictly speaking, a metaphysical concept, this seems to be an appropriate place to address the question.

The Christian faith, like other religious faiths, essentially contains claims about reality, which are either true or false. Moreover, competing worldview truth claims often have very different consequences for life. As C.S. Lewis put it,

> We are now getting to the point at which different beliefs about the universe lead to different behavior. Religion involves a series of statements about facts, which must be either true or false. If they are true, one set of conclusions will follow about the right sailing of the human fleet; if they are false, quite a different set.[20]

---

[19] Jn 18:38. Pilate's question was probably asked in a skeptical mood; we're asking it seriously.

[20] C.S. Lewis, Mere Christianity (New York: Macmillan, 1960), 58.

Many today seem to adopt Pilate's skeptical attitude and inveigh against the notion of objective truth.[21] In his consequential book *The Closing of the American Mind,* Alan Bloom bemoans, "There is one thing a professor can be absolutely certain of: almost every student entering the university believes, or says he believes, that truth is relative. The relativity of truth is a moral postulate, the condition of a free society, or so they see it."[22]

Nor are those who eschew objective truth solely among those who profess to be outside the Christian community.

---

[21] While philosophers sometimes draw technical distinctions between absolute and objective, we will use the terms interchangeably. The idea is this: an objective (absolute) truth is one that is true even in true absence of any minds that believe it to be true. It is "made true" by the way the world is, not by what any individual or group thinks about the world.

[22] Alan Bloom, The Closing of the American Mind (New York: Simon & Schuster, 1987), 25.

In a volume on Christian apologetics and postmodernism, Philip D. Kenneson titled his chapter "There's No Such Thing as Objective Truth, and It's a Good Thing, Too."[23]

So what do we mean when we say that a proposition is true? Answers to that question generally reflect three quite different theories of truth. *Metaphysical theories* answer that truth is a property of a proposition, and a proposition is made true by a fact. Something about the way the world is determines the truth of a proposition, so truth is determined by a relation between a proposition and the world. (The theory of truth we shall defend—the classical correspondence theory—is a metaphysical theory.) *Epistemic theories* also answer that truth is a property of a proposition, but they

---

[23] Philip D. Kenneson, "There's No Such Thing as Objective Truth, and It's a Good Thing, Too," in Christian Apologetics in the Postmodern World, ed. Timothy R. Phillips and Dennis L. Ockholm (Downers Grove, IL: InterVarsity Press, 1995), 156-70.

claim that the truth of a proposition (whether the proposition has the property of truth) consists in having the right kind of reasons for asserting or believing the proposition—whether the proposition is justified for us. Note carefully that epistemic theories do not merely state what would be obvious to many—namely, that having the right kinds of reasons provides good grounds for thinking that the proposition is true. (On this nonepistemic view, truth is one thing, reasons are another, and the latter provide the basis for the former.) Rather, according to epistemic theories, the truth of a proposition is its warranted assertability. Thus, truth consists in a relation between a proposition and some criterion in our mind. (Coherence theories of truth, as well as postmodern approaches that make truth relative to a narrative, are all epistemic theories.)

THEORIES OF TRUTH

Metaphysical theories: Truth is a property of a proposition—namely, its correspondence to reality.

> **Epistemic theories:** Truth is a property of a proposition—namely, its warranted assertability.
>
> **Deflationary theories:** Truth is not a property of a proposition; rather, saying a proposition is "true" is either redundant or signals that the proposition is a useful instrument for gaining power, for making accurate predictions, or for some other purpose.

Deflationary theories deny that truth is a property. Certain deflationary theories claim to give a logical analysis that is purported to show that adding the phrase is true to a statement (e.g., "The proposition that grass is green is true") is redundant. Claiming the statement is true does not attribute a real property to the proposition; it merely restates it. Other versions claim that when we say of a proposition, "That's true," we are performing a "speech act"; that is, we are merely endorsing or consenting or agreeing to an assertion. Thus truth is determined by what we want to do with a proposition. (The pragmatic theory of truth turns out to be a deflationary theory, as do those postmodern approaches that identify assertions of truth with attempts to exercise power.)*

[* Some content in this section is adapted from J.P. Moreland and Garrett DeWeese, "The Premature Report of Foundationalism's Demise," in Reclaiming the Center, ed. Millard J. Erickson, Paul Kjoss Helseth, and Justin Taylor (Wheaton, IL: Crossway, 2004), 83-84, 86-87. Used by permission of Crossway, a publishing ministry of Good News Publishers, Wheaton, IL 60187, www.crossway.org.]

How should we decide which kind of theory is correct? Several lines of reasoning lead us to reject epistemic and deflationary theories. To begin with, in rejecting deflationary accounts, we note three things. First, the purported logical analyses of sentences containing *is true* do not do what it is claimed they do: they do not analyze the meaning of *is true* but only analyze the use of the phrase. There is a significant difference, and a theory of truth must first of all give an account of the concept itself, what we mean by *is true*, not merely how we use the concept. Second, all pragmatically oriented theories falter on the recognition that (1) some truths have no pragmatic use (e.g., "There is no largest prime number"); (2) some truths are unknowable to us (e.g., it is either true or false that "The number of protons in the universe is even," but, apart from divine revelation, that is not something any person can ever know); and, what is worse, (3) some falsehoods have pragmatic value (e.g., "I did not have sexual relations with that woman"). Third, it would come as a great surprise to millions of competent language speakers to learn that when they added *is true* to a proposition, they were merely reasserting the original proposition and not making a further claim about the proposition itself. Such a counterintuitive result should not be accepted in the absence of compelling arguments, and the absence of such arguments is notable.

This counterintuitive result also applies to postmodern assertions that claims of truth are merely disguised exercises of power. Now it might sometimes be the case that insisting on the truth of a proposition (or an ideology) is, in fact, an attempt to gain or exercise power. But it does not at all follow that in a frank exchange between persons of good will, a spirited claim, "Yes, it's true!" is in any way a disguised power play. If we reflect honestly on the occasions when we ourselves have claimed truth for one or another proposition, the postmodernist claim seems patently false.

We also reject epistemic accounts of truth because they seem to conflate the issues of (1) knowing (or justifiably believing) that a proposition is true and (2) a proposition's being true. Justification is a very important issue in epistemology and will consume most of the remainder of this chapter. But why should we think that the concept of truth can be equated to the concept of justification? Indeed, many theories of justification are concerned to show that justification is truth-conducive; that is, if we have the right kind of reasons or evidence for holding a belief, then the belief likely is true. Epistemic theories of truth make the truth of a proposition a matter of our having the right kind of reasons for believing it. But that can't be correct: we often have justified false beliefs, beliefs about the world that turn out not to be the case.

Relativism about truth is also unacceptable. Note that relativism amounts to this: a proposition is made true simply by our believing it for the right kind of reasons, where those reasons might include such things as our sincerity, our cultural/linguistic/socioeconomic background, or the beliefs of the majority of those in our cultural community. Or in the case of scientism, the right kind of reasons would be the beliefs of a majority of practicing scientists or the ultimate deliverances of an ideal scientific community. But surely all these reasons can give rise to, sustain, and justify beliefs that turn out not to be the case and so are inadequate accounts of truth.

It seems, then, that a correct theory of truth will be metaphysical. It will explain what the relation is between a proposition and the objective world in virtue of which a proposition is true. Classically, that relation has been taken to be correspondence. In its simplest form, the *correspondence theory* of truth says that a proposition is true just in case (that is, if and only if) it corresponds to reality; that is, what it asserts to be the case is the case.

To be sure, some difficult problems are involved in spelling out exactly how the relation of correspondence works. Fortunately the difficulties that occupy professional epistemologists can be bypassed here. To make sense of the correspondence relation, all that is necessary is that we recognize that propositions represent (that is, that they are of or are about) some state of affairs and that *correspondence* means only that the state of affairs actually is as the proposition represents it to be. So the proposition "Grass is green" is true if and only if it corresponds to—accurately represents—the actual state of affairs of the grass's being green. As Aristotle famously said, "To say of what is that it is, and of what is not that it is not, this is true."[24]

---

24 Aristotle, Metaphysics 4.6.1101b28.

To summarize, for someone to know a proposition it is necessary that the proposition be believed and that it be true. But while necessary, these two conditions are not sufficient for knowledge.

Justification. This brings us to the justification condition for knowledge. Everyone who believes something believes it for a reason. The justification condition requires that the reason must meet a certain standard if the belief is to count as knowledge, even if true. The intuition behind this condition is that even true beliefs must be properly grounded. A person who holds a true belief based purely on a feeling or a hunch or a lucky guess can't be said to know it—feelings, hunches, and guesses are the wrong kind of reasons to ground knowledge. The lottery winner who proclaims, "I knew my lucky numbers would win" certainly knew no such thing (assuming a fair lottery). The quiz show contestant who confidently proclaims, based solely on a feeling or hunch, "C, and that's my final answer" certainly doesn't know the answer, even if it turns out that C is the correct answer after all. Or (to continue an example from above), you ask your friend what time it is. She looks at her watch and confidently replies, "Quarter after ten." Now, let's say she believes that it is 10:15 and, furthermore, that it is true that it's 10:15, and she believes it because her watch, which has always been very reliable, says it's 10:15. But suppose that, unbeknownst to her, her watch stopped at 10:15 last night (she hasn't checked it yet today), so it was simply a matter of luck that her stopped watch showed the correct time. Does she know the correct time (even though she has a true belief)? It surely seems not. For it seems, intuitively, that no one who bases a belief about the time on a stopped watch could ever be said to know the time. Stopped watches can't serve as grounds of justified beliefs about the current time.

One further general point to note about justification is this: justification comes in degrees. Say you ask a friend, "What is twenty-seven times thirteen?" and he immediately answers, "Three hundred fifty-one." You know he's good at math, so your belief that the answer is correct has some justification. But you also might reason like this: *27x10 is 270; 27x3 is, well, 25x3, 75, plus 2x3, 6; so the answer is 270+75+6,* and conclude, *351.* Clearly, having done the math, you have greater justification. And if, in addition, you work out the product on a trustworthy calculator, your degree of justification is even higher.

> ## THEORIES OF JUSTIFICATION
>
> **Foundationalism:** A belief is justified if and only if it is properly basic or is based on a properly basic belief.
>
> **Coherentism:** A belief is justified if and only if it coheres with a person's other justified beliefs.

A true belief must be justified if it is to count as knowledge. The obvious question is, What counts as justification? Two main theories of justification are current among epistemologists: *coherentism* and *foundationalism*. (Each has, of course, a number of subspecies, which for our purposes we will largely ignore.)

Coherentism. Let the term *noetic structure* refer to the ensemble of all of a person's beliefs together with the relations that hold between those beliefs, and between the beliefs and the person. Coherentism as a theory of justification amounts to the claim that a proper noetic structure is one in which all beliefs cohere with—are related to—other beliefs in an acceptable way. (To avoid confusion, you must distinguish between coherentism as a theory of justification and as a theory of truth, discussed in the previous section.) For any belief to be justified, it must cohere with other beliefs that a person is justified in holding.

It is clear that we hold a great many of our beliefs because we hold other beliefs; that is, the reason we believe p is that we believe q and r and s, and we believe that q and r and s entail p. For example, we believe that Jim is either in his apartment or at the library, and we believe he is not in his apartment, so we believe he is at the library. Or we believe that smoking causes lung cancer because we believe that the statistical correlation between smokers and lung cancer victims is far too high to be mere coincidence, or perhaps just because we believe that the surgeon general wouldn't lie about something like that. Or we believe that even though that person at the far table in the restaurant looks just like Jane, it isn't her, because we believe she left for Paris on Saturday, and no one can be in two places at once. These are all examples of beliefs that cohere with other beliefs: they are based on or fit with other beliefs, and they do so in the right kind of way, a way that is logically correct, so that if the other beliefs are true, then so is the new belief.

No doubt coherence is an important feature in a noetic structure. But we believe there are good reasons to doubt that it is an adequate theory of justification. Two questions will bring this out. First, is coherence sufficient to indicate the truth of the beliefs? Second, is coherence the only permissible relation in a proper noetic structure?

Is coherence sufficient to indicate the truth of beliefs in a noetic structure? No. Any well-written novel will contain a coherent system of propositions (or else it just doesn't hang together). But surely no one who believes all propositions contained in a good novel will believe truth, no matter how coherent his beliefs. In fact, theoretically, there is an infinite number of fully coherent belief systems, only one of which corresponds to—accurately represents—reality. So coherence alone is insufficient to indicate truth.

Is coherence the only permissible relation in a proper noetic structure? Again, the answer is no. But to explain the negative answer, we need to look more closely at the notion of coherence. All agree that coherence involves at least logical consistency. That is, a set of beliefs does not cohere if two (or more) of them are contrary or contradictory. Beyond that, there are a number of ways to understand the coherence requirement. One way would be that if a belief coheres with a set of previously accepted beliefs, then that positive coherence confers justification.

Yet if a belief fails to cohere with an accepted set, then that negative coherence results in the belief being unjustified. (Think about the significant differences between these positions.)

Then there is the view that coherence is linear; that is, all the beliefs in a coherent set could be lined up in a chain with each belief being supported by one (or perhaps a very few) other belief(s). Such a system will be circular since every belief must be supported by another belief, but such circularity might not be a problem, provided the circle is large enough. Conversely, coherence could be holistic, in which each belief is supported by all (or perhaps a very great number) of other beliefs, so that the result is not a circular chain but a crosshatched web of mutually supporting beliefs. There is something right about linear and holistic coherentism; indeed, we think both notions play a role in justification, and we'll return to these ideas below. For now, our concern is with whether coherentism is the correct overall theory of justification.

Whether positive or negative, linear or holistic, coherentism requires beliefs to be justified by their relation to other beliefs. But it certainly seems that we hold a number of beliefs—and regard them as justified—which do not depend on other beliefs. When you step outside and see a high-contrast pattern of light and shadow and feel warmth on one side of your face, you simply believe the sun is shining. It would be far-fetched in the extreme to say you infer that the sun is shining, but even if you did infer that conclusion, it seems you would infer it from your sensory experiences and not from other beliefs. If you get a headache while studying for a test, you simply believe your head hurts; you do not infer that from other beliefs. In fact, if all beliefs had to be based solely on other beliefs, it is hard to see how we could ever let in the deliverances of sensory experiences, of memory, of introspective awareness, or of rational intuition, to mention just a few of the main sources of beliefs. Just think about the beliefs you now hold: a good number of them are not, after all, based on other beliefs but are based on nondoxastic (that is, nonbelief) evidence. So if coherentism is true, then none of those beliefs can be justified. But clearly that is not the case, so coherentism must be false.

Foundationalism. Rejecting the image of circles or webs of justification, foundationalism holds that a properly constructed noetic structure has a foundation. That is, while some beliefs can be based on other beliefs, ultimately the chain comes to rest in a belief that is not based on other beliefs but is based on some nondoxastic grounds. Foundationalism is a family of theories about what kind of grounds confer justification, and all versions hold the following theses:

1. A proper noetic structure is foundational, composed of properly basic beliefs and nonbasic beliefs, where nonbasic beliefs are based either directly or indirectly on properly basic beliefs, and properly basic beliefs are not based on other beliefs.
2. A properly basic belief is a belief that meets some condition *C* (where the choice of *C* marks

different versions of foundationalism).²⁵

There are two main varieties of foundationalism. Classical foundationalism holds that condition *C* is indubitability: the ground of the belief must guarantee the truth of the belief. (Cartesianism, the epistemological project of René Descartes and his followers, is the paradigm example.)

Modest foundationalism holds that condition *C* is something weaker than indubitability: the ground of the belief must be truth-conducive. (Further restrictions on condition *C* will mark the difference between different versions of modest foundationalism.)

It is recognized in nearly all quarters that classical foundationalism is too ambitious: even granted that there are

---

[25] A third condition is that the basing relation, which confers justification, is irreflexive and asymmetrical. This rather technical condition ensures that the foundational noetic structure is not circular. We do not discuss this condition in the chapter, assuming that our criticisms of coherentism suffice.

some indubitable beliefs, there simply aren't enough of them to ground our entire noetic structure. Further, it certainly seems that some beliefs that are not indubitable are properly basic. And more, classical foundationalism is motivated largely by the belief that certainty is a necessary condition of knowledge or that one must know that one knows in order to have knowledge. But these conditions are either too strict or lead to an infinite regress.

However, recognition of the failure of classical foundationalism has led too many thinkers to assume that no form of foundationalism can succeed. For some the dismissal of modest foundationalism along with its classical cousin is motivated by a prior commitment to a different theory of justification (such as coherentism), to a postmodern view of truth, or to some other theoretical commitment. But for others, we suspect, the dismissal is due more to a suspicion that a reasonable account of properly basic belief cannot be given—that is, that condition *C* cannot be successfully cashed out. We would claim that, while the details are beyond the scope of this book, it is quite possible to give a satisfactory account of condition *C*. To see the way this might work, we need to explore the notion of grounds in greater detail.

We can say that the ground of a belief is an indicator of the truth of a belief, that the right kind of ground provides justification for a belief. Thus, the ground should be understood as epistemic rather than causal or pragmatic: the ground of a belief confers justification if it makes it probable that the belief is true, not if it causes a belief or if it shows the belief is useful in some way.

In this discussion let us stipulate our use of two familiar terms to differentiate two kinds of grounds. We'll use *evidence* to refer to nondoxastic grounds and *reasons* to refer to doxastic grounds. This seems a natural usage since in ordinary language *evidence* generally connotes something physical or otherwise external to an investigator, which is indicative of something else, whereas *reason* connotes some kind of inferential notion that is internal to the investigator's cognition. So we'll say that properly basic beliefs have evidence as their grounds and nonbasic beliefs have reasons as theirs.

In the case of nonbasic beliefs, the relation of reasons to nonbasic beliefs is relatively straightforward. Inference from a (possibly) true belief provides reasons for another belief, and if the former belief is justified and the inference is valid, then the latter belief is also justified. In essence this would amount to linear coherentism. But we could also regard a belief as justified because it "fits" well with a number of other justified beliefs, in the model of holistic coherentism, if at least one of those other beliefs is a basic belief.

The nature of evidence, however, and its relation to properly basic beliefs are more complicated. To get at this issue, let's begin by identifying particular cases that we would regard as being cases of properly basic beliefs (and remember, a basic belief is one that is not grounded on other beliefs). We could begin with those beliefs that are indubitable—which cannot rationally be doubted. Such beliefs fall into three classes: (1) self-evident, (2) incorrigible, or (3) evident to the senses. Self-evident beliefs are those that, on inspection, we see cannot be false. This class would include simple propositions of mathematics (e.g., 3+4=7) and logic (e.g., *modus ponens:* "If *p,* then *q;p;* therefore *q*"). Merely to understand such propositions is to see that they could not be false. (2) Incorrigible beliefs (like incorrigible teens) cannot be corrected. Introspective awareness of one's own mental states is generally regarded as incorrigible. If you tell me you are in pain, I can't correct you about that. I can't say, "No, you're wrong. You're mistaking being tickled for being in pain." Only you can say if you are in pain. Of course, you might be mistaken about the cause or location of your pain—think of the amputee's phantom limb pain—but you cannot be mistaken about the fact that you are in pain. (3) Beliefs about perceptual experience are also, and a bit more controversially, regarded as indubitable. But we need to be careful here, for the claim is not that you are actually seeing (hearing, touching) something. The claim is that a belief about a perceptual experience itself cannot be wrong, not that a belief about what is being perceived is actually as it is perceived to be. So my belief that "I am having a visual experience of a red-rose-shaped blotch in my visual field" cannot be wrong, although the derivative belief that "I am seeing a red rose" might be. (Of course, we almost never form beliefs of the first type; we almost always directly form the second type of belief. But the point here is that the first type of belief is indubitable.)

The three classes of indubitable beliefs are basic in that they are grounded not on other beliefs but directly on nondoxastic evidence. To say they are properly basic is to say they are justified beliefs, that they are grounded in the right way on the right kind of evidence. These three classes of indubitable beliefs are the same foundational beliefs accepted by classical foundationalism. But as we noted above, there are good reasons to accept modest foundationalism. That would mean broadening the foundation of the noetic structure, accepting into the foundation beliefs that are not indubitable—that is, which are defeasible (meaning it is possible that they could be defeated—shown possibly to be false). How can we characterize the nature of evidence and its relation to beliefs that are not indubitable, evidence that is truth-conducive in such a way as to confer justification on the beliefs?

Again, the way to approach the question is by looking at particular cases. Take memory, for example. Memories themselves, whatever they may be, are not beliefs; they ground memory beliefs. But memory beliefs are defeasible. In general, the more distant the event remembered, the more insignificant it was; and the less "normal" our mental state at the time (e.g., if we were tired, drunk, depressed), the less trustworthy our memory. Nevertheless, we surely are justified in taking some memory beliefs as properly basic. I clearly remember eating cereal for breakfast. I don't infer this from beliefs about an empty cereal box on the kitchen counter or about a distinctive aftertaste (although, perhaps, I could form my belief that way). No, I just remember, quite clearly, having cereal for breakfast this morning.

Similarly, I clearly remember being married thirty-six years ago. I don't infer this from the belief that the ring on my finger or the picture on the wall must mean I am married. My belief, based directly on memory and not inferred from something else, clearly is justified.

Again, I don't infer (most) perceptual beliefs from other beliefs. I don't, for example, infer the belief that there is a rose in the garden from the belief that I'm seeing a rose, which in turn I infer from beliefs about my perceptual experience (that I'm being appeared to red-rose-ly). I just believe there's a rose there because I see a rose (or, more precisely, because I'm having the perceptual experience of seeing a rose). Of course, some perceptual beliefs are false, so perceptual beliefs are not indefeasible. But with time and some skill developed from trial and error, we can weed out most of our false perceptual beliefs. We see what looks like water on the road, but know we're driving across the Mojave on I-15, so it's very probable that it's a mirage. We hear a voice that sounds like Jane's, but we don't form the belief that it's her, because we know she's in Paris.

Since memory and perception are the right kinds of evidence to ground memory beliefs and perceptual beliefs, respectively, such beliefs are properly basic, according to modest foundationalism. To generalize, if it can be shown that there are kinds of evidence that (nondoxastically) ground certain kinds of beliefs in a way that assures the likelihood of the truth of those beliefs, then those beliefs will be properly basic beliefs for the modest foundationalist. That is, condition *C* is met in those cases where it can be shown that a certain kind of evidence is conducive to forming (mostly) true beliefs. (To spell this out in more detail would take us much deeper into epistemological theory than we can go here. For those who still have doubts about the viability of modest foundationalism, we'll simply note that in recent years the number of professional philosophers who hold to foundationalism has been growing, aided by the defection of some very respected epistemologists from the coherentist camp to foundationalism.)

Internalism, externalism, and Reformed epistemology. Epistemologists debate among themselves over whether, and to what degree, someone must be aware of the reasons that justify her belief. Some hold that as long as the chain from evidence to Lisa's belief is reliable, her belief is justified; it doesn't matter whether Lisa is aware of the reliability of the chain. Since the factors relevant to justifying her belief are external to Lisa, this position is called *externalism*. Others hold that, at least to some extent, Lisa must be aware of the factors that justify her belief, or, at least in principle, she must be able to become aware of them. Since in this case the factors relevant to justification are or can be internal to Lisa's cognitive process, this position is *internalism*.

We cannot enter into the debate between internalists and externalists; the issues are beyond the scope of this book. But we must make the following observation. Suppose Lisa is faced with an inescapable life-or-death decision.

Suppose further that through some process unknown to us, a process that is in fact reliable and that we would recognize as reliable if we knew of and understood it, Lisa forms a belief that a certain course of action is the correct one in this situation. But suppose also that Lisa understands she cannot give any reasons that justify her belief and that she may even be aware of some reasons which would count against its truth. Now surely it is not rational to act (especially in a life-or-death situation) on a belief that you have no reason to think is true and even have reasons to think is probably false. But if externalism is correct, then either epistemic justification must be divorced from rational decision-making or some completely novel account of rationality must be given that would make Lisa's decision to act on her belief rational after all. This seems to us to be a very tall order to fill and suggests that the internalist account is most likely correct.

In recent years the respected Christian philosopher Alvin Plantinga has popularized the distinction between *justification* and *warrant.* For Plantinga, warrant is an externalist notion, while justification is an internalist notion. For the externalist (such as Plantinga), Lisa's belief will have warrant if (roughly) the entire belief-forming process is functioning properly, whether Lisa is aware of that process or not.[26] For the internalist, Lisa must be aware (or be able to become aware) that the belief is based on reasons or evidence which make it probable that it is true, if it is justified for her. Since Plantinga and a few colleagues active in formulating and defending the externalist conception of warrant are Calvinists, their position has become widely known as *Reformed epistemology*.

Reformed epistemology has brought an interesting position into contemporary epistemology. But it is often misunderstood. The Reformed

---

[26] Alvin Plantinga's full specification is that a belief has warrant if it is produced by a belief-forming faculty functioning properly in a congenial epistemic environment according to a design plan successfully aimed at truth.

epistemologist is not, as he is sometimes characterized, advocating fideism (believing with no reasons or in spite of defeaters for the belief). Rather, the Reformed epistemologist believes it is not necessary for a person to have direct, first-person access (even in principle) to the reasons that confer warrant on her position.

As we said, we don't propose to enter the debate about Reformed epistemology or about internalism and externalism in general. But we will note what seems to us to be an important point. The difference between internalism and externalism, justification and warrant, has led to a distinction in Christian apologetics between Reformed epistemology and evidential apologetics. As usually characterized, a Reformed apologist believes Christian belief is warranted even if the Christian cannot give any reasons for holding his belief. (Indeed, the Reformed epistemologists argue that belief in God is properly basic.)

By contrast, the evidentialist apologist believes a Christian can be aware of good reasons that justify his belief. It is not clear that these positions are so very different, and we think the distinction is often overstated. We would agree that a youngster growing up in a Christian home and regularly attending Sunday school, church, and maybe even a Christian school might simply find herself believing in Jesus as her Savior. Perhaps she comes to faith based on an innate inner sense of God (Rom 1:18-20, what Plantinga, following John Calvin, called the *sensus divinitatis*).

In either case, she might not be aware of why her belief is justified. But the internalist might maintain that in principle she could become aware, and that is all the internalist requires for justification. Similarly, the Reformed apologist would agree that when that girl enters college, encounters significant intellectual objections to the Christian faith, meets sincere practitioners of other religions, and studies arguments for and against the existence of God in her philosophy of religion class, she might have sufficient defeaters to seriously weaken her previously warranted belief. Now she can study the objections and rebuttals to the objections by Christian philosophers. She can read Christian apologetics and learn of the many lines of evidence supporting Christian faith and so—by becoming aware of the evidence that grounds her belief—reacquire justification for her belief. In other words, the Reformed apologist, as an externalist, does not deny that a person can, and in some cases should, be aware of the evidence grounding her belief.

Virtue epistemology. In recent years a position has emerged in epistemology that actually reaches back to Aristotle and St. Thomas Aquinas for inspiration. Known as *virtue epistemology,* the view holds that having knowledge, or justification, depends on exercising the proper intellectual virtues.

The basic idea of virtue epistemology is that if a person faithfully employs certain intellectual virtues, the noetic structure so constructed will be proper; that is, it will contain (mostly) true beliefs. The intellectual virtues are dispositions such as open-mindedness, honesty, curiosity, courage, humility, fairness, carefulness, and sound judgment. Aristotle believed that a person exercising such virtues would discover the truth. Aquinas added the insight that the intellectual and moral virtues form a seamless whole (can someone really be intellectually courageous without being morally courageous, intellectually fair without being morally fair, etc.?) so that both intellectual and moral virtue is needed to arrive at truth.

It is not entirely clear whether virtue epistemology is best regarded as a theory of knowledge (that is, a replacement for the standard K = JTB analysis of knowledge), or as a theory of justification (that is, an explanation of what constitutes having the right kind of reasons for holding a belief), or as something else. As Christians we applaud the emphasis on virtue—especially Aquinas's emphasis on the unity of the virtues—and believe that teaching critical thinking apart from considerations of moral and intellectual virtues will be defective. But we tend to think that virtue epistemology is best taken as describing certain dispositions, certain habits of thought and behavior, the possession of which puts a person in a good position to form true beliefs. It describes constraints on the character and methodology of the person who is searching for truth, not on an alternative theory of justification or knowledge.

The Gettier problem. At the beginning of our discussion we noted that knowledge was "approximately" justified true belief. The time has come to explain the need for the qualification. In 1963 Edmund Gettier published a very short paper in which he showed that it was possible for a person to have a justified true belief that really shouldn't be counted as knowledge. Gettier posed two problem cases, which went something like this:

1. Two men, Smith and Jones, are applying for the same job. The company president told Smith that Jones would get the job. Further, just a few minutes ago, Smith gave Jones two quarters, which he saw Jones put in his pocket (suppose he was repaying Jones for the soda he had bought for Smith). So Smith has very good reasons to believe

A: the person who will get the job has two quarters in his pocket. Now, surprisingly, at the last minute the president decides to give the job to Smith, the two quarters fall through a hole in Jones's pocket, and Smith actually has two quarters in his other pocket that he had forgotten about. So as it turns out, *A* is true. But intuitively, Smith has true, justified belief that *A* shouldn't be counted as knowledge. Something has gone wrong.

2. Sam and Sallie are coworkers. Sallie has often heard Sam brag about the Jaguar he owns and describe the fun he has in his Jaguar owners' club. She has seen him arrive at work and depart in a Jaguar and has occasionally accepted a ride to lunch from Sam in his Jaguar. So, naturally, Sallie forms the belief *B:* one of her coworkers owns a Jag. Now it happens that Sam is overly image-conscious. He doesn't own a Jag after all, but leases one. However, Sean, a very modest coworker of Sallie and Sam, does own a Jag, but he never talks about it or drives it to work. So Sallie's belief that *B* is justified and true, but again, something seems to

have gone wrong. Her justified true belief can't be knowledge.

The problems Gettier raised, and many like them that have surfaced since, are admittedly rather artificial. But the nature of thought experiments is such that they often do seem artificial. Yet if they succeed in raising a possible counterexample to an analysis, then they show the analysis to be flawed. And the Gettier-style problems do indeed seem to raise possible counterexamples to the K = JTB analysis. In the fifty-plus years since Gettier's paper was published, a number of strategies have been suggested to try to patch up the analysis. They range from dismissing the problem as ill-conceived, to placing restrictions on what counts as justification, to adding a fourth condition to the analysis (K = JTB+?), to jettisoning the traditional analysis altogether. No consensus has been reached among epistemologists, so we won't propose to solve the problem here. But the absence of a general solution, which takes care of all versions of the Gettier problem, does not, in our view, undermine our initial claim, which was that knowledge is (approximately) justified true belief. And if we are careful to develop our own critical thinking skills along with intellectual (and moral) virtues, we can be confident that we'll largely avoid Gettier-style traps.

THE PROBLEM OF SKEPTICISM

The skeptic is someone who challenges certain or all knowledge claims. Chances are we have all met what we might call the naive skeptic. He claims to know that you can't know anything. Of course, if he were correct, then he couldn't know that, so this naive form of skepticism is self-defeating. Even when this is pointed out to him, the naive skeptic often dogmatically maintains his position. We have found from experience that if he is holding to his skepticism as an act of intellectual rebellion or from an ideological commitment to academic anarchy (such people are often college undergraduate students), there is not much point in arguing with him. ("Do not answer a fool according to his folly," Prov 26:4.) If, however, he is willing to engage in serious discussion, we'll ask him for reasons why he believes it is true that no one can know anything. Depending on his answer to this line of questioning, he will fall into one or the other of the two remaining varieties of skepticism.

A more sophisticated form of naive skepticism, *academic skepticism*, also holds that there can be no knowledge but offers reasons for this belief. (Academic skepticism takes its name from the development of Plato's Academy several centuries after his death. It was this form of skepticism that St. Augustine targeted in his book *Contra academicos.*) Often the reasons hang on the claim that certainty is required for knowledge but is impossible to attain. Sometimes appeal is made to humility, pointing out that in the face of so much widespread disagreement about so many things, any claim to know must be grounded in arrogance. It seems that the academic skeptic is working with a different conception of knowledge than the one we have developed. The academic skeptic's view of knowledge flies in the face of common sense as well as reasonable philosophical analysis of the concept of knowledge.

The most serious form of skepticism is what we'll call *justification skepticism.* A skeptic of this variety agrees with the K = JTB analysis but claims that the justification condition can never be met; or, perhaps more judiciously, the justification condition cannot be met for certain very important kinds of knowledge claims; or, more cautiously still, we cannot know that the justification condition has been met for certain kinds of knowledge claims. Perhaps this skeptic will allow that, for example, I can know that I exist, that I am in pain, or that 7+5=12. But I cannot know, because I cannot have adequate reasons for believing, that grass is green, that there is a table in the next room, or even that the external world exists at all.

We will admit that justification skepticism can pose very difficult and subtle problems that demand quite sophisticated responses. But—and this is a very important point—it is crucial to get things in the right order here. If we begin with skeptical arguments, we might never get beyond them. One way to think about this is a version of what has been called *the problem of the criterion*. We can distinguish two different questions relevant to the human quest for knowledge. First, we can ask, "What is it that we know?" This is a question about the specific items of knowledge we possess and about the extent or limits of our knowledge. Second, we can ask, "How do we decide in any given case whether we have knowledge in that case? What are the criteria for knowledge?" This is a question about our criteria for knowledge.

Suppose we wish to sort all of our beliefs into two groups—the true or justified ones and the false or unjustified ones—in order to retain the former and dispose of the latter in our entire set of beliefs. Such a sorting would allow us to improve our rational situation and grow in knowledge and justified belief. But now a problem arises regarding how we are able to proceed in this sorting activity. It would seem that we would need an answer to at least one of our two questions above in order to proceed. But before we can have an answer to our first question about the extent of our knowledge, we would seem to need an answer to our second question about our criteria for knowledge. Yet before we can have an answer to the second question, we seem to require an answer to our first question. This is the problem of the criterion.[27] If we don't know how we know things, how can we know anything at all or draw limits to human knowledge? But if we don't know some things before we ask ourselves how we can have knowledge in the first place, on what basis will we answer that question?

---

[27] See Roderick Chisholm, The Problem of the Criterion (Milwaukee, WI: Marquette University Press, 1973); and Robert P. Amico, The Problem of the Criterion (Lanham, MD: Rowman & Littlefield, 1993).

It seems we are trapped in a vicious circle here. The skeptic concludes there is no good solution to the problem and, thus, there is no knowledge. But two positive alternative solutions are available to us.

The *methodist* (no relation to the Protestant denomination) tries to discover a method, a procedure, by which to supply or demonstrate or test the justification of knowledge claims; this approach has been advocated by such notable philosophers as René Descartes and John Locke. The *particularist* begins from the conviction that we do have some beliefs that constitute knowledge and looks for the kind of justification that can be offered for those knowledge claims; advocates of this approach include Thomas Reid, G.E. Moore, and Roderick Chisholm. Another way to put this is to say that the methodist takes a third-person perspective on knowledge, while the particularist takes a first-person perspective.

There is great value in the methodist approach when we consider questions such as what kind of investigation, what kind of experiments or observations or statistical samplings, and what patterns of inference are most likely to get to the truth of certain matters. (This kind of investigation is often carried out under the rubric of "the philosophy of x," where x would be, e.g., science or education or history. And note: this is indeed philosophy, for science, education, and history in themselves cannot offer this detached, third-person perspective on their own methods.)

However, it seems clear that the methodist approach is not the way to begin in epistemology. Simply put, methodism leads to an infinite regress: we will need a criterion for our method, but that will demand another criterion, and so on, ad infinitum. We need instead to ask the first-person question. According to particularists, we start by investigating specific, clear items of knowledge: that I had eggs for breakfast this morning, that there is a tree before me (or, perhaps, that I seem to see a tree), that 7+5=12, that mercy is a virtue, and so on. I can know some things directly and simply without having to have criteria for how

I know them and without having to know how or even that I know them. We know many things without being able to prove that we know them or without fully understanding them. We simply identify clear instances of knowing without having to possess or apply any criteria for knowledge. We may reflect on these instances and go on to develop criteria for knowledge—conditions of justification—consistent with them, and then use these criteria to make judgments in borderline cases of knowledge. But the criteria are justified by their congruence with specific instances of knowledge, not the other way around.[28]

In general we start with clear instances of knowledge, formulate criteria based on those clear instances, and extend our knowledge by using those criteria in borderline, unclear cases. Given that we surely seem to have knowledge, what reasons do we have that the beliefs in question are

---

[28] See also J.P. Moreland, Love Your God with All Your Mind, rev. ed. (Colorado Springs, CO: NavPress, 2012).

true? How is it that those reasons provide adequate justification to counter the skeptic's challenge? For us, the answer to that question takes us right back to the foundationalist epistemology described above.

As Christians we have even more reason to be skeptical of the skeptic's claims. For over and over in Scripture we are told that we can know things (the word *know* in its various forms occurs over 1,300 times in the Old and New Testaments). What seems obvious to us is that even if we can give no knock-out argument against the skeptic, we can offer an epistemology that is eminently reasonable and indeed much more plausible than the skeptic's claim that we cannot know.

THE EPISTEMOLOGY OF PEER DISAGREEMENT

In recent years, a new branch of epistemology has come into focus: the epistemology of peer disagreement.[29]

---

[29] For additional reflections on peer disagreement, see J.P. Moreland and

What do the demands of rationality require one to do when faced with an epistemic peer—roughly, a cognitive, educational equal who is equally competent as you and familiar with the same evidence—who disagrees with your conclusions? There are different viewpoints about the right way to approach such situations, but two have risen to prominence—the *conformist* and the *steadfast* views.

The conformist/conciliatory/equal-weight view. According to this position, peer disagreement has enormous epistemic significance. For example, it is plausible to think that equally trained, competent philosophers disagree about the existence of God. Unless one has a reason independent of the peer disagreement itself to prefer one's own view (say the theist philosopher has the evidence of powerful, personal experience of God and answers to

---

William Lane Craig, Philosophical Foundations for a Christian Worldview, 2nd ed. (Downers Grove, IL: Inter Varsity Press, 2017), 90-93.

prayer that the atheist lacks and, moreover, fails to weigh properly since he or she has never had such an experience before), one of two things follow. Either the person cannot rationally hold to P if the peer believes $\sim P$ (so one must withhold belief about P) or, alternatively, the two peers must split the difference to take into account not only their different views but the different degrees of certainty they have. So, if one is 80%/20% certain that P and the other peer is 30%/70% that P (i.e., 70% certain that $\sim P$), they each should adjust and be 55%/45% certain that P. In either case, equal weight should be given to each peer, and they cannot have a *rational* disagreement with each other.

Several arguments have been proffered for the conformist view, but we present three important ones here. First, if one disagrees with an expert on another field for which one is not an expert, then one should lower one's epistemic certainty. However, in principle, there is no difference between this case and disagreeing with a peer in one's own field, and, for consistency's sake, when this happens, one ought to adjust one's view as stipulated by the conformist position.

In many cases, this does seem to be a reasonable approach to disagreement with an expert in another field. But there are two exceptions. For one thing, if one can find sociological, spiritual, or ethical reasons for why the expert holds his view, or if one can find evidence that it is to the expert's advantage (e.g., financially, for promotion) to hold the view, then one can be reasonable in taking the expert to hold his view on irrelevant bases besides those that qualify him as an expert. Furthermore, Thomas Kuhn noted years ago that it is often new scientists to a field, or even those completely outside the field, who have the necessary sort of sociological, epistemic distance to look at an issue from a different angle and identify problems and solutions that are hard to see for those who have been living with an internalized perspective held by the majority of practitioners in that field. In this case, it may actually be a disadvantage to be such an expert, and the non-expert may have reasons for his view that the expert has not considered or taken seriously.

Second, that fact of peer disagreement presents second-order evidence that defeats the strength of first-order evidence. Thus, the conformist view seems to take account of the second-order evidence better than the steadfast view. In response, some argue that the presence of second-order evidence of peer disagreement relates to both peers equally and thus cancels out and warrants refocusing on the first-order issues. Also, the second-order evidence of disagreement does not require two disagreeing peers to withhold belief about their topic of disagreement. Rather, it simply introduces another layer for argumentation. Thus, while disputants should continue to formulate new arguments about and rededicate themselves to treating fairly the first-order issues, they should also see if they can find evidence to support the claim that the peers on the other side are not dealing with the evidence fairly. More on this below.

Third, it has been argued that the *uniqueness thesis* supports the conformist view. This thesis states that for a given body of evidence and given propositions in dispute, there is at most one level of rational confidence that is warranted by the evidence, even though there is a dispute as to who has achieved that level of rationality, and I have no reason to think that I'm not the one who has responded improperly to the evidence. As we will see below, that actual situation may be that I have reason to think that it is I, not my epistemic peer, who has treated the evidence properly.

Besides arguments for the conformist view, three arguments have been raised against it. If successful, they also count in favor of the steadfast view. First, the position seems to be self-refuting in this way. Conformists say that when epistemic peers disagree about P, then both sides ought to withhold belief regarding P. But, of course, epistemic peers disagree over the principle of disagreement itself along with what should be taken to follow from it. So we should withhold our belief in the alleged implications of the principle as stated by the conformist view. Some respond that the conformist dictate of revision of belief holds for all areas of peer disagreement except for the principle of disagreement itself. But this seems to be a highly question-begging claim for which evidential support is scant, to say the least.

Second, some claim that it is hard to establish that two people are, in fact, epistemic peers. Perhaps one disputant has a weaker education than the other, does not care about the issue as much, has not read as widely on the topic, and so on. In principle, this does seem to be true. But it's not clear what follows from it. If one disagrees with what appears to be an epistemic peer or even with someone who is very close to being an epistemic peer, this would seem to be all that the conformist view needs to justify its approach.

Third, if one can make a good case that one's epistemic peer has not dealt fairly and honestly with the evidence, has not approached the topic while exhibiting epistemic virtues, and does not really hunger to know the truth of the matter, then one can disregard the impact of the peer's view since it is not based on his being an expert or a peer. Failure of the unbeliever to deal honestly with the evidence often happens the closer the topic of dispute approaches moral or spiritual teachings at the center of Christianity. Christianity teaches that fallen humans often do not approach ethical or theological topics with an honest hunger to find and obey the truth. As atheistic philosopher Thomas Nagel admitted, the *cosmic authority problem*—not wanting there to be a God, not wanting to live in a universe where God has the authority to tell us what to do—has strongly influenced his own atheism and the treatment of the evidence for theism, and he suspects that this problem is a widespread factor affecting many atheists. Moreover, if the sociology of a field of study is such that conformity to the main paradigm accepted in that field provides respect, acceptance, prestige, and connection with others in the field, this second-order evidence is fair game in providing warrant for dismissing the impact of widespread peer disagreement with one's own view, even if it is in the minority. We suspect that this plays an important factor in explaining why intelligent design theory cannot get a significant foothold among evolutionary biologists.

Finally, the conformist view says two peer disputants should withhold belief about the topic of dispute unless one side has independent evidence for his view not available to the other side. But Christians will say they do have such independent evidence in the testimony of the Holy Spirit in their lives, the existence of miraculous religious experience including specific answers to prayer and God's speaking to a person or giving a word of knowledge that could not have been coincidence and that turned out to be true.

In our opinion, arguments one and three have real force against the conformist position.

The non-conformist, steadfast/extra-weight view. The steadfast view is basically the negation of the conformist view. Here, one can be justified in continuing to hold to one's view with the same degree of justification even in the presence of peer disagreement. One should, as it were, stick to one's guns. Thus, *rational* disagreement among epistemic peers is possible.

The main reasons for the steadfast view are the alleged force of the criticisms of the conformist position. Besides these, we present two further arguments for the steadfast outlook.

First, two epistemic peers may be using different principles or appealing to different types of evidence. In this case, there is no way to consider the disputants as true epistemic peers since they are not disagreeing about the same principles or evidence, and one should steadfastly hold to one's position despite disagreement. In response, one must be careful that this principle does not degenerate into a form of relativism according to which two disputing peers or communities of peers are incommensurable, because, among other things, principles of rationality are themselves paradigm dependent and thus cannot provide common ground for engaging in rational dialog. Besides being self-refuting, such a view simply cannot account for the actual nature of much of peer disputes.

However, if one person or side has adopted a question-begging or even self-refuting epistemology, and the other side has accepted a more pluralistic epistemology in which different canons of evidence and rationality are suited to different fields of study, then this argument has teeth. For example, many if not most atheists have adopted some version of scientism (science is either by far the best approach to knowledge we have or the only approach we have) to warrant their atheism. But the stronger versions of scientism are self-refuting, and the weaker versions are, arguably, false. Why should we think that rational principles in discovering truths in math, logic, physics, history, psychology, theology, art, and so on should all be the same? It is much more reasonable to conform one's epistemology to the nature of the objects studied in a given field.

Second, I have first-person acquaintance with my own treatment of the evidence, not with yours, and thus I am in a better place to know if I was fair or not. If I reexamine my approach to the evidence, as well as the evidence itself, and if I judge I have been appropriate in my approach, then I should stick to my guns because I have far less certainty that my disputant has been fair and so on. Now, one can be mistaken about one's own reasoning processes, but in general, this seems to be a good argument.

In sum, if the conformist view is taken not as an absolute, objective truth but as a mere rule of thumb, then it may be helpful in causing one to reexamine one's own evidence and intellectual competence and integrity, especially if the topic (1) is not one for which one side has an independent source of evidence and knowledge, (2) is at some distance from the core ethical and theological claims of Christianity, or (3) is something for which neither side particularly has an axe to grind or sociological reasons for preferring one view. But rules of thumb are not universal truths, and it seems that, on balance, the steadfast view is preferable to the conformist position.

CONCLUDING APPLICATIONS

In our view, the belief condition and the truth condition are quite straightforward (although revisionist theories of truth must be recognized and rejected). It is the nature of justification that raises important questions. We would urge Christians to realize that the inadequacies of classical (Cartesian) foundationalism do not infect all forms of foundationalism. If modest foundationalism is rejected in addition to its classical cousin, then the Christian is thrown back to a pragmatic or coherentist version of justification. But it is clear to us that this entails serious consequences. How can a Christian make a persuasive case for Christianity if his justification for holding to his faith is nothing more than that it fits with his other beliefs? How is that different from any sincere Mormon or Muslim? How can a Christian challenge the worldview of a Buddhist or a naturalist, since any proposition about Christian theism he argues for will not cohere with their noetic structures?

Perhaps more disturbing, what happens to biblical authority on a coherentist model? Presumably the Holy Spirit uses the written Word of God to challenge us in our beliefs, attitudes, and actions (see, e.g., Phil 3:15; 2 Tim 3:16). But unless we can ground our belief in the truthfulness and authority of God's Word somehow independent of the coherence of our other beliefs, then the coherence of those other beliefs will usually be sufficient to cause us to reject as unjustified any new propositions we discover as we study Scripture. Further, other sources we have come to accept as authoritative (e.g., the natural or social sciences or ecclesiastical tradition) can assume such a central place in our web of beliefs that new insights into the Bible gained through study, which fail to cohere with them, will generally be rejected. Is this perhaps why a good bit of contemporary preaching seems to offer justificatory reasons by telling stories or quoting polls or popular figures rather than by demonstrating that the original author of the passage intended his message to be understood in a particular way?

Well, enough. So far we have considered what is real and how we know. Perhaps the most important question to ask in light of this is how we should live, so in the next chapter, we turn to the subject of ethics.

4

HOW SHOULD I LIVE?

Ethics

The moralities accepted among men may differ—though not, at bottom, so widely as is often claimed—but they all agree in prescribing a behavior which their adherents fail to practice. All men alike stand condemned, not by alien codes of ethics, but by their own.
C.S. LEWIS, *THE PROBLEM OF PAIN*

Keep your laws off my body.
BUMPER STICKER

[The Gentiles] show that the requirements of the law are written on their hearts, their consciences also bearing witness, and their thoughts sometimes accusing them and at other times even defending them.
ROMANS 2:15

When teaching philosophy at a large public university, I (Garry) would usually begin class on the first or second day by asking, "How many of you would agree with this statement: There is no such thing as absolute truth; rather, what is true varies from person to person, from culture to culture, from age to age?" Somewhere between 75 and 80 percent of the students would raise their hands. I'd usually look at one student and ask, "Is that true? Absolutely?" and watch the intellectual squirming as the student tried to avoid the obvious self-refutation.

Then I'd write on the board,

$5+7=12$

and claim that was true for all people in all cultures at all times.

"Well, we didn't think you meant mathematics," someone would say.

"Fair enough," I'd reply, "but at least there's one kind of statement that is absolutely true."

Next I'd write on the board,

Electrolyze $H_2O \rightarrow 2H + O$

and claim that was true even if the culture didn't know about electricity or the atomic theory of matter, or even if the people believed water was a living spirit.

"We didn't think you meant science," the students would say.

"Fine, but there's another example of a kind of absolute truth. Now, what about this?" And I'd write,

> It is always wrong to torture babies for fun.

"I claim that's true for every person in every culture at every time." Now hands would go up around the room.

"What if they didn't think it was wrong?" "How can it be wrong for them if they don't think it's wrong?" And what someone thought was the trump card: "Who are you to say?"

"Okay," I'd say, "think about this," and I write,

$$e^{i\pi} + 1 = 0$$

"For those who aren't math majors, e is an irrational number, a non-ending, nonrepeating fraction that is the base of natural logarithms, approximately 2.71828...; i is an imaginary number, the square root of -1; and π is another irrational number, 3.141592653589 ... Now, this says that e raised to the power of *i* times π plus 1 equals 0. Isn't that amazing?"

After a few on-cue murmurs of amazement, I ask, "Why isn't anyone asking, 'Who are you to say?' The reason, I think, is that you know what it is to think mathematically. You know how mathematical proofs go, you believe there is such a thing as mathematical truth. But the problem is, no one has taught you how to think morally, how ethical arguments go, what moral truth is like. So you challenge the possibility of moral truth without knowing what it is you're reacting to. And that's part of what we'll be thinking about this semester!"

And that's what we'll be thinking about in this chapter.

Every day we are confronted with opinions and choices that have important consequences. We need to know how to judge whose opinion is correct; we need to know how to make the right choices. And intuitively we know that the "right" choice, the "correct" opinion is in many cases not merely a matter of what works best or what the company we keep will approve of. Some choices and opinions are clearly moral in character.

Consider the following statements:
1. You should never pass the football on first down.
2. Use the smaller fork for the salad.
3. Drive on the right side of the road.
4. You should never lie on a job application.

Statement 1 states an opinion that, for a given team in a given game, might be good pragmatic advice, but nothing moral hangs on the decision. Statement 2 says something about etiquette, about behavior that is acceptable in certain contexts but does not have the force of a moral command. Statement 3 expresses a rule that has become law, and while it might be morally wrong to violate it in the United States, it would be morally wrong to obey it in Great Britain. The particular rule itself is not a moral rule. Statement 4 states a rule that seems different from the others. We know intuitively that there is a difference between the kind of judgment expressed by (4) and the judgments expressed by (1), (2), and (3).

Just what makes one judgment a moral judgment and another judgment merely good advice? Just what makes certain behavior ethical (or unethical) and other behavior simply a matter of preference?[30] It is difficult to specify a precise set of necessary and sufficient conditions that are met by all and only moral judgments. Still, we can point to a set of characteristics common to all or most ethical claims, characteristics that serve to set off the ethical from the non-ethical.

METAETHICS

There are several distinct ways to approach the study of ethics. *Descriptive ethics* seeks to describe the ethical standards and behaviors of a group or a culture without making judgments as to the correctness of the standards and behaviors, and it is more properly part

---

[30] While a few philosophers distinguish moral and ethical, most do not, and we will use the two terms interchangeably.

of anthropology or sociology than of philosophy. *Metaethics* seeks to answer questions about the meaning of ethical terms, about the structure of ethical theories, and about the source and nature of moral values and obligations. *Normative ethics* attempts to explain how to make judgments about which actions or attitudes are obligatory, permitted, or prohibited under different ethical theories and, in consequence, to explain ascriptions of moral praise or blame. And *applied ethics* explores the ethical requirements of normative theory in a particular area, such as environmental, business, or biomedical ethics.

We will begin by doing a bit of metaethical thinking. Metaethics helps us slice the pie of different ethical theories so we can see comparisons and contrasts more easily (see fig.1). After charting the landscape of ethical theories, we'll return to consider three of the most important and widely held views about what makes actions right or wrong and how we should live.

Figure 1. Types of ethical theories

The first division is between *noncognitive* and *cognitive* theories. The difference is this: noncognitive theories do not take ethical judgments as having truth value, while cognitive theories hold that ethical judgments are either true or false. But if ethical judgments have no truth value, what do they express? Noncognitive theories fall into two general categories: *emotivism* and *prescriptivism.* These theories say, respectively, that moral statements are really either statements of emotions or prescriptions for action. And since statements of emotion ("Eeek!" "Yippee!") or prescriptions ("Take two aspirin and call me in the morning") are neither true nor false, moral judgments are neither true nor false either, even though on the surface they often look like simple declarative sentences.

Emotivist theories say simply that when someone expresses a moral judgment, he is only expressing how he feels about an action. So "Abortion is wrong" means "I really feel awful about abortion," while "Promise keeping is good" means "I like people to keep their promises." Sometimes, emotivism is characterized as the "hooray-boo theory" of morality. ("Hooray for promise keeping! Boo for abortion!")

Emotivist theorists are correct to note the emotion that often accompanies a moral judgment, but they are wrong to reduce moral judgments to mere statements of emotion. In fact, most of us intend our moral judgments to be understood as statements about moral praiseworthiness or blameworthiness of actions or agents. ("That murder was heinous." "This politician should be held accountable for that lie.") We do not believe for a minute that such statements are really nothing more than expressions of how we feel about some action or agent, and it seems to be rather arrogant for the emotivist to tell us we don't really mean what we take ourselves to be saying.

Prescriptivist theories of morality say that a moral statement is something like a doctor's prescription. If you go to your doctor and she gives you a prescription for your ailment, you may be foolish not to take the prescription as directed. If she's a good doctor, then it's good advice. Similarly, moral statements should be regarded as advice—which could be either good or bad advice, depending on the qualification of the person making the statement and other relevant circumstances. (The professor who says to his class that plagiarism is immoral is advising them not to plagiarize, which may be good advice to follow, at least on that class's term paper.) A stronger version of prescriptivism is imperativalism, according to which moral statements are imperatives that command us to do or refrain from doing something. Of course, we are confronted all the time with imperatives ("Merge left," "Sign here," "Don't miss this sale!" "Don't torture!"), and whether or not we obey them, or even regard them as binding on us, depends a lot on who issues the command, what the relevant circumstances are at the time, what the penalty for disobeying may be, and whether we regard the command as a moral imperative. In other words, we can tell the difference between a moral imperative and some other kind of imperative, which should show that moral statements cannot be reduced to simple imperatives. The person who misses the sale may wind up spending more money, perhaps even fiscally foolishly, but the person who participates in ritual torture is morally blameworthy.

In short, noncognitivist theories of morality completely fail to account for the strong intuitive sense we have of the difference between expressions of emotion, advice, or commands, on the one hand, and genuinely moral judgments, on the other. They cannot account for the different sort of disapproval society gives to those who are simply foolish or impolite and to those who are regarded as genuinely immoral. Nor can these theories begin to square with a theology that sees God as morally good and as commanding people to live morally good lives.

Legal or moral? Perhaps here would be a good place to address the relationship between morality and law. It is often said that you can't legislate morality. But in fact virtually all legislation is based on some moral principle. Traffic laws? A well-ordered traffic flow reduces injuries and deaths, and to seek such a reduction is a morally praiseworthy goal. Criminal law? Virtually all criminal law rests on moral principles such as "do not steal," "do not lie," and "do not kill." Tax law? Given that some government is necessary for a peaceful, well-functioning society, and given that government costs money, even tax law can, at least in theory, be traced to moral principles.

Now some laws are matters of convenience rather than morality (e.g., laws regulating the size, shape, and weight of letters that can be mailed without excess postage). And some laws codify prudential or pragmatic judgments rather than moral principles (e.g., laws prohibiting parking at certain times along a street to allow for street sweeping). Still, for the most part, law and morality go far together, so that in most cases a lawbreaker is also morally blameworthy for the act.

But we should realize that law and morality do diverge. There are certain acts that are not illegal but are (arguably) immoral, acts such as production or consumption of pornography, premarital sex, or vicious gossip. And the law does not attempt to regulate thoughts and attitudes, but (arguably) racial prejudice, hatred, and lust are immoral thoughts or attitudes. There may well be very good practical reasons for not declaring everything immoral to be illegal. But at the same time, we should be in no doubt as to which road to follow when law and morality do diverge.

Cognitive ethics. So if moral statements have truth value—if a moral judgment is either true or false—what determines the truth value? Cognitive theories of morality differ in giving different answers to this question. The broad division within cognitivist ethics is between subjective and objective theories. Now something is *subjective* if it depends on what is in a person's mind (thoughts, beliefs, fears, hopes, etc.), while something is *objective* if it is completely independent of anyone's thoughts, beliefs, and so on. Subjectivist ethical theories take ethical statements to be either true or false, but they locate the truth maker for the statement in the thoughts, beliefs, or other internal states of the moral subject. Ethical subjectivism can be further subdivided into *cultural relativism* and *individual relativism.* Objectivist ethical theories claim that ethical judgments are true or false because of the way the world is, irrespective of what beliefs anyone may hold about the world. Moral objectivists deny that beliefs or thoughts are relevant to the truth of a moral judgment. Ethical objectivism can be subdivided into *ethical naturalism* and *ethical nonnaturalism.*

Subjectivist ethics (relativism). Subjectivist theories of ethics agree that ethical statements have truth value, but they hold that whether a particular ethical statement is true or false depends on what people think. Cultural moral relativism is the view that the common moral beliefs of a culture are what make moral statements true or false; they determine what is moral relative to the beliefs of the culture. An act is moral within a particular culture if and only if it is judged to be moral by that culture.

Cultural ethical relativism. Because moral relativism in this cultural sense is so widely held, we want to pay close attention to the issues involved. First, what sort of arguments can be advanced to support relativism? The usual defense of the position begins with the observation that moral codes differ considerably from one culture to another and from one era to another. Anthropologists have filled volumes detailing differing moral standards in various cultures. One culture buries its dead, another burns its dead, while a third eats its dead. One culture holds bribery to be immoral, while another regards such "gifts" as a normal way of doing business. Even within our own country, views on morality have changed. Divorce, extramarital sex, and consumption of alcohol were all at one time regarded as immoral (at least by a large segment of the population), while racial segregation was not. This leads to a descriptive thesis about cultural relativism:

5. What is believed to be moral differs from culture to culture and from age to age.

While we believe a case can be made that the moral codes of different times and cultures do not differ as much as is often claimed, nevertheless, for the sake of argument, we'll grant (5). But what follows from the descriptive thesis? Most arguments for moral relativism draw a normative conclusion:

6. Therefore, what is moral differs from culture to culture and from age to age.

But it is clear, when formalized, that (6) does not immediately follow from (5). There is a missing or suppressed premise, a dependency thesis:

5A. What is moral depends on what is believed to be moral.

With (5A) included as a premise in the argument, (6) does indeed follow. But why should we believe (5A)? No one who is not already willing to accept the conclusion (6) would accept (5A), and if the argument depends on (5A), the argument clearly begs the question.

Tolerance. The most obvious way to formulate an argument for moral relativism is a failure. Why else, then, might someone want to accept (6)? Probably the most common reason today is a defective view of tolerance. Ask the average college undergraduate or the average progressive or liberal city dweller (country people tend to be more conservative, both politically and ethically), and you'll be told that it is somehow wrong to judge another person or an action to be immoral. Why? Because we must be tolerant. And the opposite of tolerant is bigoted. Furthermore, it is morally wrong to be bigoted. Tolerance has become the supreme virtue in our culture, such that the only thing that can't be tolerated is intolerance (and never mind that this is self-refuting).

Of course, the refusal to make a judgment about the morality of an action is not genuine tolerance; it's moral cowardice or intellectual laziness or plain confusion. True tolerance is the view that even if I believe that you are wrong, I will not use coercion to enforce my belief. (Of course, there are exceptions, notably for actions that harm others.) A truly tolerant person does not refrain from making judgments but rather refrains from using power to get others to change their beliefs, relying instead on persuasion.

So tolerance as an argument for ethical relativism also fails since it must rely on a defective notion of tolerance. If, then, both the argument from descriptive relativism and the argument from tolerance fail, and it is relatively easy to see that they do, why do so many persist in holding to a relativist view of morality? Perhaps it is not too far off the mark to suggest that in our society, with its emphasis on individualism, rights, and liberties, a new tacit social contract has emerged: I won't judge you if you don't judge me. This seems especially true in the case of so-called victimless crimes, notably those related to sex.

Against cultural relativism. Totally apart from the failure of arguments for ethical relativism, there are good arguments against it. We'll point out just three. First, cultural relativism makes criticism of other cultures impossible because if that culture believes action *A* is moral, it is not relevant that our culture believes *A* is immoral. When teaching at a major public university, I was often confronted in class with students who would refuse to judge Nazi Germany's Final Solution as immoral. "Well," they'd say, "of course it would be wrong for us to do that, but if they didn't think it was wrong, it wasn't wrong for them." And (appallingly) these students would maintain that position no matter what the issue was: slavery, human sacrifice, female genital mutilation, torture, terrorism—no practice was wrong if the culture didn't think it was wrong. But surely we can make judgments about different cultures. We do not need to be a perfect society ourselves before we can criticize another on moral grounds. Nazi Germany was wrong, no matter what the culture believed; female genital mutilation is wrong, no matter how entrenched the tradition may be.

(Or so we claim, and later on we'll show how such judgments can be properly grounded.)

Second, cultural relativism makes the moral reformer immoral. For if what a culture believes is moral is in fact moral, then anyone who challenges that culture's beliefs is by definition immoral. Internal criticism is impossible. The abolitionist William Wilberforce was morally wrong, as was Mahatma Gandhi and Martin Luther King Jr. But that just can't be right. If a moral theory yields such counterintuitive results, so much the worse for the theory.

Finally, cultural relativism is an unstable position and will reduce ultimately to moral anarchy. The reason is that it is not possible to give a non-question-begging definition of culture. What constitutes the relevant culture with respect to a moral judgment? Is it the particular local community? (The Supreme Court held that local community standards are relevant when considering what constitutes pornography.) Or is it a single state? (Prostitution is legal in Nevada.) Or a region? (The South, prior to the Civil War, would have regarded slavery as moral.) Or the whole nation? The so-called Western world? Or something more narrow—evangelical Christians, Ivy League sororities, CEOs earning in excess of $10 million per year? Sooner or later, the definition of culture will invoke common moral beliefs as one identifying characteristic of a culture, with the result that a "culture" consists of "those who agree." But this is not at all helpful. It amounts to the claim that something is wrong only for those who believe it is wrong, which finally amounts to individual ethical relativism or moral anarchy.

Individual ethical relativism. Is it in fact the case that individual ethical relativism is moral anarchy? Yes. It is the condition described by the book of Judges: "All the people did what was right in their own eyes" (Judg 21:25 NRSV). It is the condition described by Thomas Hobbes (1588–1679) in *Leviathan:*

> In such condition there is no place for industry, because the fruit thereof is uncertain: and consequently no culture of the

earth; no navigation, nor use of the commodities that may be imported by sea; no commodious building; no instruments of moving and removing such things as require much force; no knowledge of the face of the earth; no account of time; no arts; no letters; no society; and which is worst of all, continual fear, and danger of violent death; and the life of man, solitary, poor, nasty, brutish, and short.[31]

John Calvin (1509–1564) once said that no matter how bad a human government is, God grants that it is never so bad as anarchy. Individual relativism is unlivable. If a person believes it is not wrong for him to steal, rape, or murder, what recourse does the victim have? Even if the individual relativist approves of legislation against such things in the interests of an orderly society, how can she not feel morally wronged (not merely legally

---

[31] Thomas Hobbes, Leviathan, in The English Philosophers from Bacon to Mill, ed. Edwin A. Burtt (New York: Modern Library, 1939), 161.

wronged) if she's the victim? In short, while many may be moral relativists when "doing to," they soon become nonrelativists when "being done unto."

Objectivist ethics. We come now to the general class of objectivist ethical theories, those which hold that the truth or falsehood of moral statements does not depend on the thoughts or beliefs of any individuals or cultures. Objectivist theories fall into one of two categories, either *ethical naturalism* or *ethical nonnaturalism*. Both, though, are often labeled *moral realism* since they agree that moral properties are real features of the world and not dependent on the mental life of any creatures.

Ethical naturalism. Ethical naturalists believe that moral properties are defined in terms of, or are reducible to, properties described by the natural (and perhaps the social) sciences. Some versions of natural law theory and some accounts of natural rights are naturalist theories in this sense.

Aristotle believed (very roughly) that the necessary conditions of human flourishing could be "read off" human beings and that to withhold anything necessary for flourishing was immoral. For example, he said that humans need adequate food, shelter, clothing, and (at least a modest amount of) leisure to be able to flourish, and so people had a moral right to these things. Jeremy Bentham (1748–1832) believed it was natural, and therefore moral, for humans to minimize pain and maximize pleasure—the ethical system known as *utilitarianism.* John Stuart Mill (1806–1873) developed utilitarianism, claiming that what was moral was to seek the greatest good for the greatest number. Note that in both cases—pain and pleasure for Bentham and the greatest good for the greatest number for Mill—what counts as moral or immoral can be measured by the natural or social sciences. They are natural properties of the world. (We should mention in passing that there are versions of utilitarianism that take "the greatest good" as being that which commonly held cultural beliefs take to be the good. Such versions are subjectivist, not objectivist.)

It seems to many philosophers (us included) that ethical naturalism makes a mistake in reducing morality to natural properties. It is not at all clear that normative (moral) properties can be reduced to, or defined in terms of, natural (nonmoral) properties. For natural properties do not in themselves carry any normative notions; they just are. So something else must invest certain properties with moral qualities (e.g., causing gratuitous pain is morally wrong) while not so investing other properties (e.g., singing off-key is not morally wrong). In other words, there must be a metatheory that determines which natural properties give rise to moral properties, and it cannot itself be naturalistic, or else an infinite regress results.

Ethical nonnaturalism. In contrast to naturalist theories, ethical nonnaturalism holds that ethical properties are irreducible features of the universe. Just as there are physical facts and properties, so too there are moral facts and properties. Plato believed that goodness, justice, and the like were eternal forms that existed just as surely as redness, squareness, or the form of man. Some contemporary nonnaturalists want to avoid the language of Platonic forms but still posit the existence of irreducibly nonnatural moral properties in the universe. And religions like Christianity, which locate the source of morality in the nature of God, also yield nonnaturalist ethics.

Having completed our metaethical survey of the terrain occupied by theories of morality, we now want to turn our attention to three of the most influential theories, leaving aside the misguided moral relativism that we have already seen reason to dismiss.

NORMATIVE ETHICS

We will examine three ethical theories in this section: *consequentialism, deontology,* and *virtue ethics.* But before we get to that, we must address four preliminary matters. First, what do we expect an ethical theory to give us? Well, roughly, we want a way to tell what's the right thing to do. We want a guide to making moral decisions. Given that we accept the principle "Do what is morally good," we want to know, what is morally good?

So we expect a moral theory to help us identify what makes for moral goodness. But notice that we don't expect a moral theory to tell us why we should do the right thing. That's really a metaethical question, and we'll return to it in the final section of the chapter.

Second, as evangelical Christians, it is important to note that we emphatically do not believe that by being moral anyone can be saved. Discussions of moral theory are not discussions of soteriology (the theology of salvation). But, equally emphatically, we believe that all people ought to be moral and that we should be able to make a persuasive argument that certain actions are moral or immoral, arguments that appeal to everyone whether or not they accept the authority of Scripture.

Third, we need to sound a caution against a practice we both have seen adopted by some undergraduates in our ethics classes. This is the assumption that all that is needed in order to act morally is to find some rationale in some ethical theory for the action we're contemplating. These people become eclectic ethicists, picking and choosing among theories to find the one theory that will "give them permission" to do what they want to do anyway. But ethical theory is not like that. A moral life should not be a toolbox of different theories, each ready to be employed for a different problem, but should be a seamless, tightly woven fabric.

Finally, we must restrain ourselves. We are sorely tempted to do applied ethics, to argue about the relationship of morality to contemporary issues. But this is not, after all, a book of that sort. So with some genuine reluctance, we'll leave the application to you as homework.

Table 1. Normative ethical theories

Theory	Object of Moral Evaluation	Principle	Example(s)
Consequentialism	The outcomes of acts	The greatest good for the greatest number	Utilitarianism
Deontology	The acts themselves	Always do one's duty	Kantian ethics, divine command theory

Virtue Ethics	The moral agent	Act on virtues with sound judgment	Aristotle, Aquinas
Ethical Egoism	The acts themselves	Always seek one's own interests	Ayn Rand's "Objectivism"
Hedonism	The outcomes of acts	Always seek one's own pleasure	Epicureanism
Stoicism	The attitude of the agent	Accept one's fate; be responsible for one's own attitudes	Epictitus, Marcus Aurelius, Seneca

Only the first three are serious contenders; the last three will not be discussed in the text.

Consequentialism (outcome-based ethics). Consequentialism refers to any moral theory that judges the moral value of an action based on its outcome or consequences. We should always seek to do that action which has good consequences and to avoid those actions which have bad consequences. Of course, spelling out just what constitutes "good consequences" is no small matter, and different answers give different forms of consequentialism.

The most popular form of consequentialism is utilitarianism. As it is usually stated, the principle of utilitarianism is always to seek "the greatest good for the greatest number." Suppose that your rich, eccentric uncle summons you to his deathbed, names you executor of his will, and asks you to promise to give his entire $10 million estate to aid in relocating prairie dogs threatened by encroaching development. You promise, and he dies. That evening on the news you see a desperate plea from the government of an African nation threatened by famine; without $10 million with which to buy food, a million people will likely starve to death. Utilitarianism offers a quick and easy "calculus" to help you decide whether to keep your promise to your uncle or to break it and save a million lives. Prairie dogs are not a threatened or endangered species, and surely people's lives are worth more than prairie dogs' lives. You should break your promise and send the money to Africa.

On first consideration, the utilitarian principle seems to be a fine ethical principle: it is clear, comprehensive, and easy to apply. But further consideration reveals that it is none of these. First, it is not clear, for it involves two superlatives; and it is impossible in almost every case to maximize both good and numbers of people. The two are not strictly commensurable. Suppose you had $100,000 to distribute as you saw fit, provided that you used it to secure "the greatest good for the greatest number." Would you give one dollar to 100,000 people? Or $100,000 to one person, or...? Utilitarianism fails, after all, to give clear guidance in moral decision-making.

Second, it is not comprehensive. To see this, ask how you define the "good." We already encountered Bentham and Mill. Bentham takes "good" as maximization of sensual pleasure and minimization of pain, while Mill takes "good" as coming in degrees, where the intellectual pleasures are higher than sensual pleasures. Since Bentham and Mill, various analyses of "good" have been given by proponents of utilitarianism. But the point is that utilitarianism itself does not help at all in deciding what the good consists in, so as a moral theory it is incomplete, needing some additional theory to specify the nature of the good.

Third, it is not easy to apply. For often actions have unintended consequences, and what we think is likely to bring about good may turn out to do just the opposite. Further, how far must you look? The moral ripples of certain actions spread widely and last long, and who of us can know the comparative consequences of our actions with any degree of probability?

In response to questions such as these, utilitarianism has undergone extensive refinement and today comes in a number of varieties. We do not propose to look at the details of any, for we believe that at the end of the day, utilitarianism of any variety will turn out to be an unsatisfactory theory for individual ethical decision-making. A couple of thought experiments (which have been widely discussed in the relevant literature) will highlight the difficulties that plague any version of utilitarian theory.

First, utilitarianism can possibly lead to a perversion of justice. Say you are sheriff in a small town which has seen a recent murder that was clearly racially motivated. You have carefully investigated, but you have no leads, no idea who the murderer might be. Unrest grows, and rioting breaks out as the racial minority smells a coverup. Word reaches you through an informant that the most militant sector of the minority will themselves kill one person of the racial majority at random each night until "justice is done." Now, as sheriff, you know you have just jailed a mentally incompetent vagrant whom you could frame for the murders. Suppose you reasonably believe this would end the rioting, prevent additional killing, and restore calm. What would the utilitarian principle say is the right thing to do here? Plausibly consequentialism would tell you to frame the vagrant. This is a very counterintuitive example of the ends justifying the means, but that's just the point: consequentialism evaluates an action based on its outcome—its ends. Yet surely the nature of the action itself must have some bearing on its morality.

Second, utilitarianism may place a person in a situation that demands violating very deeply held moral principles. British philosopher Bernard Williams offers this example:

Jim finds himself in the central square of a small South American town. Tied up against the wall are a row of twenty Indians, most terrified, a few defiant, in front of them several armed men in uniform. A heavy man in a sweatstained khaki shirt turns out to be the captain in charge and, after a good deal of questioning of Jim which establishes that he got there by accident while on a botanical expedition, explains that the Indians are a random group of inhabitants who, after recent acts of protest against the government, are about to be killed to remind other possible protesters of the advantages of not protesting. However, since Jim is an honored visitor from another land, the captain is happy to offer him a guest's privilege of killing one of the Indians himself. If Jim accepts, then as a special mark of the occasion, the other Indians will be let off. Of course, if Jim refuses, then there is no special occasion and Pedro here will do what he was about to do when Jim arrived, and kill them all. Jim, with some desperate recollection of schoolboy fiction, wonders whether if he got hold if a gun, he could hold the captain, Pedro and the rest of the soldiers to threat, but it is quite clear from the set-up that nothing of that kind is going to work: any attempt of that sort of thing will mean that all the Indians will be killed, and himself. The men against the wall, the other villagers, understand the situation, and are obviously begging him to accept. What should he do?[32]

Now suppose Jim has carefully constructed his moral character around a principle of nonviolence. Williams asks why it is that Jim should be constrained by the theory of utilitarianism to

---

[32] Bernard Williams, "A Critique of Utilitarianism," quoted in Louis Pojman, Ethics: Discovering Right and Wrong, 2nd ed. (Belmont, CA: Wadsworth, 1995), 121.

perform an action that so clearly violates his moral integrity, just because someone else has set up the situation in such a way that that's how the utilitarian calculus comes out. How is it that Jim's character and the nature of the act don't enter into the ethical evaluation of the situation?

Third, utilitarianism often has the odd consequence that you should want everyone else to be a deontologist (doing their duty—see next section) while secretly you are a utilitarian. Imagine you are in London during the Battle of Britain, and the prime minister has declared that, in order to conserve coal for the industries supporting His Majesty's military, everyone should keep the heat in their apartments at 62°. Now you know that the British will certainly do their duty and keep their apartments cold. But, you reason, your overall happiness would be greatly increased if you could heat yours to 72°. No one would know the difference, and the small additional amount of coal you burned would surely not make a difference to the war effort. Utilitarian calculus says that since cheating on the temperature of your apartment would increase overall happiness, provided everyone else does their duty, you should in fact cheat and keep it private. But how is it that a moral theory can have the implication that you should want everyone else to follow a different theory, that you should keep quiet about it and break the rules?

In fairness, utilitarians have offered responses to these and other problems that have been raised, but a great many ethicists have found the responses inadequate. It seems highly doubtful that the end can justify the means (in all but the most extreme and improbable circumstances, perhaps), that outcomes are the sole object of moral evaluation, and that the nature of the action and the character of the agent have no role to play.

Before we leave our discussion of consequentialism, however, we should note that asking about the greatest good for the greatest number is often a good place to start when considering matters of public policy. Suppose you're on a city council considering a project to widen a freeway. The project is predicted to result in greatly improved traffic flow and shorter commutes for thousands (thereby saving gas and pollution), and to lower the accident rate on the freeway by 21 percent and lower accident-related deaths by eight per year. But the project also will result in 190 families being displaced from their homes. And suppose that you and a majority of the council think that the project will indeed result in the greatest good for the greatest number, so under the doctrine of eminent domain, you condemn the homes. But in going ahead, you'll encounter the problem of distributive justice. The greatest good for the greatest number almost always entails increased harm for a few. So in using a utilitarian approach to public policy, government officials must always be ready to offer just compensation—compensatory justice—to those who have been harmed by a decision.

Deontology (duty-based ethics). While consequentialism claims that the good outcomes of an act make the act morally good, deontological ethics (from the Greek *deon,* "that which is necessary or right") focuses on the nature of the act itself. Consequentialism says the end justifies the means; deontology says this is never the case. Consequentialism claims the nonmoral values (e.g., happiness, avoidance of pain) determine the moral rightness or wrongness of an act; deontology says (most) acts themselves have intrinsic moral qualities, and it is our duty to do that which is moral. Since keeping promises is moral and breaking promises is immoral, in the case above, you should keep your promise to your uncle and save the prairie dogs. The outcome—the death by starvation of a million in Africa—has no bearing on your decision. You are responsible only for doing your duty, not for altering your duty to achieve different outcomes.

Although some deontologists have focused on individual acts, most deontological theories have argued that ethical rules are the proper way to think about our moral duty. Rules such as "Tell the truth," "Keep your promises," and "Don't commit murder" are examples. What rules like this have in common is that they are universalizable;

that is, if action *A* is morally right (or wrong), then for anyone in circumstances relevantly similar, *A* would also be right (or wrong).

Two further distinctions must be mentioned here. First, deontologists differ among themselves as to how moral duties can be known. Intuitionists believe that we know moral duties through our conscience, while rationalists hold that it is through use of our reason that we discover our moral duties. It seems likely that both aspects have a place in the moral life. For our conscience certainly does serve as a source of moral knowledge (see Rom 2:15). But there seem to be many situations where the issues are so complicated—think especially of the many difficult moral choices presented to us by the advances in biotechnology—that we must apply reason carefully in analyzing the relevant moral factors before us.

The second distinction is that between *absolutism* and *objectivism.* Absolutists believe that an adequate moral theory will never produce conflicting duties, that moral principles are all of equal force and cannot be overridden. Objectivists (here used in a different sense than it's used in metaethical theory) claim that while moral duties are universal, they are not necessarily without exception. Moral duties override all other kinds of considerations, but they come in a form such that there is a hierarchy among them. The objectivist often distinguishes prima facie duties—those which at first glance seem to hold—from actual duties.

To illustrate the difference, consider the oft-discussed case of the Dutch woman who hides Jews from the Nazis. When the SS arrives at the door, the absolutist would say she has a duty to tell the truth, while the objectivist would say that the duty to save lives overrides the duty to tell the truth. The objectivist may even tell her that while truthfulness is a prima facie duty, the Nazis, because of their immoral intentions, have forfeited their moral claim to being told the truth. Note that rather than being a lesser of two evils, this is the greater of two goods.

We now need to look at two distinct versions of deontology: Immanuel Kant's *categorical imperative* and the *divine command theory of morality*.

The categorical imperative. One particular form of deontological ethics deserves a closer look. The great German philosopher Immanuel Kant (1724–1804) is perhaps best known for developing a deontological system centered on what he called the categorical imperative (CI). This principle was an imperative, a command, and so imposed a moral duty, and it was categorical—that is, it was exceptionless and unqualified. Kant offered several formulations of the CI, of which two are best known. The first says, "Act only according to that rule which you could at the same time will to become a universal law." The second puts it differently: "Act always so as to treat humanity—whether in your own person or that of any other—always as an end and never merely as means." Kant believed that these two formulations were equivalent.

In Kant's ethics the CI thus gives us a rule for testing all other moral rules. Suppose you wonder whether to cheat on an anatomy exam, rationalizing that if you do, you will be admitted to medical school and you know you could become a very compassionate doctor. But could you universalize that rule? If so, could you ever trust a doctor or a surgeon, knowing it is possible that she too had cheated in anatomy?

So far, Kantian ethics may seem quite attractive. The two formulations of the CI sound like very plausible candidates for a rule by which to judge other rules, as principles by which we should strive to live. There is even an echo of the Golden Rule, at least in the second formulation. Scholars have noted that Kant's thought was deeply influenced by his German Pietistic upbringing.

There are weaknesses in Kant's theory, however. It is an absolutist deontological system, and it turns out that such systems face great difficulty when pressed into daily service. To see this, say you have decided that the rule "Always keep your promises" meets the CI: it can be applied universally. Now suppose that a neighbor comes to you with a pistol and ammunition and asks you to keep them for him as he has no place to keep them safe from his children. He makes you promise to give them back when he asks. Months later, your friend has lost his job, his wife has left him and taken the children, his house is foreclosed and his car repossessed, and you know he is suicidal. He comes to you one night after drinking heavily and asks for his gun and ammunition back, muttering something about "ending it all." Because you're a very compassionate person and you know that his depression will pass if he gets competent counseling, it certainly seems that you should do your utmost to get him help and not facilitate his suicide. So you modify your rule: "Always keep your promise unless keeping the promise can be seen to have potentially deadly results."

But this is not permissible under a deontological conception of ethics, for the results of an action have no bearing whatsoever on your duty to perform the action. You cannot make consequentialist modifications to a categorical duty. If consequentialism is open to critique for not taking into account the nature of the act and the character of the agent, then deontology can be criticized for failing to take into account the consequences of an act or the character of the agent.

Divine command theory of morality. It's easy to see why Christians throughout the ages have found some sort of deontological ethics very amenable to their faith. And while some regard an ethical system grounded in God's commands to be a separate category, we'll treat it as a version of deontology. For if the "chief end of man is to glorify God and enjoy Him forever," as the Westminster Shorter Catechism puts it, it follows that the way to do this is by obeying God's commands. The Christian's duty is to obey.

More generally, the divine command theory (DCT) holds to three theses: First, morality depends on God. Second, any action is required (prohibited, permitted) only if it is required (prohibited, permitted) by a command of God. And third, if God does not exist, then there is no morality. (Recall the words spoken by Ivan Karamazov in Feodor Dostoyevsky's *The Brothers*

Karamazov: "If there is no God, then everything is permitted.") Under the DCT, morally right means commanded by God, while morally wrong means prohibited by God.

The DCT is faced immediately with an objection called the "Euthryphro dilemma" (named for Plato's dialogue, the *Euthryphro,* in which Socrates asks Euthryphro, "Do the gods love what is pious because it is pious, or is it pious because the gods love it?"). As an objection to the DCT, the dilemma goes like this: either *(a)* God commands action A because A is moral or *(b)* A is moral because God commands A. Presumably the theist does not want to accept *(a)* and admit that the standard of morality is external to God. Nor would the theist want to accept *(b)*. If *(b)*, allegedly, then God could command anything whatever—theft, rape, genocide—and it would be moral. Thus, morality is arbitrary.

While some Christian thinkers have taken the second horn of the dilemma *(b)*, most have held that the dilemma is a false one. If God is essentially morally perfect, then God would not—indeed, could not—command just any act whatsoever; and if God is thus understood, this modified DCT avoids the force of the Euthyphro dilemma.

But two other problems face a modified DCT. The first has to do with the specification of moral (or immoral) acts, the second with the nature of public morality. The first simply notes the great complexity of moral problems that we face in our world, problems such as stem cell research, genetic engineering, preemptive war against terrorism, and producing genetically modified foods. It is dubious that any clear command of God can be applied unambiguously to these problems, so the DCT fails to deliver on its promise. (This is not to deny that moral principles from divine revelation may be applied to complex contemporary moral issues. But the DCT supposes divine commands, not moral principles. Applying principles is quite different from obeying direct commands.)

The second problem faced by the DCT has to do with the public square. How should a religiously based morality be applied in a religiously pluralistic society? It could be argued that biblical law should be the law of the land (roughly the position argued by Reconstructionism), but we do not believe that the laws of ancient Israel are applicable in any straightforward way outside their theocratic context. And even if they were, we would land again squarely in the specification problem. We believe that a better approach is hinted at in two relevant passages in Scripture. In the first two chapters of Amos, the prophet reports the Lord's judgment on six nations surrounding Israel and then on Israel itself. The six nations, which were not recipients of the Mosaic law, are judged for what today would be called crimes against humanity, while Israel is judged for violations of this law. And in Romans 2:1-16, the Gentiles are held accountable not to the letter of the law but to the standard of their own conscience. The point is this: there is a standard of morality available to all people through their conscience and through their use of reason, apart from divine revelation (and that standard is sufficient to show their just condemnation before God and need of salvation). Thus, we think that moral arguments in the public square can and should be made based on moral intuition and natural reason, even while moral arguments among God's people may invoke the surer standards of revelation. But this argument from natural morality is not available under the DCT. So while we do not in any way wish to minimize the obligation that the moral principles and direct commands of Scripture put on believers, we do not think that the DCT is an adequate general moral theory.

Virtue ethics (agent-based ethics). Virtue theory, also called *aretaic ethics* (from the Greek word aretē, "virtue") has a long and distinguished pedigree, going back to Aristotle and Plato, running through Thomas Aquinas, and including many contemporary advocates. In contrast to both deontological and consequentialist theories, which focus on actions and outcomes, virtue ethics focuses on the character of a good person and the quality of the good life. It addresses the development of good character and emphasizes community and relationships.

Virtue theory is *teleological* (from the Greek word *telos,* "end, purpose") in that its aim is to develop dispositions that enable a person to live well. A virtue is a disposition, a skill of sorts.[33] Virtues thus are character traits that enable a person to achieve the goal of *eudaimonia,* "happiness," not in the sense of momentary pleasurable satisfaction but in the sense of flourishing, well-being, an excellent life.

Classic virtue ethics includes a commitment to essentialism, which, roughly, is the idea that human beings have an essence or nature. On this view the truth about human nature provides the grounds for understanding ideal human functioning. One who functions ideally and skillfully in life is one who functions properly in accordance with human nature. Human nature defines

---

[33] Our colleague David Horner explains that a habit is a disposition that makes it hard not to do something, while a virtue is a disposition that makes it easy to do something.

what is unique and proper for human flourishing, and a bad person is one who lives contrary to human nature. Thus, in Romans 1:26-27 Paul argues that homosexuality is wrong because it is "unnatural"; that is, it is contrary to proper human functioning in accordance with the essence of being human.

Given a correct understanding of proper human functioning, virtue ethics spells out what constitutes a good character—the sum total of dispositions to think, feel, judge, desire, and act in such a way as to flourish. Virtues go beyond the distinctly moral virtues and include "intellectual virtues," such as studiousness, intellectual curiosity, and rationality, as well as "natural virtues" such as courage (one can be a courageous crook as well as a courageous Christian). Indeed, there is a unity among the virtues, so that one who is lacking in one area cannot be truly virtuous in other areas. A person who is intellectually lazy, prejudiced, or complacent cannot be a virtuous agent any more than can the genius who is an inveterate liar. Traditionally, virtue ethics include at least the "four cardinal virtues" of prudence, justice, courage, and temperance. Christianity added the distinctively Christian virtues of faith, hope, and love.

Aristotle, in the *Nicomachean Ethics,* investigates how virtue is developed and emphasizes the role of examples and instruction, of friends and laws. For Christian thinkers the spiritual disciplines have been central to understanding character. A spiritual discipline, such as fasting, solitude, or silence, is a repeated activity aimed at developing habits that train a person in a life of virtue. Practicing a spiritual discipline is very much like practicing the scales on a piano. One does not practice the scales to get good at playing the scales. Rather, one practices the scales to form the habits necessary for becoming an excellent piano player. Similarly, one does not perform spiritual disciplines to get good at them but, rather, to get good at life. A spiritual discipline is a means to habit formation relevant to the development of character and virtue.

Virtue ethics has secured a wide following throughout the history of ethics and has enjoyed something of a revival in recent years. And it is easy to see why. Its core notions of the flourishing life, the good person, character, and virtue capture much of what is central to the moral life. Yet virtue ethics is not without its critics. Two objections are often raised against it.

The first objection is the claim that given naturalistic evolutionary theory, several notions at the core of virtue theory, while not logically impossible, are nevertheless implausible. Such things as an overarching purpose to life, genuine essences or natures, and notions of proper and improper functioning are hard to harmonize with a view that depicts humans as creatures that have evolved through a blind process of chance and necessity.

One response might be found in the work of some contemporary virtue ethicists, such as Alasdair MacIntyre, who seek to explicate virtue ethics without essentialism. Roughly, virtues are features judged to be skills relevant to the good life as that is understood relative to the narrative embodied in different traditions. A tradition is a community whose members are united by a core of shared beliefs and a commitment to them. Thus, virtues are not grounded in an objective human nature; rather, they are linguistic constructions relative to the valuations and commitments of different traditions. But we have our doubts that this approach can prove successful. In addition to being subject to the criticisms of moral relativism we noted above, we doubt that a MacIntyrean notion of virtue can make sense of moral life or our deepest moral intuitions. We have a deep conviction that there is an objective difference between a good and a bad person, between a life lived well and a life lived poorly, and that the difference is more than a matter of cultural customs.

A second response that can be made would be simply to deny that there is a logical contradiction between naturalistic evolution and virtue theory. But we grant that the two do not sit easily with each other. So perhaps this conflict (together with other problems with Darwinism) is further evidence that evolution needs serious modification if not rejection.

The second objection is that virtue ethics simply fails to give guidance in resolving moral dilemmas and in knowing what to do in various moral situations. This is especially true when virtue ethics is compared with rule-based ethical theories such as deontological ethics. Rule-based theories are far better suited for providing such guidance than is virtue ethics.

This objection is overstated if it means that virtue theory provides no guidance at all for the moral life. The role of example (asking questions such as "What would Jesus do in this situation?" or imitating virtuous people) does provide guidance for leading a morally superior life. Further, the virtuous agent will use her intellect, emotion, judgment, and desire together in evaluating her duties as well as conceivable outcomes of various actions, and then she will just do the right thing. The key to virtuous action is virtuous character.

Certainly there is much more that could be said here, but it's time to move on.

WHY BE MORAL?

In concluding our discussion of ethics, we return to the metaethical question mentioned above: Why should I be moral? Note that this is not a question that any normative theory can answer; their role is to spell out what moral or immoral actions consist in and how to go about moral decision-making. But those projects assume the obligation to live a moral life.

There really are two questions here. The first is, "Why should anyone at all be moral?" Perhaps the best answer to that question comes from such fictional portrayals as William Golding's *Lord of the Flies*. It is summarized by Hobbes in his classic *Leviathan*, in which he depicts "man in the state of nature" (i.e., as we are left to ourselves), a "state of war of every man against every other man," where there is no security, no commerce, no culture, no invention, no development, and life is "solitary, poor, nasty, brutish and short." This, as Christians, we recognize as the reign of sin. And the corrosive effects of sin must be checked by moral behavior (even though regeneration is still required for salvation).

Second, we can ask, "Why should I be moral?" This question asks, in effect, why I should adopt a moral point of view. We can understand this question in the sense Glaucon put it to Socrates in Plato's *Republic.* He asks why we should prefer to be a very moral person who is unsuccessful and is regarded as immoral and not as an immoral person who is successful and appears to be highly moral. Answering the question "Why should I be moral?" will answer why I should desire to be good even if I seem bad rather than desire to be bad but seem good.

Socrates's answer to Glaucon (to which the whole *Republic* is devoted) comes to the claim that the harmony of one's soul is incompatible with an immoral life. To ask if you should prefer to be moral or immoral is like asking if you should prefer to be healthy or unhealthy. The immoral person will not, in the end, be able to enjoy his unjustly enriched life. But it isn't at all clear that there might not be people with such amoral character that they could enjoy their ill-gotten gains anyway. And don't we all know good people who are quite unhappy? We have found that even if Socrates's answer seems attractive to students, they have very little difficulty imagining someone else for whom it is false. So perhaps, in arguing that each of us should be moral, we need another argument.

We might immediately offer the religious answer. God commands us to be good, and the penalty for evil is God's judgment. But of course the religious answer will seem compelling only to someone who believes in a God of a certain type—the Judeo-Christian God—and will have no force for atheists or many agnostics. So we need to find a secular answer to the question that can persuade a secular person to adopt the moral point of view.

Think again about the question "Why should I be moral?" Is the *should* a moral or a practical *should?* If the answer is that it is a moral *should,* then it assumes that the moral point of view has already been adopted: it is moral to be moral. But that is trivial for the person who has already adopted the moral point of view and will not help at all for the one who hasn't. So we should (in the practical sense!) take the *should* in the question to be a practical or rational *should*. In this sense the question asks what practical or rational justification can be given for being moral.

Let's put it differently. Why should I incorporate the moral point of view in my worldview? Well, as rational people, we attempt to formulate a life plan, a reasonable manner of living our lives, a consistent guide to negotiating life and living it "eudaimonistically," so that we are fulfilled as persons. And we formulate our life plan in accordance with our worldview. Clearly, if our worldview incorporates features such as right and wrong, if morality is built into the universe, as it were, then immoral actions will "go against the grain of the universe" and our lives cannot reasonably be expected to go as well as if we were to go "with the grain."

This conclusion can be reached even if the only sort of ethical notions in a person's worldview are such very weak features as "It is wrong for someone to do x to me" or "I have a (moral) right to do x." But we can go a step further. Rational people, we believe, have a moral conscience. (Indeed, the inability to tell right from wrong is a legal basis for an insanity defense.) So for a rational person the conscience must play a role in a worldview and in developing a life plan. A secularist can simply accept conscience as a brute fact about the universe, as inexplicable in terms of more basic features as the fact that there are universals and particulars. Once the nontheist grants that there are basic moral obligations in the universe to which conscience points, then the envisioning of a rational life plan must include a commitment to morality as best as it can be understood. And this will lead him to think about normative ethics.

This is rather rough and quick, but the point is clear, we think. Even nontheists have reason to be moral. And they can be good without God.

They just can't explain why they should be, since they must accept morality as a brute fact about the universe, and of course, as evangelical Christians, we believe that being good without God is insufficient for salvation. But then, as we said, moral theory is not soteriology. And it is in everyone's interests, Christian and non-Christian alike, to live in a world in which most people are moral most of the time.

5

WHAT AM I?

Philosophical and Theological Anthropology

I think we ought to hold not only that man has a soul, but that it is important that he should know that he has a soul.
GRESHAM MACHEN, *THE CHRISTIAN VIEW OF MAN*

Recently the police were accused of excessive force in squelching a riot in Los Angeles. One woman complained, "The police don't need to treat us like animals! We're human beings!" Sadly, our culture's acceptance of naturalistic evolutionary theory implies just that—humans are mere animals. Questions about what we are and how we function abound today. What is a human being? Is there a soul, or are we just complex computers? Is there free will, and if so, what is it? In this chapter we will investigate two main topics: Is a human being merely physical or a combination of the physical and immaterial? and, What does it mean to say that human beings have free will?

PHILOSOPHY OF MIND

Historically, most people have been substance dualists and believed in a soul of some kind. According to substance dualism, one's various conscious states (feelings, sensations, thoughts, desires, intentional choices) are immaterial and not physical states, and the thing that contains consciousness (the I, self, ego, soul) is not the brain but rather is an immaterial subject. Many philosophers who deny dualism admit that it is the commonsense view. Throughout church history, we see the same thing. Most Christians have believed in the souls of men and beasts; more specifically, they have believed that a human has a body and a soul. The human soul, while not by nature immortal, is capable of entering an intermediate disembodied state upon death and, eventually, of being reunited with a resurrected body.

Surprisingly, some Christians reject substance dualism and embrace physicalism. According to physicalists, a human being is a physical thing—a body or a brain—and all of a human being's features are either entirely physical (that is, they can be completely described in the language of the hard sciences) or they emerge from and depend entirely on one's physical states. Their reasons are varied, but two are prominent. First, the rise of modern science has supposedly called into question the reality of a substantial soul. Allegedly, neurophysiology demonstrates the radical dependence and, in fact, identity between mind and brain. Second, some assert that biblical revelation depicts the human person as a holistic unity, whereas dualism is a Greek concept falsely read into the Bible. Christians, we are told, are committed to monism and the resurrection of the body, not to dualism and the immortality of the soul.

Neither claim is convincing. Regarding the dependence of mental functioning on the brain, the dependence is actually a two-way street, with brain functioning also being influenced by mental functioning. And just because one thing depends on another, it does not follow that they are identical or that they are composed of the same sort of stuff. The physical universe depends on God for its functioning, but it does not follow that the physical universe is immaterial or that God is material.

Regarding the claim that dualism is the result of projecting Greek thought into the Bible, this is simply false. The case for Old Testament anthropological dualism rests on two lines of evidence. First, while admitting of a wide range of meanings, two key anthropological terms, *nefesh* (soul) and *ruakh* (spirit), have clear cases where they mean an immaterial center of thought, desire, and emotion—a continuing locus of personal identity that departs at death, reunites with a resurrection body, and is that which God adds to the body to make a living person (Gen 35:18; 1 Kings 17:21-23; Ps 146:4; Ezek 37). In this sense *nefesh* and *ruakh* are used of disembodied spirits (angels) and of God himself. Second, *refaim* is the Old

Testament term for the dead in Sheol, and it frequently refers to disembodied persons there (Ps 88:10-12; Is 14:9-10). Old Testament affirmation of a disembodied intermediate state explains Old Testament warnings about necromancy (communicating with the dead; cf. Deut 18:11; 1 Sam 28).

Turning to the New Testament, the evidence for some form of substance dualism is quite powerful. Death is referred to as a giving up of the spirit (*pneuma*) in Matthew 27:50 or soul (*exepsyxen*) in Acts 5:10. The dead in the intermediate state are described as spirits or souls (Heb 12:23; Rev 6:9-11) prior to the resurrection of the body. Jesus himself distinguished the body and soul (Mt 10:28), taught that the patriarchs continued to be alive after their burial (Mt 22:23-33), and promised the thief on the cross that he would be in paradise that very day (Lk 23:42-43). Paul affirmed a naked (that is, disembodied) intermediate state such that to be absent from the body was to be with the Lord (2 Cor 5:1-10), and he believed that during a visionary experience he may well have been temporarily disembodied himself (2 Cor 12:1-4).

Granting that Christianity seems to teach some form of dualism, we may still wonder what the extrabiblical evidence says. In what follows, we will defend property and substance dualism, respectively; examine objections against dualism; and critique three forms of physicalism.

CONSCIOUSNESS AND PROPERTY DUALISM

The nature of consciousness. At least five kinds of conscious states exist. A *sensation* is a state of awareness or sentience—for instance, a conscious awareness of sound or pain. Some sensations are experiences of things outside me, like a tree. Others are awarenesses of states within me, like pains. Emotions are a subclass of sensations and, as such, are forms of awareness of things. I can be aware of something in an angry way. A *thought* is a mental content that can be expressed in an entire sentence. Some thoughts logically imply other thoughts.

For example, "All dogs are mammals" entails "This dog is a mammal." If the former is true, the latter must be true. Some thoughts don't entail but merely provide evidence for other thoughts. For example, certain thoughts about evidence in a court case provide grounds for the thought that a person is guilty. A *belief* is a person's view, accepted to varying degrees of strength, of how things really are. A *desire* is a certain felt inclination to do, have, or experience certain things. An *act of will* is a choice, an exercise of power, an endeavoring to act, usually for the sake of some purpose.

Are properties (such as being a pain or a thought) and the events composed of them (a pain or thinking event) genuinely mental, or are they physical? Property dualists argue that mental states are not physical since they possess *five* features not owned by physical states:

1. There is a raw qualitative feel or a "what it is like" to have a mental state such as a pain.
2. At least many mental states have intentionality—*ofness* or

aboutness—directed toward an object.
3. Mental states are inner, private, and immediate to the subject having them.
4. They require a subjective ontology: namely, mental states are necessarily owned by the first-person sentient subjects who have them.
5. Mental states fail to have crucial features (e.g., spatial extension, location) that characterize physical states and, in general, cannot be described using physical language.

We cannot undertake a defense of the mental nature of all five of these features. Rather, we shall examine three important arguments for property/event dualism.

Three arguments for the view that consciousness isn't physical. First, given an accurate description of consciousness (see above), it becomes clear that mental properties/events are not identical to physical properties/events. Mental states are characterized by their intrinsic, subjective, inner, private, qualitative feel, made present to a subject by first-person introspection. For example, a pain is a certain felt hurtfulness. The true nature of mental states cannot be described by physical language, even if through study of the brain one can discover dependency relations between mental/brain states. In addition to having the first four features listed above, mental states have some or all of the following features, none of which is a physical feature of anything. Some sensations are vague: for example, a sensation of an object may be fuzzy or vague, but no physical state is vague. Some sensations are pleasurable or unpleasurable, but nothing physical has these properties: for instance, a cut in the knee is, strictly speaking, not unpleasurable; it is the pain event caused by the cut that is unpleasurable. Mental states can have the property of familiarity (e.g., when a desk looks familiar to someone), but familiarity is not a feature of a physical state. Since mental states have these features and physical states do not, mental states are not identical to physical states.

> ## FIVE KINDS OF CONSCIOUS STATES
>
> ***Sensation:*** A state of awareness or sentience
>
> ***Thought:*** A mental content that can be expressed in an entire sentence
>
> ***Belief:*** A person's views of how things really are
>
> ***Desire:*** A felt inclination to do, have, or experience certain things
>
> ***Act of will:*** A free choice; an exercise of power, usually for the sake of some end

A second argument for property/event dualism is called the *knowledge argument.* Suppose that Mary, a scientist blind from birth, knows all the physical facts relevant to acts of perception. When she suddenly gains the ability to see, she gains knowledge of new facts. Since she knew all the physical facts before recovery of sight and since she gains knowledge of new facts, these newly acquired facts must not be physical facts; moreover, given

Mary's situation, they must be mental facts.

To appreciate the argument, recall the distinctions we made in chapter three between three kinds of knowledge. (1) *Knowledge by acquaintance:* One has such knowledge when one is directly aware of something—for example, when one sees an apple directly before him. One does not need a concept of an apple or knowledge of how to use the word *apple* to have knowledge by acquaintance of an apple. (2) *Propositional knowledge:* This is knowledge that a proposition is true. For example, knowledge that "the object there is an apple" requires having a concept of an apple and knowing that the object under consideration satisfies the concept. (3) *Know-how:* This is the ability to do certain things, for example, to use apples for certain purposes. Generally, knowledge by acquaintance provides grounds for propositional knowledge, which in turn provides grounds for genuine know-how. It is because one sees the apple that one knows that it is an apple, and it is in virtue of one's knowledge of apples that one has the skill to do things to or with them.

By way of application, for the first time Mary comes to have a specific mental property—a sensation of red. In this way, Mary gains six new kinds of knowledge: she gains knowledge by acquaintance, propositional knowledge, and skill both with regard to the color red and her sensation of red. Mary now knows by acquaintance what redness is. On further reflection and experience, she can now know things like "Necessarily, red is a color." She also gains skill about comparing or sorting objects on the basis of their color (of how to arrange color patterns that are most beautiful or natural to the eye, etc.). Assuming that the color red is in the external world (e.g., on the surface of an apple) and not inside the mind itself, we may say that the three kinds of knowledge just listed are not themselves knowledge of mental facts but are forms of knowledge (in this case, of redness itself) that can be gained only by having the relevant mental states (in this case, by having a sensation of red).

Further, Mary gains knowledge about her sensation of red. She is now aware of having a sensation of red for the first time and can be aware of a specific sensation of red's being pleasurable, vague, and so on. She also has propositional knowledge about her sensations. She could know that a sensation of red is more like a sensation of green than it is like a sour taste. She can know that the way the apple appears to her now is vivid, pleasant, or like the way the orange appeared to her (namely, redly) yesterday in bad lighting. Finally, she has skill about her sensations. She can recall them to memory, re-image things in her mind, adjust her glasses until her sensations of color are vivid, and so on.

Physicalists respond to the argument in this way:[34] When Mary gains the ability to see red, she gains no knowledge of any new facts. Rather,

---

[34] David Papineau, Philosophical Naturalism (Cambridge, MA: Blackwell, 1993), 103, 114; and Paul M. Churchland, Matter and Consciousness (Cambridge, MA: MIT Press, 1984), 33-34.

she gains new abilities, new behavioral dispositions, new know-how, new ways to access the facts she already knew before gaining the ability to see. Before the experience, Mary knew all there was to know about the facts involved in what it is like to experience red. From a third-person perspective, she could imagine what it would be like for some other person to experience red. She could know what it is like to have an experience of red due to the fact that this is simply a physical state of the brain and Mary had mastered the relevant physical theory before gaining sight. But now she has a *prelinguistic representation* of redness, a *first-person* ability to image redness or *re-create* the experience of redness in her memory. She can *reidentify* her *experience of* red and *classify* it according to the type of experience it is by a new *"inner" power of introspection.* Prior to the experience, she could merely recognize when someone else was experiencing red "from the outside" (that is, from observing the behaviors of others). Thus, the physicalist admits a duality of types of knowledge but not a duality of facts that are known.

For two reasons, this response is inadequate. First, it is false that Mary gains a new way of knowing what she already knew instead of gaining knowledge of a new set of facts. Previously listed are some of Mary's new factual knowledge, and it seems obvious that Mary failed to have this factual knowledge prior to gaining the ability to see.

Second, when physicalists describe Mary's new know-how, they help themselves to a number of notions that clearly seem to be dualist ones (listed in italics above): *prelinguistic representation, image, first-person introspection*, and so forth. These dualist notions are the real intuition pumps for the physicalist rejoinder. Remove the dualist language and replace it with notions that can be captured in physicalist language, and the physicalist response becomes implausible.

The third argument for property/event dualism is based on intentionality: some (perhaps all) mental states have intentionality. No physical state has intentionality. Therefore, (at least) some mental states are not physical. Intentionality is the "ofness" or "aboutness" of various mental states. One has a sensation *of* the door, a thought *about* summer, a belief *about* abortion.

Many physicalists, especially those called *functionalists* (see following), depict humans as computers and consciousness as software. Accordingly, they identify intentionality with physical causal/functional relations. Functionalists describe mental properties/states in terms of bodily inputs, behavioral outputs, and other mental-state outputs. For example, for a computer to think "about" math is just for it to receive certain inputs from a keyboard (2+2) and give certain outputs through the printer (4). The software is whatever state is in the computer that gives the correct output when it receives certain input. Applied to mental states like pain, this model holds that a pain is whatever "software" state is produced by pin sticks and so forth and causes a tendency to grimace and desire pity. The state of desiring pity is, in turn, spelled out in terms of other mental states and bodily outputs. Mental properties are like software; they are functional kinds. A pain is not a state with a certain intrinsic quality (namely, hurtfulness); rather, it is a function an organism performs. Thus, a completely inanimate computer can be "conscious," for example; it can have a thought or be in pain if it performs the right outputs (produces "Ouch!" given the correct input, e.g., a pin prick).

Dualists respond by pointing out that computers function as though they have mental states about various things, but they do not really have such states. Computers have artificial intelligence, not real intelligence. Just because a computer or a brain can function according to the right inputs and outputs, this does not mean that a computer or brain actually has thoughts *about* adding, beliefs *about* various data, sensations *of* different objects. Real mental states have intentionality—they are literally of or about various things—but mere functional devices, whether computers or brains, do not; they merely imitate intentionality.

We have seen reasons to affirm property dualism: consciousness and conscious states are mental and not physical. But what about the bearer of consciousness? Is it immaterial or something physical, like the brain or body?

THE SELF AND SUBSTANCE DUALISM

In this section we argue for substance dualism—namely, that the owner of consciousness (the soul or self) is immaterial. Substance dualists are also property dualists because substance dualists believe that both the ego and consciousness itself are immaterial. But one can be a mere property dualist without being a substance dualist if one accepts the immateriality of consciousness but holds that its owner is the body or, more likely, the brain. In contrast with mere property dualism, substance dualists hold that the brain is a physical thing which has physical properties and that the mind or soul is a mental substance which has mental properties. When I am in pain, my brain has certain physical properties (electrical, chemical), and my soul or self has certain mental properties (the conscious awareness of pain). The soul is the possessor of its experiences. It stands behind, over, and above them and remains the same throughout one's life. The soul and the brain can interact with each other, but they are different particulars with different properties.

We offer three arguments for some form of substance dualism.

Our basic awareness of the self. When we enter most deeply into ourselves, we become aware of a very basic fact: we are aware of our own self (ego, I, center of consciousness) as being distinct from our bodies and from any particular mental experience we have, and as being an uncomposed, spatially unextended center of consciousness. I simply have a basic, direct awareness of the fact that I am not identical to my body or my mental events; rather, I am the immaterial self that *has* a body and a conscious mental life.

An experiment may help convince you of this. Right now I am looking at a chair in my office. As I walk toward the chair, I experience a series of chair representations. That is, I have several different chair experiences that replace one another in rapid succession. As I approach the chair, my chair sensations vary. If I pay attention, I am also aware of two more things. First, I do not simply experience a series of sensory images of a chair. Rather, through self-awareness, I also experience the fact that it is I myself who has each chair experience. Each chair sensation produced at each angle of perspective has a perceiver who is I. An *I* accompanies each sensory experience to produce a series of awarenesses: *I am experiencing a chair sense image now.*

I am also aware of the basic fact that the same self that is currently having a fairly large-chair experience (as my eyes come to within twelve inches of the chair) is the very same self as the one who had all the other chair experiences preceding this current one. Through self-awareness, I am aware of the fact that I am an enduring *I* who was and am (and will be) present as the owner of all the experiences in the series.

These two facts—I am the owner of my experiences, and I am an enduring self—show that I am not identical to my experiences. I am the conscious thing that has them. I am also aware of myself as a simple, uncomposed, and spatially unextended center of consciousness. (I am "fully present" throughout my body; if my arm is cut off, I do not become four-fifths of a self.) In short, I am a mental substance.

Unity and the first-person perspective. A complete physicalist description of the world would be one in which everything would be exhaustively described from a third-person point of view in terms of objects, properties, processes, and their spatiotemporal locations.[35] For example,

---

[35] Some material in this and the following section are adapted from J.P. Moreland and Scott B. Rae, Body and Soul: Human

a description of an apple in a room would go something like this: "There exists an object three feet from the south wall and two feet from the east wall, and that object has the property of being red, round, sweet and so on."

The first-person point of view is the vantage point that I use to describe the world from my own perspective. Expressions of a first-person point of view utilize what are called *indexicals:* words like *I, here, now, there,* and *then.* Here and now are where and when I am; there and then are where and when I am not. Indexicals refer to me, myself. *I* is the most basic indexical, and it refers to myself that I know by acquaintance with my own self in acts of self-awareness. I am immediately aware of my own self, and I know to whom *I* refers when I use it: it refers to me as the self-conscious, self-reflexive owner of my body and mental states.

According to physicalism, there are no irreducible, privileged first-person

---

Nature and the Crisis in Ethics (Downers Grove, IL: InterVarsity Press, 2000).

perspectives. Everything can be exhaustively described in an object language from a third-person perspective. A physicalist description of me would say, "There exists a body at a certain location that is five feet eight inches tall, weighs 160 pounds," and so forth. The property dualist would add a description of the properties possessed by that body, such as "the body is feeling pain" or "the body is thinking about lunch."

But no amount of third-person descriptions captures my own subjective, first-person acquaintance of my own self in acts of self-awareness. In fact, for any third-person description of me, it would always be an open question as to whether the person described in third-person terms was the same person as I am. I do not know myself *because* I know some third-person description of a set of mental and physical properties and also know that a certain person satisfies that description. I know myself as a self immediately through being acquainted with my own self in an act of self-awareness. I can express that self-awareness by using the term

I, which refers to my own substantial self. It does not refer to any conscious experience or bundle of such experiences I am having, nor does it refer to anybody described from a third-person perspective.

A related argument has been offered by William Hasker.[36] The argument is an attempt to show that the unity of consciousness cannot be explained if one is a brain, because a brain is just an aggregate of different physical parts. It is only if the self is a single, simple subject that the unity of consciousness is adequately accounted for.

To grasp the argument, consider one's awareness of a complex fact, say, one's own visual field, consisting of awareness of several objects at once, including a number of different surface areas of each object. One's entire visual field is composed of several different experiences: for example, an awareness of a desk toward one's left side and an awareness of a podium in the center of

---

[36] William Hasker, The Emergent Self (Ithaca, NY: Cornell University Press, 1999), 122-46.

one's visual experience of an entire classroom. Corresponding to such an experience, thousands of different light waves are bouncing off different objects (and off different locations on the surface of the same object, say, different areas of the desk's top side); they all interact with the subject's retinas, and they all spark signals that terminate in myriads of different parts of the brain. Accordingly, a physicalist may claim that such a unified awareness of the entire room by means of one's visual field consists in the fact that there are a number of different physical parts of the brain, each of which terminates a different wavelength and each of which is aware only of part of and not the whole of the complex fact (the entire room). However, this will not work, because it cannot account for the fact that there is a single, unitary awareness of the entire visual field. It is the very same self that is aware of the desk to the left, the podium at the center, and, indeed, each and every distinguishable aspect of the room. But there is no single part of the brain that is correspondingly activated as a terminus for the entire visual field. Only a single, uncomposed mental substance can account for the unity of one's visual field or, indeed, the unity of consciousness in general.

The modal argument. Thought experiments have rightly been central to this debate in which two persons switch bodies, brains, or personality traits or in which a person exists disembodied. In these thought experiments, someone argues in the following way: Because some situation S (e.g., Smith's existing disembodied) is conceivable, this provides justification for thinking that S is metaphysically possible. Now if S is possible, then certain implications follow about what is or is not essential to personal identity (e.g., Smith is not essentially a body). We all use conceiving as a test for possibility/impossibility throughout our lives. I know that life on other planets is possible (even if I think it is highly unlikely or downright false) because I can conceive it to be so.

Let us apply these insights about conceivability and possibility to the modal argument for substance dualism.

People know that disembodied life after death, even if false, is at least a possibility. When people hear of near-death experiences or ponder surviving the destruction of their bodies, they easily believe these things *could possibly* be so because they can conceive of them. But it is obvious that their brains and bodies could not survive in a disembodied state! Since something is true of them (they are disembodiable), not of their body/brain, they cannot be the same as their bodies/brains. The same is true of a person's mental life and character. A person could exist with a different set of memories and character traits, so a person is not the same thing as his or her memories or character. Rather, a person is what has a body/brain and has a mental life and character.

A parallel argument can be advanced in which the notions of a body and disembodiment are replaced with the notions of physical objects in general. (It is not hard to conceive that one could exist even if the entire material world were destroyed.) So understood, the argument would imply the conclusion that one has good grounds for thinking that one is not identical to a physical object and that being physical is not essential to one's identity. A parallel argument can also be developed to show that possessing the ultimate capacities of sensation, thought, belief, desire, and volition are essential to one; that is, one is a substantial soul or mind.

We cannot undertake a full defense of the argument here, but it would be useful to a say a bit more about our knowledge of ourselves. There are a number of things about ourselves and our bodies of which we are aware that ground what we can and cannot conceive of ourselves. For example, I am aware that I am unextended (I am fully present at each location in my body, as Augustine claimed) and that I am neither a complex aggregate of separable parts nor the sort of thing that can be composed of physical parts. Rather, I am aware that I am a basic unity of inseparable faculties (of mind, volitions, emotion, etc.) that sustains absolute sameness through change and that is not capable of gradation (I cannot become two-thirds of a person).

In near-death experiences, people report themselves to have been disembodied. They are not aware of having bodies in any sense. Rather, they are aware of themselves as unified egos that have sensations, thoughts, and so forth. Moreover, Christians who understand the biblical teaching that God and angels are bodiless spirits also understand by direct introspection that they are like God and angels in the sense that they are (1) spirits with the same sorts of powers God and angels have but that they also have bodies and (2) the New Testament teaching on the intermediate state is intelligible in light of what they know about themselves, and it implies that we will and therefore can exist temporarily without our bodies. In 2 Corinthians 12:1-4, Paul asserts that he may actually have been disembodied. These factors ground people's ability to conceive of themselves as existing in a disembodied state, and this provides grounds for thinking that this is a real possibility (even if it is false, though, of course, we do not think it is false). Thus, one cannot be one's body, nor is one's body essential to him.

OBJECTIONS TO DUALISM

We have seen that a good case can be presented on behalf of property and substance dualism. But what are the arguments against dualism? Three have been especially prominent.

Two philosophical objections to dualism. First, physicalists claim that on a dualist construal of a human being, mind and body are so different that it seems impossible to explain how and where they interact. How could a soul, totally lacking in any physical properties, cause things to happen to the body or vice versa?

This objection assumes that if we do not know *how* A causes B, then it is not reasonable to believe *that* A causes B, especially if A and B are different. But this assumption is not a good one. We often know that one thing causes another without having any idea of how causation takes place, especially when the two items are different. Even if one is not a theist, it is not inconceivable to believe it possible for God, if he exists, to create the world or to act in that world, even though God and the material universe are very different. Even if we grant that there is no God, if the idea of a spiritual God causing things to happen in a material world is not in itself unintelligible, then it is hard to see why a similar idea that a human soul can exercise free will and raise an arm is problematic. In the case of mind and body, we are constantly aware of causation between them. Episodes in the body (being stuck with a pin, having a head injury) can cause things in the soul (a feeling of pain, loss of memory), and the soul can cause things to happen in the body (worry can cause ulcers, one can freely and intentionally raise his arm). With such overwhelming evidence *that* causal interaction takes place, there is no sufficient reason to doubt it.

Furthermore, it may even be that a "how" question regarding the interaction between mind and body cannot even arise. A question about how *A* causally interacts with *B* is a request for an intervening mechanism between *A* and *B* that can be described. One can ask how turning the key starts a car because there is an intermediate electrical system between the key and the car's running engine that is the means by which turning the key causes the engine to start. The "how" question is a request to describe that intermediate mechanism. But the interaction between mind and body may be, and most likely is, direct and immediate. There is no intervening mechanism, and thus a "how" question describing that mechanism does not even arise.[37]

The second objection involves the problem of other minds: if dualism is true, we can never know that other people have mental states because those states are private mental entities to which outsiders have no direct access. In this regard dualism implies skepticism in two ways: it leaves us

---

[37] See also J.P. Moreland, "The Argument from Consciousness," in The Rationality of Theism, ed. Paul Copan and Paul Moser (London: Routledge, 2003), 204-20.

skeptical as to whether other minds exist in the first place; and even if they do, it leaves us skeptical as to what other persons' mental states are like. Perhaps they have reversed quality experiences compared to me: for example, they sense redness and joy when I sense blueness and pain, and vice versa. When my daughter was in fifth grade, she actually asked me how we knew that it wasn't the case that when her mother saw a red object, she saw it as blue but used the word *red* to talk about it, while everyone else saw it as red and used the word *red* just like mom did! If dualism is true, the objector continues, we could never know.

The dualist problem of other minds has been greatly exaggerated. For one thing, dualism does, in fact, imply the following: from what we know about a person's brain, nervous system, and behavior, we cannot logically deduce his or her mental states. But, again, far from being a vice, this implication seems to be the way things really are. In fact, this truth about people was central to the knowledge argument for dualism. That the dualist is correct here is so commonsensical that even young children occasionally wonder if they may sense colors in a way different from others. In general, it *is* logically possible for one person to be in one kind of mental state and another person to be in a different kind of mental state even though their physical states are the same.

Second, the logical possibility just mentioned does not imply skepticism about other minds. We do not know something only if it is logically impossible that we be wrong about it. We all know many things—for example, that we had coffee this morning—even though it is logically possible that we may have been mistaken. Regardless of how we explain our knowledge of other minds, we do, in fact, have such knowledge, and the mere logical possibility that we are wrong about the mental states of another is not sufficient to justify skepticism.

A scientific objection to dualism. It is well known that one of the driving forces behind physicalism is evolutionary theory. Evolutionist Paul Churchland makes this claim:

> The important point about the standard evolutionary story is that the human species and all of its features are the wholly physical outcome of a purely physical process. If this is the correct account of our origins, then there seems neither need, nor room, to fit any nonphysical substances or properties into our theoretical account of ourselves. We are creatures of matter. And we should learn to live with that fact.[38]

Since humans are merely the result of an entirely physical process (the processes of evolutionary theory) working on wholly physical materials, then humans are wholly physical beings. Something does not come into existence from nothing; and if a purely physical process is applied to wholly physical materials, the result will be a wholly physical thing, even if it is a more

---

[38] Churchland, Matter and Consciousness, 21.

complicated arrangement of physical materials!

Dualists could argue that this objection is question begging. To see this, note that the objection can be put into the logical form known as *modus ponens* (that is, if *P,* then *Q;* and *P;* therefore, *Q*):

> If humans are merely the result of naturalistic, evolutionary processes, then physicalism is true. Humans are merely the result of naturalistic, evolutionary processes. Therefore, physicalism is true.

However, the dualist could adopt the *modus tollens* form of the argument (that is, if *P,* then *Q;* and not-*Q;* therefore, not-P):

> If humans are merely the result of naturalistic, evolutionary processes, then physicalism is true. But physicalism is not true. Therefore, it is not the case that humans are merely the result of naturalistic, evolutionary processes.

In other words, the evolutionary argument begs the question against the dualist. The dualist could say that the *modus tollens* form of the argument should be embraced, not the *modus ponens* form.

In fact, the existence of finite minds can be used as evidence for the existence of God. If we grant what Churchland acknowledges—namely, that there is no scientific explanation for the origin of mind, including no evolutionary explanation—and if scientific and theistic explanations are the best live alternatives, then we can explain the origin of finite minds best by appealing to a divine mind as its most adequate cause. If we limit the alternatives to what are live options for most people in Western culture, in the beginning were either the particles or the *logos* (mind). It is easier to see how finite mind could come from a universe that is fundamentally Mind (God being more basic in reality than matter) than it is to see how mind could come from particles.

A CRITIQUE OF PHYSICALIST ALTERNATIVES TO

DUALISM REGARDING CONSCIOUSNESS

Type-identity physicalism. Currently there are three main versions of physicalism: *type-identity physicalism, functionalism,* and *eliminative materialism.* Type-identity physicalists claim that mental properties/types are identical to physical properties/types. Moreover, identity statements asserting the relevant identities are construed as contingent identity statements (true statements that, nevertheless, could have turned out to be false) employing different yet co-referring expressions. For example, the statement "Red is identical to wavelength x" is contingently true (while true, it could have been false, unlike "2+2=4," which is a necessary truth), and the terms *red* and *wavelength x* both refer to the same thing (namely, a specific wavelength), even though the terms do not have the same dictionary definition. Likewise, the statement "Painfulness is identical to a C-fiber firing pattern" is allegedly a contingent identity statement. The truth of these identity statements is an empirical discovery that could have turned out to be false.

Two main objections seem decisive against type-identity physicalism.[39] First, it is obvious that mental and physical properties are different from each other (see above), and physicalists have not met the burden of proof required to overturn these deeply ingrained intuitions.

Physicalists respond that in other cases of identity (e.g., heat is mean molecular kinetic energy), our intuitions about nonidentity turned out to be wrong, and the same is true in the case of mental properties. But for two reasons, this response fails. For one thing, these other cases of alleged property identities are most likely cases of correlation of properties. Second, we can easily explain why our intuitions

---

[39] The rest of this section has been adapted from J.P. Moreland, "The Soul and Life Everlasting," in Philosophy of Religion: A Contemporary Reader, ed. William Lane Craig (New York: Rutgers University Press, 2002), 429-46.

were mistaken (granting that they were mistaken for the sake of argument) in the other cases, but a similar insight does not appear in the case of mental properties. Since there is a distinction between what heat is (mean molecular kinetic energy) and how it appears to us (as being warm), our intuitions about nonidentity confused appearance with reality. But since mental properties such as painfulness are identical to the way they appear (a pain just is the way it seems to us, viz., as a hurtful state), no such source of confusion is available. Thus, intuitions about their nonidentity with physical proper ties remain justified.

THREE VERSIONS OF PHYSICALISM

Type-identity physicalism: Mental properties (e.g., painfulness) are identical to physical properties (e.g., being a C-fiber firing).

Functionalism: Types of mental states are "software states" identical to (1) bodily inputs, (2) behaviors, and (3) other mental states as outputs. Types of mental states are functional roles realized by particular brain states. A pain-type state is identical to (1) a state of being caused by things like pin sticks, (2) a state of causing one to grimace and shout "ouch!," and (3) a state of causing one to want pity.

Eliminative materialism: Mental states do not exist, and mental terms belong to an outmoded theory called *folk psychology*.

The second difficulty with type-identity theory is called the *multiple realization problem:* humans, dogs, Vulcans, and a potentially infinite number of organisms with different physical type states can all be in pain, and thus the mental kind, being painful, is not identical to a particular physical kind.

Functionalism. Largely in response to this last problem, a different version of physicalism, called *functionalism,* has risen to prominence. Functionalists treat the mental life like software and describe mental properties/states in terms of bodily inputs, behavioral outputs, and other mental state outputs. Such a characterization depicts a mental state in terms of its functional role in behavior (a pain is whatever state is produced by pin sticks, etc., and which causes a tendency to grimace and desire pity), not in terms of its intrinsic attributes (a pain is intrinsically something that hurts). Type-identity physicalism is a hardware view; functionalism is a software position. For the functionalist, the mental life is not something a person has; it is something a person does.

There are at least two serious difficulties with functionalism in its various formulations. First, there are problems regarding absent or inverted *qualia*. A *quale* (plural, *qualia*) is a specific sort of intrinsically characterized mental state, such as seeing red, having a sour taste, or feeling a pain. If a Vulcan realized the correct functional role for pain but exemplified the causal intermediary of being appeared to redly while feeling no hurtfulness at all, the functionalist will say the Vulcan is in pain. But it seems obvious that the

Vulcan is not in pain but rather is experiencing the mental state of an appearing-of-red, and this supports property dualism. Qualia arguments turn on the observation that mental kinds are essentially characterized by their intrinsic properties and accidentally characterized by their extrinsic functional relations. Thus, property dualism correctly captures the essence of mental properties, and functionalism fails on this score.

Second, functionalism fails to account for first-person knowledge of one's own mental states by introspection. On a functionalist interpretation, what makes a specific pain event a pain has nothing whatever to do with its intrinsic features. What makes for a specific kind of mental event is entirely a matter of its extrinsic relations to inputs from the environment and to bodily and other mental outputs. The same brain event that realizes pain in one possible world could realize any other mental state in a different world with a different functional context. Thus, there is no way for a subject to know what mental state he is having by being conscious of it. In fact, since bodily outputs are essential to the mental event's very identity, one would have to wait until he observed his own behavior to see what mental state he was in! Any view that implies this absurdity is surely false!

Eliminative materialism. The third major alternative to dualism is eliminative materialism. On this view mental terms like *pain* do not get their meaning from a subject's own first-person experience of pain. Rather, they get their meaning from their role in *folk psychology,* a commonsense theory designed to explain the behaviors of others (grimacing) by attributing mental states (pain) to them; and, like flat-earth theories, folk psychology will eventually be abandoned and replaced with some neurophysiological theory. Thus, the various mental terms of folk psychology fail to refer to anything that actually exists (e.g., there is no such thing as a flat earth and there is no such thing as a belief or a thought) and should be eliminated. Some eliminative materialists apply the view to all mental states (including sensations such as pain), while others limit it to propositional states such as beliefs and thoughts.

Eliminative materialism has not garnered widespread acceptance. First, dualism is not primarily a theory, much less a replaceable one; rather, it is a descriptive report of the mental self and its states with which one is acquainted through introspection. Second, it simply seems implausible to say that no one has ever actually had a sensation or belief. Third, some have argued that, in effect, eliminative materialism is self-refuting in that it advocates the belief that there are no such things as beliefs. Some eliminative materialists have responded that self-refutation can be avoided because, while their view does in fact reject the existence of beliefs, it does allow for a physical replacement that plays the same role as beliefs, and this replacement is what the theory advocates. But many critics remain skeptical of this response on the grounds that if an entity is found that actually plays the same role as a belief, it will be a belief by another name. If it plays a different role, then self-refutation may be avoided only at the expense of proffering an inadequate revisionism.

In sum, it needs to be said that it is not science but philosophical naturalism that supports physicalism. The mind-body problem is not primarily a scientific one. Though briefly presented, these arguments provide solid philosophical grounds for rejecting physicalism and accepting property and substance dualism. As Christians have affirmed for centuries, human persons are both body and soul.

TWO PHYSICALIST ALTERNATIVES TO SUBSTANCE DUALISM REGARDING THE HUMAN PERSON

In the previous section, we evaluated the main physicalist views about consciousness and our mental states (e.g., sensations, thoughts, beliefs). In this section, we turn to an evaluation of physicalist views—not of consciousness but of the "self," the human person, the possessor/unifier of consciousness. While there are a handful of physicalist alternatives to substance dualism regarding the identity of a human being or human person, two are of special interest—animalism and the brain view. In what follows, we will present each followed by a critique.[40]

ANIMALISM

The view. According to animalism, we are essentially identical to animals, biological *organisms,* bodies. As such, we are substantial continuants that sustain absolute identity through accidental change even though we are made up entirely of matter and may gain and lose parts over time.

What explains an animal's ability to retain literal sameness through part replacement? The answer is that animals

---

[40] For more in this, see J.P. Moreland and William Lane Craig, Philosophical Foundations for a Christian Worldview, 2nd ed. (Downers Grove, IL: InterVarsity Press, 2017), 280-86, 292-94.

have lives, or, more accurately, lives "have" animals. A *life* is a self-organizing, self-sustaining event that enables the organism to sustain its internal structure despite material turnover. A life is a vast array of biological events/processes. How does a life provide the ability for an organism to retain identity through part replacement? In this way: Consider organism O_1 at time t_1 composed of all and only the parts called "the ps." Each part is constantly undergoing events, changes, and biological processes. Let us call the set of all the events of the ps at t_1 "the es." Now consider an organism O_2 at a later time t_2. Let all and only its parts at t_2 be called "the qs" and let us call the set of all the events of the qs at t_2 "the ks." Now we can state persistence conditions for organisms/animals in this way:

P_o: O_1 at time t_1 is identical to O_2 at time t_2 just in case the es are caught up into or constitute life L_1 at t_1, the ks are caught up into or constitute life L_2 at t_2, and L_1 is identical to L_2.

Put more simply, if the activities of an organism's parts and those of "another" organism's parts are both caught up into the same life, then the "two" organisms are actually identical. The idea is that the event called "a life" is ontologically more fundamental than an organism, and the life is the organism's career such that the life—a special kind of event, that is, the sum of the metabolic activities of the organism's parts—sustains the delicate, complicated structure among the organism's parts. A life is a homeodynamic storm of atomic simples (a dynamic set of processes over time that draw in and expel parts while maintaining its structure), a self-maintaining, well-individuated, jealous event. An organism persists just in case the metabolic process that is its life continues to impose its characteristic organization on new parts.

Moreover, what is it for a set of entities—the xs—to count as parts? The xs compose (are parts of) some y (and y will always be an organism) if and only if the activities of the xs constitute a life. Finally, while we are essentially animals, we are accidentally persons. Being a person is like being a teenager—a phase we go through when certain psychological criteria are met (e.g., capable of reasoning, forming goals and developing ways to achieve them). Thus, you exist at conception, but since you are merely an animal, you have little value; eventually you become a person for a while, and if, at the end of life, you fail to satisfy the relevant psychological criteria for personhood, you continue to exist, but now as a nonpersonal animal. Key animalists are Eric Olson, Peter van Inwagen, and Trenton Merricks.[41]

Assessing animalism. Besides the fact that animalism allows one to avoid what some take to be problematic substance dualism, the main argument for animalism is that it solves *the thinking animal problem.* Suppose we

---

[41] See Eric Olson, What Are We? (Oxford: Oxford University Press, 2007); Peter van Inwagen, Material Beings (Ithaca, NY: Cornell University Press, 1990); Trenton Merricks, Objects and Persons (Oxford: Oxford University Press, 2001).

see Bob sitting in a chair. Now there seems to be a thinking animal in that chair—a living organism/body with a mental life indistinguishable from Bob's and this living body is intimately related to Bob. Since the thinking animal and Bob are indistinguishable—they are like each other physically and mentally—it seems obvious that we should just identify Bob and the thinking animal. Otherwise, we have to believe there are (at least) two thinkers in the same chair—the thinking animal and Bob. But this is to multiply entities without warrant, and animalism solves the problem nicely.

Many philosophers offer two responses to this argument. First, the intuition on which the argument is built—there seems to be a thinking animal in that chair—is just plain false. Except for a small handful of Western intellectuals who have accepted physicalism (and most physicalists are not animalists), the overwhelming majority of people throughout the world today and since Neanderthals have been dualists regarding the self. This is evidenced by the widespread belief throughout human history that when we die, we leave our bodies and continue conscious existence in an afterlife. Almost no one looking at Bob in the chair would think that he qua living body is a conscious, thinking being. No, apart from many Western intellectuals, virtually everyone would think that if Bob were shot dead in that chair, he would leave his body and continue to think and be conscious. When a television show comes on that features near-death experiences, virtually everyone, including skeptics of their validity, will say something like this: "I am skeptical about these near-death experience claims, but I'll admit they *could* be true, and whether or not they are veridical is a matter of the quality of the evidence for and against them."

No one would say this about the search for evidence of square circles in Montana. We all know such things cannot be found because a square circle is broadly logically impossible. We don't have to look for evidence one way or another by trudging through Montana! The fact that people are willing to look at the evidence means they take disembodied existence to be broadly logically possible; they would not believe this if they were animalists since an animalist holds that we are essentially living, physical organisms. As such, an organism existing in a disembodied state is broadly logically impossible. No search for evidence is needed to rule out disembodied existence. Because disembodied existence is metaphysically possible, this entails that we are not essentially physical beings as animalists would have it. The claim that most people see Bob as a thinking animal is simply false.

Second, if animalism is true, then it is hard to see how the problems of the reality of free agency and the unity of consciousness can be solved. The former problem will be discussed in the next section, and the latter was treated earlier in the chapter, so we won't go into detail here except to note that they present difficulties for those who think that a living, physical organism thinks and has free will. It seems, then, that the main argument for animalism does not succeed. Are there strong arguments against animalism? We believe so, and the following set of arguments form a cumulative case against animalism that, in our view, makes it untenable.

Objection one. For animalists, lives are ontologically basic or primitive, and an organism is a derived entity that gets its existence and identity from the relevant living event. But this seems backward. Lives do not "have" organisms in the animalist sense; organisms have lives. According to contemporary biology, lives are not self-sustaining but organisms are. In fact, life is characterized as a set of certain activities that occur within an organism. Thus, organisms are primitive and lives are derivative. This is the overwhelming majority view since Aristotle, and surely the burden of proof is on the animalist to overturn this burden. But so far as we can tell, there are no arguments—surely no sufficient arguments—for flip-flopping lives and organisms, and thus the burden of proof has not been met.

Objection two. While *mereological essentialism* may hold for a mere collection of cells, animalists assert that it is just false when applied to living organisms. Unfortunately, things aren't that simple. Admittedly, the vast majority of us have strong intuitions that living beings sustain absolute sameness even if they undergo part replacement. But, as we discussed in chapter two, given the atomic theory of matter and the reduction of living things to *mereological aggregates,* it is hard to see how such organisms could survive part replacement. It seems to us that the best explanation for why organisms are literal continuants involves appeal to some form of substance dualism. So, while animalists seem correct about organisms being continuants, their ontological analysis of organisms undermines this possibility. Biological structure and a life are themselves in constant flux and thus are not metaphysically robust enough to ground the identity of organisms through part replacement. The animalist ontology cannot provide a metaphysical analysis of organisms that avoids treating them as mereological aggregates subject to mereological essentialism.

Appealing to a life won't help the animalist here. At any given moment, a life is a collection of numerous activities, and from moment to moment, those activities change. When an organism sleeps, runs, loses an organ, and so forth, different living activities obtain. A life, then, is an extended event that is composed of a waxing and waning flux of very different subevents. Thus, a life in the animalist view is not the same from one moment to the next. Some animalists claim that as a primitive fact, life itself is a continuant that is wholly present at each moment the life exists. But besides the fact that this move seems to turn a life into a substance and not an event, there is no evidence for this claim. We know that "life" is reducible to a set of living activities that occur at a time, and a moment later they are over and replaced with other activities in serial succession. In sum, life as animalists construe it is not itself a continuant; it is in constant flux and thus cannot serve as the ground for an organism's being a continuant.

Objection three. Some argue that animalism gets the wrong answer to how many living beings there are, because animalism tracks biological features instead of the more preferable psychological traits. To see this, consider two conjoined twins fused from the upper to lower region of the chest area. How many living beings are there? It is clear that there are two living organisms/bodies and two persons, each with his own stream of consciousness.

So far so good. Now consider the fictitious case of Arnold. Let us assume Arnold is a living human person in some sense or other. Arnold has only one living body, but miraculously there are two completely independent streams of consciousness and subjects of those streams. When a single living animal such as you has thoughts like "I am hungry" and "I am tired," it is appropriate to say that the animal has the conjunct-thought "I am hungry and tired."

But this is not so with Arnold. One stream/subject thinks "I am hungry" and the other thinks "I am tired," but we cannot infer from this that there is a thinking being with the conjunct-thought. It seems clear that there are two living, thinking things—in this case, persons—and not one. If we track biological traits like the animalist does, we will say that there is just one living, thinking animal. After all, there is just one living body. But if we track psychological traits, there are two streams of consciousness/two subjects of experience and therefore two unified persons present. According to some, by emphasizing biological life instead of unified consciousness, animalism selects the wrong criterion for counting the number of living, thinking beings.

Objection four. Animalism suffers from a *sorites paradox* (sometimes called the paradox of the heap). Grant that one hundred thousand grains of sand piled on one another is a heap of sand. If we remove one grain of sand, it seems it still is a heap. If we remove just one more grain of sand it still is a heap, and so on and so on. It seems that we could get down to one grain of sand and still call it a heap, which is absurd, or admit that there is some seemingly arbitrary point such that if you remove one particular grain of sand at that point, the heap goes out of existence. Many have solved this particular sorites paradox by claiming either that heaps don't really exist in the first place or that our concept of being a heap is a vague, unclear one that we use for various purposes but is not precise enough to spell out exactly how many grains of sand one needs for a heap. "Heap" like "baldness" are loose, vague concepts.

Unfortunately, neither of these options is available for animalism. There clearly are (according to animalism) living organisms, and thinking ones at that. And lives that give existence and identity to organisms are self-maintaining, well-individuated (ontologically speaking, for any part, it either is or is not part of the organism as a whole; organisms are not ontologically vague), and jealous ("desiring" to retain their structure and identity) events. But now the sorites paradox seems to present a very serious problem for animalism. If we remove one tiny part (and thus its activities) from an organism, does the organism still exist and retain its identity? Clearly, the animalist will say yes. If we remove one more tiny part, do we still retain the same organism in existence? Yes. But we know that if we reach a point at which, say, we have just five tiny particles jumping around, the organism no longer exists.

These facts raise two uncomfortable problems for animalists. First, it seems odd to say that at some point the removal of just one tiny atomic simple causes the entire organism to go out of existence. Such a tiny cause is hardly adequate to explain such a significant metaphysical effect. Second, the removal of that one, specific atomic simple seems entirely arbitrary for causing the organism to pop out of existence. Why not the atomic simple removed just before the correct one? Why not the one removed after the correct one? Any answer to this question will have an air of arbitrariness and ad hocness about it. And this counts strongly against animalism.

THE BRAIN VIEW

The view. The brain view is most likely the position held by most practicing scientists—especially neuroscientists—who are physicalists. The position is fairly easy to characterize: I am identical to a brain. Now, as stated, the view is clearly false because many parts of the brain have no direct connection to consciousness (e.g., certain tissues, blood in the brain), and certain nonbrain parts do have direct connection to consciousness (e.g., certain parts of the nervous system like the optic nerve). Moreover, as stated, the view does not explain why one would select the brain as opposed to, say, the liver, the lungs, or the heart. Thus, the brain view (I am a brain) must be supplemented with two other principles.

Thinking Subject Maximalism. A thinker's (a conscious person's) parts are all and only those directly involved in thinking (i.e., consciousness). This explains why the brain is chosen and why certain brain parts are ruled out and certain nonbrain parts are ruled in (e.g., the nervous system). But Thinking Subject Maximalism (TSM) leads to a difficulty with the brain view. It leads to many different selves because different subregions of the brain have parts such that all and only those parts are directly involved in different, isolated states of consciousness (e.g., sensing color, sensing shape, feeling empathy). Thus, "I" actually turn out to be a collection of selves: a color-sensing self, a shape-sensing self, and so on. So the TSM principle must be supplemented with the following principle to unify the brain into one person and rule out the problem of subsystems.

The Psychological Individuation Principle. Conscious states belong to the same person if and only if they causally interact with each other and with no other person's thoughts. It should be clear how this principle is supposed to unify all the brain's subsystems into one person. For example, certain sensations such as a feeling of thirst can cause a desire for a drink of water. This desire can, in turn, cause a thought that the desire can be satisfied by using the drinking fountain nearby. Note that these are three very different conscious states that would be directly related to different subsystems of the brain—a sensation, a desire, and a thought. But since there is causal interaction among the three states, according to the Psychological Individuation Principle, they are all states of the same person.

In sum, this is a brief but accurate depiction of the brain view.

Assessing the view. However popular the brain view may be, it suffers from very significant difficulties. First, it suffers from all the difficulties mentioned in regard to other physicalist views (it cannot explain near-death experiences and the metaphysical possibility of disembodied existence, it cannot permit libertarian free will, it cannot avoid mereological essentialism, and so forth).

Second, it needs TSM and the Psychological Individuation Principle (PIP) to avoid problematic entailments mentioned above. Take TSM. The phrase *directly involve with* is extremely vague and most likely means "that directly cause conscious states." But this seems to violate two key roles for any entity taken to be the human person: (1) the owner of consciousness and (2) the possessor of a point of view. The brain view seems to depict various brain states as subvenient causes for emergent mental properties/states. Thus, TSM becomes "A thinker's (a conscious person's) parts are all and only those that cause emergent conscious properties/states." But in general, if x causes y, y does not belong to x nor does x own y. When fire causes smoke, lightning causes thunder, exposing sodium to oxygen causes a flame, the effects may be produced by their respective causes, but those effects are independent entities that do not belong to their causes.

In order for the entity that is a human person to possess consciousness, that entity must exemplify consciousness, and that is not what the brain does if it causes emergent properties/states. Moreover, the principle seems backward. A thinker's (separable) parts are not all and only those that cause consciousness. No, the reason some (inseparable) parts cause consciousness and others do not (e.g., digestive juices) is that the former are parts of a thinker. Things do what they do because of the parts and properties they have, not vice versa.

Now take PIP. First of all, PIP is not necessary. One can have a brief idle thought that belongs to him but has no causal relation whatever to other thoughts. Again, while some mental states (a feeling of pain) do cause others (a desire for pain medication), this is not always the case. When one thinks through a syllogism (e.g., If *P*, then *Q;P;* therefore *Q*), one undergoes a sequence of three different thoughts. But the first two do not cause the thought of conclusion. No, they entail the thought of the conclusion, and the thinker freely draws that conclusion by having an insightful awareness of the first two thoughts and their logical relations. In general, the stages of rational deliberation are not sequences in which earlier insights cause later ones. The earlier insights give evidence for later ones. Finally, in near-death experiences, a very high percentage of the millions of people who have had such experiences (and the tens of thousands who have been studied and researched about their experiences) claim that communication is direct between God and the person or persons having a near-death experience. In these cases, no intermediate sentences or assertions are needed; communication is a form of telepathy. But if in these cases (and surely these are metaphysically possible even if one thinks—irrationally—that they are all false) another person directly causes someone to have a thought, PIP is not satisfied, yet the thought is still the recipient's.

Second, PIP is backward. The reason it is generally (but not universally) true that one's conscious states causally interact with each other and no one else's is because those states belong to a specific person ontologically prior to their causal interaction with other states.

Third, the brain view cannot avoid or accommodate certain indexical facts. According to the brain view, I am identical to a brain. But which one? No exhaustive third-person description of all the brains in the world will provide us an answer. Why? Because we would have to already know that the brain we are third-person describing is mine or else we would not know whose brain was being described.

Nor can the brain view adjust itself and say that I am identical to *my* brain. There are two problems lurking in the neighborhood. First, *my* is classified as either a possessive adjective or possessive noun (as the word *mine*). In either case it is derivative of the first-person indexical *I* (e.g., "*I* have *this* brain," where the italicized words are *indexicals*). So there is an indexical fact about the owner of the brain being a specific I that is not captured by third-person physicalist language. In addition, if I am my brain, then saying "my brain" is like "my thumb" or "my car." In all cases, I am not identical to the thing I possess; I am its owner. Thus, "I am my brain" implies that I am not identical to my brain; rather, I am the thing that has a brain.

Fourth, the brain view suffers from the problem of too many thinkers. As mentioned above, there are various subsystems to the brain that are involved with their own isolated sort of conscious states, and therefore we should consider the brain view to entail several selves, not one. And given that TSM and PIP are failures, the brain advocate cannot appropriate them to avoid this problem.

Fifth, brains are divisible and can be present in percentages, as can brain functioning, but persons are all or nothing and cannot exist as a percentage of a person. In certain operations, over half of the brain is removed and a certain amount of functioning is lost, but there is still a complete person present. This would not be the case if a person is identical to a functioning brain.

For these reasons, we believe the brain view must be rejected.

FREEDOM AND DETERMINISM

General comparison. All Christians believe we have free will, but they differ about how free will is to be understood. Determinism is the view that for every event that happens, there are conditions such that, given them, nothing else could have happened.[42] Every event is caused or necessitated by prior factors such that, given these prior factors, the event in question had to occur. Libertarians embrace free will and hold that determinism is incompatible with it. Compatibilists hold that freedom and determinism are compatible with each other and thus the truth of determinism does not eliminate freedom. As we will see, compatibilists have a different understanding of free will from the one embraced by libertarians.

Compatibilism. For compatibilists, if determinism is true, then every human action (e.g., raising one's hand to vote) is causally necessitated by events that obtained prior to the action, including events that existed before the person acting was born. That is, human actions are mere happenings, parts of causal chains of events leading up to them.

---

[42] This section is adapted from J.P. Moreland, "Complementarity, Agency Theory, and the God-of-the-Gaps," Perspectives on Science and Christian Faith 49 (March 1997): 2-14.

But freedom properly understood is compatible with determinism.

Libertarianism. Libertarians claim that the freedom necessary for responsible action is not compatible with determinism. Real freedom requires a type of control over one's action—and, more importantly, over one's will—such that, given a choice to do *A* (raise one's hand and vote) or *B* (refrain from voting, leave the room), nothing determines that either choice is made. Rather, the agent himself must simply exercise his own causal powers and will to do one alternative, say, *A*. When an agent wills *A*, he also could have chosen *B* without anything else being different inside or outside of his being. He is the absolute originator of his own actions. When an agent acts freely, he is a first or unmoved mover; no event causes him to act. His desires, beliefs, and so on may influence his choice, but free acts are not caused by prior states in the agent.

We can delve more deeply into compatibilist and libertarian accounts of freedom by looking at three areas central to an adequate theory of free will.

Three areas of comparison between compatibilism and libertarianism.

The ability condition. In order to have the freedom necessary for responsible agency, one must have the ability to choose differently from the way the agent actually does. Compatibilists and libertarians agree that a free choice is one where a person *can* will to do otherwise, but they differ about what this ability is. Compatibilists see this ability as a hypothetical ability. Roughly, this means that the agent would have done otherwise had some other condition obtained—for instance, had the agent desired to do so. We are free to will whatever we desire even though our desires are themselves determined. Freedom is willing to act on your strongest preference.

Libertarians view hypothetical ability as a sleight of hand and as not sufficient for the freedom needed for responsible agency. For libertarians, the real issue is not whether we are free to do what we want but whether we are free to want in the first place. A free act is one in which the agent is the ultimate originating source of the act. Freedom requires that we have the categorical ability to will to act. This means that if Smith freely wills to do *A,* she could have refrained from willing to do *A* without any conditions whatever being different. No description of Smith's desires, beliefs, character, or other things in her makeup and no description of the universe prior to and at the moment of her choice to do *A* is sufficient to entail that she did *A.* It was not necessary that anything be different for Smith to refrain from choosing *A.*

The libertarian notion of categorical ability includes a dual ability: if one has the ability to exert his power to do *A,* one also has the ability to refrain from exerting his power to do *A.* By contrast, the compatibilist notion of hypothetical ability is not a dual ability. Given a description of a person's circumstances and internal states at time t, only one choice could obtain at t, and the ability to refrain is not there; its presence depends on the hypothetical condition that the person had a desire (namely, to refrain from acting) which was not actually present.

The control condition. Suppose Jones raises his hand to vote. Compatibilists and libertarians agree that a necessary condition for the freedom of this act is that Jones must be in control of the act itself. But they differ radically as to what control is.

In order to understand compatibilist views of the control condition, recall that compatibilists take cause and effect to be characterized as a series of events making up causal chains with earlier events together with the laws of nature (either deterministic or probabilistic) causing later events. The universe is what it is at the present moment because of the state of the universe at the moment before the present together with the correct causal laws describing the universe. A crude example of such a causal chain would be a series of one hundred dominos falling in sequence from the first domino on until the one hundredth domino falls. Suppose all the dominos are black except numbers forty through fifty, which are green. Here we have a causal chain of events that progresses from domino one to one hundred and that "runs through" the green dominos.

Now, according to compatibilism, an act is free only if it is under the agent's own control. And it is under the agent's own control only if the causal chain of events—which extends back in time to events realized before the agent was even born—that caused the act (Jones's hand being raised) "runs through" the agent himself in the correct way. But what does it mean to say that the causal chain "runs through the agent in the correct way"? Here compatibilists differ from each other. But the basic idea is that an agent is in control of an act just in case (that is, if and only if) the act is caused in the right way by prior states of the agent himself (e.g., by the agent's own character, beliefs, desires, and values). This idea is sometimes called a *causal theory of action.*

Libertarians reject the causal theory of action and the compatibilist notion of control and claim that a different sense of control is needed for freedom to exist. Consider a case where a staff moves a stone but is itself moved by a hand that is moved by a man. In *Summa Contra Gentiles,* St. Thomas Aquinas states a principle about causal chains that is relevant to the type of control necessary for libertarian freedom:

> In an ordered series of movers and things moved [to move is to change in some way], it is necessarily the fact that, when the first mover is removed or ceases to move, no other mover will move [another] or be [itself] moved. For the first mover is the cause of motion for all the others. But, if there are movers and things moved following an order to infinity, there will be no first mover, but all would be as *intermediate movers....* [Now] that which moves [another] as an instrumental cause cannot [so] move unless there be a principal moving cause [i.e., a first cause, an unmoved mover].[43]

---

[43] Thomas Aquinas, Summa Contra Gentiles 1.13 (emphasis added).

Suppose we have nine stationary cars (A-I) lined up bumper to bumper and a tenth car (T) runs into the first car (A), causing each to move the next vehicle until car nine on the end (I) is moved. Suppose further that all the cars are black except cars E through H, which are green. Now what caused the ninth car (I) to move? According to Aquinas, cars B to H are not the real cause of motion for car I. Why? Because they are only *instrumental causes;* each of these cars passively receives motion and transfers that motion to the next car in the series. Car T is the real cause since it is the first mover of the series. It is the source of motion for all the others. Only first movers are the sources of action, not instrumental movers that merely receive motion passively and pass that on to the next member in a causal chain.

For libertarians, it is only if agents are first causes, unmoved movers, that they have the control necessary for freedom. An agent must be the absolute, originating source of his own actions to be in control. If, as compatibilists picture it, an agent is just a theater through which a chain of instrumental causes passes, then there is no real control. Further, the control that an unmoved mover exercises in free action is a dual control: it is the power to exercise his own ability to act or to refrain from exercising his own ability to act.

Table 2. Compatibilist and libertarian freedom compared

Condition	Compatibilist	Libertarian
Ability	1. The ability is hypothetical. One could have done otherwise if one had different desires and beliefs. 2. The ability is one-way. At any time, one could not refrain or do otherwise.	1. The ability is categorical. It is not conditional on anything changing in order to obtain a different result. 2. The ability is two-way. At any time, one can either do something or refrain—both are genuine metaphysical possibilities.
Control	3. Freedom relies on a causal theory of action; that is, an action is under one's control if it was caused in the right way by appropriate prior mental states (not unlike dominos falling). 4. The control is one-way.	3. Freedom requires a first, unmoved mover to originate action. Aristotle, for example, says that if a stone is moved by a staff, the staff is moved by a hand, and the hand is moved by a man, then the man is the efficient cause and the rest are instrumental causes. 4. The control is two-way.
Rationality	5. Reasons are efficient causes; that is, that by means of which an effect is produced. They are temporally prior to or simultaneous with a given effect. When Jones raises his hand to vote, the compatibilist says that a belief/desire state in Jones has caused his hand to raise to vote. It is useful to note that on this view, Jones does not actually do anything; he is merely a container of beliefs and desires. There are no actions on this view, only happenings.	5. Reasons are a final goal; that is, that for the sake of which an effect is produced. They are a desired future state.

The rationality condition. The rationality condition requires that an agent have a personal reason for acting before the act counts as a free, rational one. Consider again the case of Jones's raising his hand to vote. In order to understand the difference between the two schools in how to handle this case in light of the rationality condition, we need to draw a distinction between an *efficient* and a *final cause.* An efficient cause is that by means of which an effect is produced. One ball moving another is an example of efficient causality. By contrast, a final cause is that for the sake of which an effect is produced. Final causes are teleological goals, purposes for which an event is done; the event is a means to the end that is the final cause.

Now a compatibilist will explain Jones's voting in terms of efficient and not final causes. According to this view, Jones had a desire to vote and a belief that raising his hand would satisfy this desire, and this state of affairs in him (the *belief/desire set* composed of the two items just mentioned) caused the state of affairs of his hand going up. On this view, a reason for acting turns out to be a certain type of state in the agent, a belief/desire state, that is the real efficient cause of the action.

Persons as substances do not act; rather, states within persons cause latter states to occur.

Many libertarians respond by saying that our reasons for acting are final and not efficient causes. Jones raises his hand in order to vote or, perhaps, in order to satisfy his desire to vote. In general, when person *S* does *A* in order to *B*, *B* states the reason (e.g., a desire or a value), which is the teleological purpose for the sake of which *S* freely does *A*. Here the person acts as an unmoved mover by simply exercising his powers in raising his arm spontaneously. His beliefs and desires do not cause the arm to go up; he himself does. But *B* (the desire to vote) serves as a final cause for the sake of which *A* (raising his hand) is done. Thus, compatibilists embrace a belief/desire psychology (states of beliefs and desires in the agent cause the action to take place), while at least many libertarians reject it and see a different role for beliefs and desires in free acts.

THEOLOGICAL IMPLICATIONS OF THE FREE WILL DEBATE

The issues we've just discussed have a direct bearing on theological debates over the freedom of the will between Augustine and Pelagius, John Calvin and Martin Luther and Jacobus Arminius, and between their many theological heirs. Over the centuries, the issues have become diffused, vocabulary has changed, and the points of many of the historical disputes are obscure to all but the historical theologians. We will not even begin to resolve the many issues involved; nevertheless, we would like to note three points.

First, these days the issue is often cast in terms of God's sovereignty. If God is not sovereign of all, it is said, he is not sovereign at all. As an argument, if God does not control everything, then he is not sovereign. But if humans have libertarian freedom, then God does not control everything. Therefore, if humans have libertarian freedom, God is not sovereign. But we doubt any reasonable Christian libertarian would deny that at all times God is in control of everything. What they deny is that he actually exercises active control in everything. The libertarian maintains only that some morally significant actions are free in a libertarian sense, not that all are; and a Christian libertarian will maintain that God has granted a limited freedom to humans, that he can and sometimes does intervene to assure that his will is accomplished, but that this does not entail that he always intervenes. Just as God need not continually exercise all his powers to do anything in order to remain omnipotent, so too he need not exercise his sovereign control at all times to remain sovereign.

Second, a libertarian can consistently maintain both that humans have (delegated) libertarian freedom and that no human can freely decide to trust Christ. That is, the inward work of the Holy Spirit is necessary if a person is to trust Christ for salvation, yet that person can still enjoy the sort of freedom which the libertarian believes is essential to moral accountability. On this view, a person has genuine freedom to do good or evil, but no matter how much good the person does, it will not suffice for salvation (for which faith in Christ is necessary, faith that is due to the working of God's Spirit).

Third, many compatibilists are guilty of posing a false dilemma when they argue that if an action is not caused by a person's character or desires or reasons (or some such thing), then the action is random. As we said above, libertarians believe that reasons are not efficient causes and that a free agent is a first cause herself. An agent acts, and no set of individually necessary and jointly sufficient antecedent conditions determine the action. Yet since the agent is a person, the action is not random, the product of chance quantum events in the motor regions of the brain (or some such thing).

Again, as with all these issues, there is much more to say, but we must leave matters here. One thing should be clear at the end of this chapter: it is of paramount importance that we know what we are as human persons. If we don't, the effects may well be catastrophic on how we relate to other persons and other things in creation as well as on how we relate to God himself.

6

HOW SHOULD CHRISTIANS THINK ABOUT SCIENCE?

Philosophy of Science

The theorist who maintains that science is the be-all and end-all—that what is not in science textbooks is not worth knowing—is an ideologist with a peculiar and distorted doctrine of his own. For him, science is no longer a sector of the cognitive enterprise but an all-inclusive world-view. This is the doctrine not of science but of scientism. To take this stance is not to celebrate science but to distort it.

NICHOLAS RESCHER

Science is a crucial component of the modern world. People who lived during the Civil War had more in common with Abraham than with us. From DNA research to computer science, ours is a world of science.

For Christians this comes as no surprise. We believe in a rational God who created the world and human faculties such that we could gain knowledge from our exploration of his world. Christians celebrate scientific knowledge. Unfortunately, as the above quote from Nicholas Rescher warns, ours is a culture that frequently distorts rather than celebrates science. To see what we mean by this, consider the following.

In 1989, California issued a new science framework to provide guidance for the state's public school science classrooms. It contained advice about how to handle students who approach teachers with reservations about evolution:

> At times some students may insist that certain conclusions of science cannot be true because of certain religious or philosophical beliefs they hold.... It is appropriate for the teacher to express in this regard, "I understand that you may

have personal reservations about accepting this scientific evidence, but it is scientific knowledge about which there is no reasonable doubt among scientists in their field, and it is my responsibility to teach it because it is part of our common intellectual heritage."[44]

Christians cannot afford to read this statement with a surface analysis of what it indicates about our culture. Its real importance lies not in its promotion of evolution over creation, though that is no small matter. No, its real danger resides in *the picture of knowledge it presupposes:* the only, or at least the most reliable, knowledge we can have about reality—and, thus, the only claims that deserve the backing of public institutions—is empirical knowledge (knowledge in some way or another testable by the five senses, allowing for instruments like microscopes that extend the senses) gained by the hard sciences. Nonempirical claims outside

---

[44] Cited in Mark Hartwig and Paul Nelson, Invitation to Conflict (Colorado Springs, CO: Access Research Network, 1992), 20.

the hard sciences, such as those at the core of ethics, political theory, and religion, are not items of knowledge but rather matters of private feeling.

Notice the words associated with science: *conclusions, evidence, knowledge, no reasonable doubt, intellectual heritage.* These deeply cognitive terms express the view that science alone exercises the intellectual right of defining reality. By contrast, religious claims are described in distinctively noncognitive language: *beliefs, personal reservations.*

In such a culture we now live and move and have our being as disciples of Jesus. Like leaven, this attitude toward scientific knowledge relative to alleged nonempirical fields such as theology has begun to permeate the church. For example, Christian scholar Karl Giberson claims that "Science, after all, is but one limited perspective on the world, although I would argue that it is the most epistemologically secure perspective that we have."[45] For thinking

---

[45] Karl Giberson, "Intelligent Design on Trial: A Review Essay," Christian Scholar's

Christians, this perspective is unacceptable. Christians are in the knowledge business, imparting theological, ethical, and political knowledge to others and providing tools necessary to obtain it. We are not in the "belief" business, passing on mere beliefs or a religious "tradition" from one generation to the next. As we noted above, Christianity is about knowledge. So we must think carefully about science and its relationship to a Christian worldview, and philosophy is the field in which such reflection takes place. Let's get started.

WHERE DO WE GO FOR HELP?

In 2002 a conference on intelligent design took place in Kansas City. Representatives from all sides of the

---

Review 24 (May 1995): 469; cf. Karl Giberson, Worlds Apart (Kansas City, MO: Beacon Hill, 1993); and J.P. Moreland, "Theistic Science and the Christian Scholar: A Response to Giberson," Christian Scholar's Review 24 (May 1995): 472-78.

issue were present, including a number of scientists and science teachers who oppose creationism and intelligent design theory. During the conference, those scientists repeatedly claimed that because the scientific method requires that one explain data by appealing to natural laws and natural processes, creationism was a religious perspective and not a scientific one. Even if creationist explanations were true, they said, once a person appeals to God, that person has stopped doing science and entered the field of religion.

Interestingly, a number of pastors and lay Christians regularly deferred to the scientists as the proper authorities to make this sort of claim about the scientific method. However, as we will see in this section, this claim about science and a number of similar claims are not scientific assertions at all but are philosophical claims about science. If this is correct, then a scientist as a scientist is no more of an authority on the issue than is a pastor or layperson who has done some serious reading in philosophy of science. Let's delve more deeply into this issue.

Philosophy is, in part, a second-order discipline that studies the assumptions, concepts, and argument forms of other disciplines, including science. By contrast, science is a set of first-order disciplines. In philosophy of science, we investigate questions *of* philosophy *about* science. Philosophers and historians of science, and not scientists themselves, are authorities trained to deal with these types of questions. In science we investigate questions *of* science *about* a specific realm of scientific study. Here scientists are the authorities.

Here are first-order questions scientists formulate: What is a covalent bond, and how does it work? What is the structure of a methane molecule? What makes an ecosystem stable? Scientists are the experts regarding these questions. By contrast, here are second-order philosophical questions about science for which philosophers and historians, not scientists, are the experts: What is science? Are there clear necessary and sufficient conditions that some intellectual activity must have to count as science? Is there such a thing as the scientific method, and, if so, what is it? How do scientific theories explain things?

Unfortunately, controversy rages over which field is the proper place to turn in order to seek professional expertise in resolving these second-order questions. Consider this statement by J.W. Haas Jr., editor of the influential *Perspectives on Science and Christian Faith:* "The place of the philosopher in the practice of science has long been controversial. Whether philosophers should (can?) be the arbiters of what constitutes science remains problematic for the working scientist."[46] Along similar lines, Giberson rejects "the traditional viewpoint that practicing scientists find so annoying, namely that philosophers are the relevant, competent and final authorities to determine the rules of science."[47]

---

[46] J.W. Haas Jr., "Putting Things into Perspective," Perspectives on Science and Christian Faith 46 (March 1994): 1.

[47] Giberson, "Intelligent Design," 460.

Actually the issue is not controversial at all, since the central topics do not involve how to *practice* science (which requires familiarity with instrumentation, procedures, etc.) but how to *define* science and *distinguish* it from nonscience. But as we have seen, these and related matters are largely philosophical in nature. This is not to say that scientists and others cannot be a part of this discussion; it is merely to affirm that when they participate, they will be largely dealing with philosophical issues for which they are not professionally trained.

The fact that these issues are philosophical and not primarily scientific can be seen from the following: Read the relevant debates and discussions and ask what scientific experiment or scientific procedure one would use to resolve the dispute. Or get any college catalog and look at the course descriptions in different branches of science. You will discover that almost nowhere in an undergraduate or graduate program in any branch of science are the relevant topics discussed, except perhaps in the first week of freshman chemistry. By contrast, entire graduate programs in the history or philosophy of science are devoted to definitions of science and similar second-order issues. By way of application, those pastors and laypersons at the Kansas City conference who had done some reading in the relevant literature in philosophy of science actually had more authority to speak on many topics being debated than did the scientists who had not read the philosophical literature.

SHE BLINDED ME WITH SCIENCE (SCIENTISM)

Scientism is the view that science is the very paradigm of truth and rationality.[48] If something does not square with currently well-established scientific beliefs, if it is not within the

---

[48] This section is adapted from J.P. Moreland, introduction to The Creation Hypothesis: Scientific Evidence for an Intelligent Designer, ed. J.P. Moreland (Downers Grove, IL: InterVarsity Press, 1994), 14-17.

domain of entities appropriate for scientific (that is, empirical) investigation, or if it is not amenable to scientific methodology, then it is not true or rational. Everything outside of science is a matter of mere belief and subjective opinion, of which rational assessment is impossible. Science, exclusively and ideally, is our model of intellectual excellence.

Actually there are two forms of scientism: *strong scientism* and *weak scientism*. Strong scientism is the view that some proposition is true or rational to believe if and only if it is a scientific proposition—that is, if and only if it is a well-established scientific proposition that, in turn, depends on its having been successfully formed, tested, and used according to appropriate scientific methodology. There are no truths apart from scientific truths, and even if there were, there would be no reason whatever to believe them.

Advocates of weak scientism allow for the existence of truths apart from science and are even willing to grant that they can have some minimal, positive rationality status without the support of science. But advocates of weak scientism still hold that science is the most valuable, most serious, and most authoritative sector of human learning. Every other intellectual activity is inferior to science. Further, there are virtually no limits to science. There is no field into which scientific research cannot shed light. To the degree that some issue outside science can be given scientific support or can be reduced to science, the issue becomes rationally acceptable. Thus, we have an intellectual obligation to try to use science to solve problems in other fields that heretofore have been untouched by scientific methodology. For example, we should try to solve problems about the mind by the methods of neurophysiology and computer science.

If either strong or weak scientism is true, this would have drastic implications for the integration of science and theology. If strong scientism is true, then theology is not a cognitive enterprise at all and there is no such thing as theological knowledge. If weak scientism is true, then the conversation between theology and science will be a monologue, with theology listening to science and waiting for science to give it support. For thinking Christians, either of these alternatives is unacceptable. What, then, should we say about scientism?

To begin, strong scientism is self-refuting. Strong scientism is not itself a proposition *of* science but rather a second-order proposition *of* philosophy *about* science to the effect that only scientific propositions are true and/or rational to believe. And strong scientism is itself offered as a true, rational belief. Self-refuting propositions (e.g., "There are no truths") don't just happen to be false though they could have been true. They are necessarily false: it is not possible for them to be true. Thus, no amount of scientific progress in the future will have the slightest effect on making strong scientism more acceptable.

There are two more problems that count equally against strong and weak scientism. First, scientism (in both forms) does not adequately allow for the task of stating and defending the necessary presuppositions for science itself to be practiced (assuming scientific realism). Thus, scientism shows itself to be a foe and not a friend of science.

Science cannot be practiced in thin air. It requires a number of philosophical theses that must be assumed if science is going to get off the runway. Each assumption has been challenged, and the task of stating and defending them falls to philosophy. The conclusions of science cannot be more certain than the presuppositions it rests on and uses to reach those conclusions.

Strong scientism rules out these presuppositions altogether because neither the presuppositions themselves nor their defense are scientific matters. Weak scientism misconstrues their strength in its view that scientific propositions have greater cognitive authority than those of other fields, like philosophy. This would mean that the conclusions of science are more certain than the philosophical presuppositions used to justify and reach those conclusions, and that is absurd. In this regard the following statement by John Kekes strikes at the heart of weak scientism:

A successful argument for science being the paradigm of rationality must be based on the demonstration that the presuppositions of science are preferable to other presuppositions. That demonstration requires showing that science, relying on these presuppositions, is better at solving some problems and achieving some ideals than its competitors. But showing that cannot be the task of science. It is, in fact, one task of philosophy. Thus the enterprise of justifying the presuppositions of science by showing that with their help science is the best way of solving certain problems and achieving some ideals is a necessary precondition of the justification of science. Hence philosophy, and not science, is a stronger candidate for being the very paradigm of rationality.[49]

---

[49] John Kekes, The Nature of Philosophy (Totowa, NJ: Rowman & Littlefield, 1980), 158.

Here is a list of some of the philosophical presuppositions of science:
- the existence of a theory-independent, external world
- the orderly nature of the external world
- the knowability of the external world
- the existence of truth
- the laws of logic and mathematics
- the reliability of our cognitive and sensory faculties to serve as truth gatherers and as sources of justified beliefs in our intellectual environment
- the adequacy of language to describe the world
- the existence of values used in science (e.g., "test theories fairly and report test results honestly")
- the uniformity of nature and induction

Most of these assumptions are easy to understand. It may be helpful, however, to say a word about the last one. Scientists make inductive inferences from past or examined cases of some phenomenon (e.g., "All observed emeralds are green") to all cases, examined and unexamined, past and future, of that phenomenon (e.g., "All emeralds whatever are green"). The *problem of induction* is the problem of justifying such inferences. It is usually associated with David Hume. Here is his statement of it:

> It is impossible, therefore, that any arguments from experience can prove this resemblance of the past to the future, since all these arguments are founded on the supposition of that resemblance. Let the course of things be allowed hitherto ever so regular, that alone, without some new argument or inference, proves not that for the future it will continue so. In vain do you pretend to have learned the nature of bodies from your past experience. Their secret nature, and consequently, all their effects and influence, may change without any change in their sensible qualities. This happens sometimes, and with regard to some objects. Why may it not happen always, and with regard to all objects? What logic, what process of argument secures

you against this supposition? My practice, you say, refutes my doubts. But you mistake the purport of my question. As an agent, I am quite satisfied in the point; but as a philosopher who has some share of curiosity, I will not say skepticism, I want to learn the foundation of this inference.[50]

We cannot look here at various attempts to solve the problem of induction except to note that inductive inferences assume what has been called the *uniformity of nature:* the future will resemble the past. And the uniformity of nature principle is one of the philosophical assumptions of science.

There is a second problem that counts equally against strong and weak scientism: the existence of true, reasonable beliefs outside of science. The simple fact is that true, rationally justified beliefs exist in a host of fields outside of science. Many of the issues

---

[50] David Hume, An Inquiry Concerning Human Understanding (1748; repr., Indianapolis: Bobbs Merrill, 1965), 51-52 (section 4.2 in the original).

in this book fall in that category. Strong scientism does not allow for this fact, and it is therefore to be rejected as an inadequate account of our intellectual enterprise.

Moreover, some propositions believed outside science (e.g., "Torturing babies for fun is wrong"; "I am now thinking about science") are better justified than some believed within science (e.g., "Evolution takes place through a series of very small steps"). Some of our currently held scientific beliefs will be revised or abandoned in one hundred years, but it would be hard to see how the same could be said of the extrascientific propositions just cited. Weak scientism does not account for this fact. In sum, scientism in both forms is inadequate. There are domains of knowledge outside and independent of science; and while we have not shown this here, theology is one of those domains. How, then, should the domains of science and theology be integrated?

INTELLIGENT DESIGN AND METHODOLOGICAL NATURALISM

The main area where the debate about the integration of science and theology has been focused is in the creation/evolution controversy, so let's use that controversy to spell out the broader question of integration.

Theological options in the creation/evolution controversy. *Evolution* has several meanings. First, it may mean "change over time." This sense of evolution is uncontroversial if taken to mean that *microevolution* has occurred—that is, that organisms can and have changed in various ways within certain limits. Second, it may mean the thesis of common descent: all organisms are related by common ancestry. This is sometimes called *macroevolution,* especially when coupled with the third meaning of evolution: the blind watchmaker thesis. This is a thesis about the mechanism of evolution, an explanation of how evolution in the first two senses has occurred. The thesis states that the processes of evolution are nonintelligent, purposeless, and completely naturalistic (e.g., through mutation, natural selection, genetic drift).

There are three main camps among Christians regarding the creation/evolution controversy. First, there are *young earth creationists.* Advocates contend that God's work of creation took place in six literal, consecutive days of twenty-four hours each and that the original creation of the universe took place recently, say, ten to twenty thousand years ago. Moreover, most young earth creationists hold that the flood of Noah, understood as a universal deluge, is a major key for understanding the earth's geological column.

> ## THREE SENSES OF EVOLUTION
>
> ***Microevolution:*** Organisms change over time.
>
> ***Thesis of common descent:*** All organisms are related by common ancestry.

> ***The "blind watchmaker" thesis:*** The processes of evolution are nonintelligent, purposeless, and completely naturalistic.

Second, there are *progressive creationists* (sometimes called *old earth creationists*) who hold that theistic evolution is scientifically and biblically inadequate, contending that there is strong scientific and biblical evidence that God has miraculously acted to create at various times. Progressive creationists differ over how often God has done this, but many say that God directly created each "kind" of organism, and most agree that God directly created "the heavens and earth," first life (especially animal life), and Adam and Eve. Progressive creationists do not take the days of Genesis to be consecutive, literal twenty-four-hour periods, preferring instead to take them as long, unspecified periods of time or as six twenty-four hour periods separated from each other by long periods of time. Either way, they view the age of the universe and earth in terms of billions of years, though most progressive creationists hold that Adam and Eve are recent creations. They are divided as to whether Noah's flood was a universal or a local flood, but they all agree that the flood is not the major factor to be consulted in understanding the earth's geology.

Finally, most *theistic evolutionists* claim that theology is complementary to science, that Scripture is not a science textbook, and that methodological naturalism (see following) is the correct posture to take while doing science. Thus, theistic evolution is the proper view to take regarding origins. Accordingly, the general theory of evolution is to be taken as approximately true. Most theistic evolutionists accept all three senses of evolution listed above, except they would modify sense three. They would hold that naturalistic processes were, indeed, operative in the creation of all life and these are complementary to God's creative and providential activity. Some theistic evolutionists hold that when God created the world in the beginning, he caused it to have functional integrity: the created world has no gaps, no functional deficiencies that would require God to "intervene" miraculously. Rather, God implanted potentialities in his original creation such that all the various kinds of creatures would arise through normal processes as these potentialities unfold. Others hold that God simply guides and sustains the widely accepted processes of evolution and creates through secondary causation solely by means of those processes.

The main debate between young earth and progressive creationists is over the use of the Hebrew word *yom* (day) in Genesis and thus over the age of the universe and earth and over the usefulness of the flood for doing geology. They are agreed, however, that the general theory of evolution is false and that some sort of *intelligent design* is appropriate. Conversely, theistic evolutionists usually hold that science presupposes methodological naturalism, that science and theology are complementary to each other, and that evolution is a problem for Christians only when it is coupled with *philosophical naturalism* as a broad worldview. Thus, the dialogue among these groups is not merely one about scientific fact. It never has been, because beginning with Darwin himself, the creation/evolution controversy has significantly been a debate about philosophy of science: Should theology directly interact with and enter into the very fabric of science, or should science adopt methodological naturalism?

Intelligent design. The idea behind intelligent design is simple. When Christians engage in any intellectual activity, including science, they should consult all they know that is relevant to that activity, and theological beliefs should be among those consulted. Moreover, some theological propositions are clearly relevant to the practice of science and thus should be part of the Christian's scientific practices. Intelligent design can be considered as an approach to science that includes a commitment to the idea that (1) God, conceived of as a personal agent of great power and intelligence, has through direct, primary agent causation and through indirect, secondary causation created and designed the world for a purpose and has directly intervened in the course of its development at various times, and (2) the commitment expressed in proposition (1) can appropriately enter into the very fabric of the practice of science and scientific methodology.

To understand this description of intelligent design, it is important to grasp the distinction between primary and secondary causal actions by God. Roughly, what God did in parting the Red Sea was a primary causal act—an extraordinary, direct, discontinuous "intervention" by God. What God did in guiding and sustaining that sea before and after its parting involved secondary causal acts by God. Such acts are God's usual way of operating, by which he sustains natural processes in existence and employs them as intermediate agents to accomplish some purpose.

For example, theological propositions that the universe had a beginning, that human beings (and animals) have souls and are not merely physical entities, that humans are fallen, that they arose within a certain time frame in the

Middle East, that the basic kinds of life were directly created by God, and that the flood of Noah was universal could all be used to form hypotheses with testable implications; to serve as background knowledge to evaluate the plausibility of various, especially competing scientific hypotheses; and to explain certain things that are scientifically accessible. Thus, intelligent design endorses the use of the insights of theology, where appropriate, for doing science.

When discussing intelligent design, it is appropriate to mention what is called the *intelligent design* (ID) movement. Major participants in the ID movement are Phillip E. Johnson, Michael Behe, William Dembski, Paul Nelson, and Stephen Meyer. What makes the ID movement unique is that, while there may be slight variants of this approach, all ID advocates believe that intelligent design can be discovered in science, and the inference to an Intelligent Designer from such discoveries is a scientific inference. Thus, the ID movement refocuses the use of design as an argument for God's existence from philosophy to science itself. The movement also rejects methodological naturalism and is committed to the legitimacy of the intelligent design perspective described above. The ID movement is an entire approach to science, and, as such, it goes far beyond the topic of evolution. However, when applied to evolution, with a certain qualification to be mentioned shortly, the ID movement does not map neatly onto the three views mentioned above. In principle, advocates of young earth and progressive creationism are participants of the ID movement. But the converse is not true. Not all participants of the ID movement are young earth or progressive creationists. There is room for a qualified version of theistic evolution within the ID movement. To understand these issues more fully, we must probe more deeply the central intellectual commitments of the ID movement.

According to ID proponents, the central debate about evolution is not over the age of the universe, it is not whether the history of the cosmos and life contains gaps due to the primary causal activity of God in creating various kinds of life, and it is not primarily about science and theology. Regarding evolution, ID proponents are committed to two central claims. First, the central issue is between an intelligent design hypothesis and the blind watchmaker thesis. According to the blind watchmaker thesis, there is no scientific evidence for appealing to an intelligent designer in order to explain the history of life or the existence and nature of living things and their parts. Rather, nonintelligent, purposeless naturalistic processes are fully adequate to explain all the relevant scientific facts. Advocates of ID demur and believe an intelligent design model is superior to the blind watchmaker thesis. Second, as noted above, the facts that justify an inference to an intelligent designer and the inference itself are properly construed as being within the domain of science. ID proponents reject methodological naturalism and accept intelligent design.

In light of these two commitments, it becomes possible to clarify in what sense theistic evolution is and is not consistent with the ID movement. If theistic evolution is construed such that it includes a commitment to the thesis of common descent, a commitment to the functional integrity of creation (that is, subsequent to the initial creation of the universe, there are not gaps and God does not act in natural history by way of primary causal miracle), and a commitment to methodological naturalism, then theistic evolution is not compatible with ID theory. However, if theistic evolution is taken to include the first two commitments and not the third, then theistic evolution and ID theory are compatible.

The central aspect of ID theory is the idea that the designedness of some things which are designed can be identified as such in scientifically acceptable ways.[51] Dembski, the main

---

[51] The following four paragraphs are adapted from J.P. Moreland, "Duhemian and Augustinian Science and the Crisis in Non-Empirical Knowledge," in Life and Learning XII, ed. Joseph W. Koterski (Washington, DC: University Faculty for Life, 2003), 201-2.

figure in developing this aspect of ID theory, analyzes cases in which insurance employees, police, and forensic scientists must determine whether a death was an accident (that is, there was no intelligent cause) or was brought about intentionally.[52] According to Dembski, whenever the following three factors are present, scientific investigators are rationally obligated to draw the conclusion that the event was brought about intentionally: the event was contingent (that is, even though it took place, it did not have to happen), the event had a small probability of happening, and the event is capable of independent specifiability.

To illustrate, consider a game of bridge in which two people receive a hand of cards. Let one hand be a random set of cards—call it hand *A*—and the other be a perfect bridge hand dealt to the dealer himself. Suppose further that the dealer had announced prior to

---

[52] William Dembski, Intelligent Design (Downers Grove, IL: InterVarsity Press, 1999).

the deal that he was going to receive a perfect hand. Now if that happened, we would immediately infer that while A was not dealt intentionally, the perfect bridge hand was and that, in fact, it represents a case of cheating on the part of the dealer. What justifies our suspicion?

First, neither hand had to happen. There are no laws of nature, logic, or mathematics that necessitate that either hand had to come about in the history of the cosmos. In this sense each hand and, indeed, the very card game itself are contingent events that did not have to take place. Second, since hand A and the perfect bridge hand have the same number of cards, each is equally improbable. So while necessary, the small probability of an event is not sufficient to raise suspicions that the event came about by the intentional action of an agent.

The third criterion makes this clear. The perfect bridge hand can be specified as special independent of the fact that it happened to be the hand that came about, but this is not so for hand A. Hand A can be specified as "some random hand or other that someone happens to get." Now that specification applies to all hands whatsoever and does not mark out as special any particular hand that comes about. So understood, A is no more special than any other random deal. But this is not so for the perfect bridge hand. This hand can be characterized as a special sort of combination of cards by the rules of bridge quite independent of the fact that it is the hand that the dealer received. It can also be characterized as a specific hand marked out as special by the dealer's prediction; thus, this deal of cards is special apart from the simple fact that it is the deal the dealer himself received. It is the combination of contingency (this hand did not have to be dealt), small probability (this particular arrangement of cards was quite unlikely to have occurred), and independent specifiability (according to the rules and the dealer's prediction, this is a pretty special hand for the dealer to receive) that justifies us in accusing the dealer of cheating.

Dembski and other ID theorists argue that the fine-tuning of the universe, the biological information in living organisms, and other phenomena justify the scientific inference to an intelligent designer. Thus, ID theorists accept intelligent design and reject methodological naturalism. Their opponents disagree.

Natural science and methodological naturalism. Many believe that intelligent design and ID theory violate the very nature of science itself. Atheist Michael Ruse claims that "even if Scientific Creationism were totally successful in making its case as science, it would not yield a *scientific* explanation of origins. Rather, at most, it could prove that science shows that there can be *no scientific* explanation of origins."[53] Elsewhere, Ruse states that "the Creationists believe the world started miraculously. But miracles lie outside of science, which by definition

---

[53] Michael Ruse, Darwinism Defended (Reading, MA: Addison-Wesley, 1982), 322.

deals with the natural, the repeatable, that which is governed by law."[54]

Ruse's opinion was affirmed by Judge William Overton in the 1981 creationism trial held in Little Rock, Arkansas. Overton judged that scientific creationism could not be taught in public school science classes because creation science (which is a specific version of ID theory) is a religious and not a scientific notion. In his ruling, Overton presented the alleged essential characteristics of science—a line of demarcation between science and other fields consisting of a set of necessary and sufficient conditions that some activity must exhibit to count as a scientific activity—and claimed that creation science failed to satisfy these characteristics. In short, science must conform to methodological naturalism (see following). Here was Overton's line of demarcation:

---

[54] Ruse, Darwinism Defended, 322; cf. David Hull's review of Phillip Johnson's Darwin on Trial in Nature 352 (August 8, 1991): 485-86.

More precisely, the essential characteristics of science are: (1) It is guided by natural law; (2) It has to be explanatory by reference to natural law; (3) It is testable against the empirical world; (4) Its conclusions are tentative, i.e., not necessarily the final word; and (5) It is falsifiable.[55]

Many Christians agree with Overton's assessment, claiming that in the natural sciences (defined ostensively as the sciences of chemistry, physics, biology, geology, and other branches of science usually taken to be the "hard" sciences) one ought to adopt methodological naturalism, according to which the goal of natural science is to explain contingent natural phenomena strictly in terms of other contingent natural phenomena. Explanations should refer only to natural objects and events and not to the personal choices and actions of human and divine agents. Natural science seeks knowledge of the physical

---

[55] Cited in Norman L. Geisler, The Creator in the Courtroom (Milford, MI: Mott Media, 1982), 176.

properties, behavior, and formative history of the physical world. Within science we should adopt methodological naturalism where answers to questions are sought within nature, within the contingent created order. For example, in describing how two charged electrodes separate hydrogen and oxygen gas when placed in water, the "God hypothesis" is both unnecessary and out of place. The physical universe—the world of atoms, subatomic particles, and things made of atoms—is the proper object of scientific study, and methodological naturalism is the proper method for pursuing that study. Conversely, philosophical naturalism is the philosophical doctrine that the natural world is all there is and that God, angels, and the like do not exist. Science presupposes methodological naturalism but not philosophical naturalism, and the two should not be confused.

What should we make of methodological naturalism as a philosophy of science? For two reasons, we reject it. Negatively, advocates of methodological naturalism have failed to make their case. Those advocates rely on a *line of demarcation* between science and nonscience that consists in stating a set of necessary and/or sufficient conditions for something to count as science. Overton's list is an example of this strategy. Unfortunately, no one has ever been able to draw such a line of demarcation, and such a line does not exist. Since intelligent design was regarded as science by scientists and philosophers of science throughout most of the history of science, and since intelligent design can be clearly illustrated in various ways (see following), then the burden of proof is on the one who would deny that intelligent design is a science (a second-order philosophical claim). This burden of proof has not been met, so methodological naturalism should be rejected.

Various criteria have been offered as a line of demarcation, a set of necessary and sufficient conditions for something to count as science: it must focus on the natural or physical world, be guided by natural law, explain by reference to natural law, be empirically testable, be held tentatively and not as the last word, be falsifiable, be measurable or quantifiable, involve predictions, and be repeatable. The problem is that no single criterion or set of criteria is necessary or sufficient for counting as science. There are examples of science that do not have the criterion in question (thus, it is not necessary), and there are examples of nonscience that do have the criterion (thus, it is not sufficient). For example, there are scientists who hold their views dogmatically and theologians that hold their views tentatively. Again, there are aspects of science that are not quantifiable (e.g., certain theories about viruses and how they work) and aspects of literary studies that are quantifiable (e.g., quantitative treatments of word frequency in determining how an author uses a word). And on it goes.

Remember, it is one thing to argue that while ID theory is, indeed, a scientific theory, it should be rejected for one reason or another (e.g., because it doesn't explain the facts or yield good predictions). This is a first-order claim of science. But it is another thing altogether to make the second-order philosophical claim that ID theory isn't even science in the first place. It is this philosophical claim that we reject. The inadequacy of methodological naturalism and the genuine scientific nature of ID theory are widely acknowledged by philosophers of science, even among those who are atheists and who believe ID theory is actually false.

Positively, several areas of science employ explanations of various phenomena that appeal to the actions, motives, beliefs, and intentions of an intelligent agent, not to natural physical processes and laws. For example, SETI (the search for extraterrestrial intelligence), archeology, forensic science, psychology, and sociology use personal agency and various internal states of agents (desires, willings, intentions, beliefs) as part of their descriptions of the causal entities cited in their explanations of the things they try to explain. This is especially true in the historical sciences as opposed to the empirical sciences. Thus, there is nothing nonscientific about appealing to divine agency in creationist explanations of certain phenomena such as the origins of the universe, first life, and humankind. At the very least, such an appeal cannot be faulted as nonscientific on the grounds that it involves an agent causal explanation and not an explanation in terms of some natural law like the law of gravity. Moreover, such an appeal to divine agency may be especially (but not solely) appropriate where there are theological reasons to believe God acted through primary and not secondary causes.

It may be objected that such appeals are permissible in the human sciences but not in the so-called natural sciences like biology or paleontology. But this response is clearly question begging in that it is an attempt to define and classify examples of so-called natural science by smuggling methodological naturalism into the definition rather than by using neutral ostensive definitions of natural science. It also distorts the history of at least some of the natural sciences. Scientists from Charles Darwin to Stephen Jay Gould have clearly seen that theological ideas can have scientifically testable implications, a fact that is not accounted for on the methodological naturalist view of scientific explanation.

For example, one often finds Darwin and other evolutionists making claims to the effect that if God were an optimal, efficient designer who was also free to use variety in his designing activities, then certain biological structures (e.g., homologous structures like the forelimbs of birds, porpoises, and humans, which have a similar structure but serve different purposes) would not be present because they are not very efficient, nor do they show much creativity. The point here is not to evaluate the strength of such arguments or to examine the appropriateness of the model of God as designer they utilize. Rather, the point is to show that the history of biology and paleontology illustrate arguments of this sort time and again. And such arguments are not merely rhetorical devices but substantive claims that show how theological ideas, adequate or inadequate, can have implications for scientific explanation, evaluation, and testing.

Some critics object that the intelligent design model utilizes an intellectually inappropriate god-of-the-gaps strategy in which one takes God to act only when there are gaps in nature; that one appeals to God merely to fill up gaps in our scientific knowledge of naturalistic mechanisms; that these gaps are used in apologetic, natural theology arguments to support Christian theism; and that because scientific progress is making these gaps increasingly rare, this strategy is not a good one.[56]

Several things may be said against this criticism. First, the model does not limit God's causal activity to gaps. God is constantly active in sustaining and governing the universe. Nature is not autonomous. Moreover, intelligent design need not have *any* apologetical aim at

---

[56] This and the next three paragraphs have been adapted from J.P. Moreland, "Theistic Science and Methodological Naturalism," in The Creation Hypothesis: Scientific Evidence for an Intelligent Designer, ed. J.P. Moreland (Downers Grove, IL: InterVarsity Press, 1994), 59-60.

all. A Christian theist may simply believe that he or she should consult all we know or have reason to believe is true (including theological beliefs) in forming, evaluating, and testing scientific theories and in explaining scientific phenomena. And even if someone uses intelligent design with apologetical intentions, creationists need not limit their apologetical case to gaps. The model merely recognizes a distinction between primary and secondary causes and goes on to assert that at least the former could have scientifically testable implications irrespective of the apologetic intentions of such a recognition.

Second, the model attempts to explain phenomena in light of God and his activities, not in order to cover our ignorance but only when good theological or philosophical reasons are present: for instance, in cases where certain theological or philosophical reasons would cause us to expect a discontinuity in nature where God acted via primary causation, or in cases where some doctrine like original sin sheds light on some psychological theory regarding human behavior. Third, even if the gaps in naturalistic scientific explanations are getting smaller, this does not prove that there are no gaps at all. It begs the question to argue that just because most alleged gaps turn out to be explainable in naturalistic terms without gaps at that level of explanation, then all alleged gaps will turn out this way. After all, what else would one expect of a gap but that there would be few of them? Gaps due to primary divine agency are miracles that are in the minority for two reasons. We have already seen that God's usual way of operating is through secondary causes and that primary causal gaps are God's extraordinary, unusual way of operating, so, by definition, these will be few and far between. Also, the evidential or sign value of a miraculous gap arises most naturally against a backdrop where the gaps are rare and unexpected and have a religious context (that is, there are positive theological reasons to expect their presence).

Fourth, the distinction between "empirical" and "historical" science is helpful for answering the god-of-the-gaps problem. Empirical science is a nonhistorical, empirical approach to the world that focuses on repeatable, regularly recurring events or patterns in nature (e.g., the relationship between pressure, temperature, and volume in a gas). By contrast, historical science is historical in nature and focuses on past singularities that are not repeatable (e.g., the origins of the universe, first life, and various kinds of life).

Advocates of this distinction claim that appealing to God's primary causal activity is legitimate in historical science even if not in empirical science because the former deals with cases where, theologically speaking, God's primary causal activity is to be found, while the latter deals with God's secondary causal activity. Now it could be argued that most cases in which we appealed to God as a cover for our ignorance of a gap were those involving issues of empirical science, not historical science. Thus, when those gaps are filled by naturalistic mechanisms, the conclusion to draw is not that God should never be appealed to as an explanatory notion of some scientifically discoverable phenomenon but rather that the notion of a primary causal act of God should be limited to cases in historical science precisely because of the differences between primary and secondary causation that are captured in the historical/empirical science distinction.

Finally, ID proponents practice intelligent design without necessarily embracing gaps in the history of the cosmos. According to ID advocates, one can use science to discover the products of intelligent design without having any idea how those products came about. Critics who raise a god-of-the-gaps objection against intelligent design fail to take into account ID theory.

THE REALISM/ANTIREALISM DEBATE

Ever since the ancient Greeks began to investigate nature, there has been a debate about these questions: What is the purpose of scientific theories? What does it mean to say a scientific theory is successful? Are successful scientific theories merely useful fictions that explain empirical observations and generate accurate predictions, or do their theoretical terms actually refer to real entities? And does a successful theory provide fairly accurate descriptions of those entities? This is the realist/antirealist debate, and it is still hotly contested. *Scientific realism* is the view that science progressively secures true, or approximately true, theories about the real, theory-independent world "out there" and does so in a rational way. For example, a realist claims that because electron theory has been successful, there actually are electrons and our current descriptions of them are at least approximately true. Let us say that a theory is successful to the degree that it harmonizes well with observations, yields accurate predictions, and generates fruitful new lines of research. The realist says that a theory is successful if and only if it is approximately true.

Antirealism, which has different forms, denies realist interpretations of science in favor of alternatives. For many antirealists, scientific theories are instruments, useful fictions that allow us to make accurate predictions and so forth. The main value of a scientific theory is its success in harmonizing with observational data, yielding accurate predictions and generating new lines of research. When a theory is successful, we can conclude that it is successful—nothing more, nothing less. The success of a theory has little or nothing to do with the theory's truth, and we cannot conclude that reality is the way the theory says it is just because the theory works. For example, we cannot reasonably say that electrons really exist just because electron theory has been successful.

Why should Christians be concerned with this debate? Besides the intrinsic intellectual value of the debate, one's views of the realism-antirealism controversy should be factored into one's understanding of the integration of science and theology. If realism is accepted as the correct view of a scientific theory (e.g., the idea that by employing the notion of imaginary time as something real, one can avoid postulating that the universe had a beginning) and if that theory seems to run counter to some theological affirmation (say, that the universe had a beginning), then Christians will have to refute that scientific theory, adjust their understanding of the theological affirmation, or adopt a different strategy. Thus, much depends on what it means for a theory to be well-established or successful. This, in turn, is related to the debate about realism and antirealism. However, if antirealism is adopted for scientific theories, then one would not take a well-established scientific theory to be approximately true, and there would be no pressure to adjust the truth of the theological affirmation. For example, if a theologian believes that all physical events have causes, and if quantum physics seems to deny this, then if quantum theory is taken in an antirealist way, there would be no need to adjust one's view of causation. Yet there may be dangers in adopting antirealism for scientific theories because it may be difficult to limit antirealism within science. For example, if one's antirealism affects one's theological assertions, then claims about God, life after death, and so forth could be interpreted as not making reference to actual entities (God, the afterlife) in the world.

Should Christians adopt realism or antirealism as a philosophy of science? This is no easy question, and responsible Christian philosophers are divided on the issue. It would seem that, insofar as Christian doctrine is concerned, each position is a live and legitimate option. However, the very presence of this debate has an important implication. When trying to decide whether some scientific entity—like electrons or DNA—really exists, it is important to keep in mind that the issues relevant to the decision are not simply the scientific ones. A defense of the existence of the theoretical entities of science is not ultimately a question of whether some scientific theory is "successful." More fundamentally, it is a question of which philosophy of science—scientific realism or some form of antirealism—is to be preferred as a characterization of success of scientific theories. This is important to keep in mind when you are trying to integrate science with your Christian faith. But just exactly what is the integration of science and theology, and how does one go about doing it?

MODELS FOR INTEGRATING SCIENCE AND THEOLOGY

To be engaged in the task of integration is to embark on a journey that is at once exciting and difficult. Integration is no easy task, and it is a lifelong project that should occur within an individual believer's life and among the various members of the Christian community working together. Part of the difficulty of this journey is due not only to the massive amount of information and vast array of studies that need to be consulted but also to the fact that there are many different aspects of and attitudes toward integration itself. It is beyond our present scope to attempt to give anything even approximating a topology of these aspects and attitudes. However, it may be helpful to list some examples where the need for integration arises as well as some of the different ways that theology (as defined above) interacts with other disciplines in the process of developing an integrated Christian worldview.[57]

Here are some cases that illustrate the need for integration:

A psychologist reads literature regarding identical twins who are reared in separate environments. He notes that they usually exhibit similar adult behavior. He then wonders if there is really any such thing as freedom of the will, and he ponders what to make of moral responsibility and punishment if there isn't.

A neurophysiologist establishes specific correlations between certain brain functions and certain feelings of pain, and she puzzles over the

---

[57] A portion of this section correlates with J.P. Moreland, "Philosophical Apologetics, the Church, and Contemporary Culture," in Evangelical Apologetics, ed. Michael Bauman, David W. Hall, and Robert C. Newman (Camp Hill, PA: Christian Publications, 1996), 3-34.

question of whether there is a soul or mind distinct from the brain.

An anthropologist notes that cultures frequently differ over basic moral principles and wonders whether this proves that there are no objectively true moral values that transcend culture.

In each of the cases listed above, there is a need for the person in question, if he or she is a Christian, to think hard about the issue in light of the need for developing a Christian worldview. When one addresses problems like these, there will emerge a number of different ways that theology can interact with an issue in a discipline outside theology. Here are some of the different ways that such interaction can take place.

The two realms view. Propositions in theology and another discipline may involve two distinct, nonoverlapping areas of investigation. For example, debates about angels or the extent of the atonement have little to do with organic chemistry. Similarly it is of little interest to theology whether a methane molecule has three or four hydrogen atoms in it.

The complementarity view. Propositions in science and theology are noninteracting, complementary approaches to the same reality that adopt very different standpoints, ask and answer very different kinds of questions (e.g., evolutionary science tells us what happened and how, whereas theology tells us who guided the process and why), involve different levels of description, employ very different cognitive attitudes (e.g., objectivity and logical neutrality in science, personal involvement, and commitment in theology), and are constituted by very different language games. These different, authentic perspectives are partial and incomplete and therefore must be integrated into a coherent whole. However, each level of description is complete at its own level without having gaps at that level for the other perspective to fill and without having the possibility of direct competition and conflict. There may be implications for theology from science or vice versa, but these are rare and should allow theology and science to remain in their own proper domains with no illicit territory encroachment from one to the other. Some form of theistic evolution is the favored model of creation/evolution integration for complementarians.

The direct interaction view. Propositions in theology and another discipline may directly interact in such a way that either one area of study offers rational support for the other or one area of study raises rational difficulties for the other. For example, certain theological teachings about the existence of the soul raise rational problems for philosophical or scientific claims that deny the existence of the soul. The general theory of evolution raises various difficulties for certain ways of understanding the book of Genesis. Some have argued that the Big Bang theory tends to support the theological proposition that the universe had a beginning.

The presuppositional view. Theology tends to support the presuppositions of another discipline and vice versa. Some argue that the presuppositions of science make sense given Christian theism but that they are odd and without ultimate justification in a naturalistic worldview. Similarly, some argue that philosophical critiques of epistemological skepticism and defenses of a correspondence theory of truth offer justification for some of the presuppositions of theology.

The practical application view. Theology fills out and adds details to general principles in another discipline and vice versa, and theology helps one practically apply principles in another discipline and vice versa. For example, theology teaches that fathers should not provoke their children to anger, and psychology can add important details about what this means by offering information about family systems, the nature and causes of anger, and so on. Psychology can devise various tests for assessing whether one is or is not a mature person, and theology can offer a normative definition to psychology as to what a mature person is.

By way of application, suppose you want to integrate some topic—say, scientific claims about the age of the earth or the genetic origins of homosexuality—with your biblical and theological views. How should you proceed? We suggest three steps.

Step one. List the main options in treating the biblical text regarding the topic. Two rules of thumb may be helpful here. First, while the history of the church is not infallible, if there is a view or set of views that have been embraced widely by respected thinkers in the history of the church, you should require a lot of evidence before going in a different direction. Second, consult biblical commentators and theologians who are widely respected in the evangelical community and, more broadly, in the larger church that embrace historic, orthodox Christianity. Beware of adopting views of biblical teaching that seem to be politically correct revisions of the Bible. A good test for such revisions is when a position on an area of biblical teaching has recently been adopted at just the time when there is ideological pressure from the larger culture to find a way to accept that viewpoint. It is more than ironic that some in the church discover for the first time in church history a view that "coincidentally" is being recommended by the church's critics.

Step two. Get clear on exactly what the scientific data show. Do the data really support a certain interpretation? If so, how strongly? Are there other ways of interpreting the scientific evidence that, even if in the minority, are reasonable? You want to be careful not to accept some view as the only reasonable option to integrate with biblical teaching just because some authorities say so. Be creative and list various ways of interpreting the data.

Step three. Given your list of biblical and scientific options for interpreting the relevant data, try to decide which of the five models of integration fits this particular problem. Your decision expresses how you think the topic should be integrated into your theological beliefs. Here's something to keep in mind in step three: given the presence of scientific naturalism and postmodernism as rival worldviews to Christian theism, these two worldviews are agreed that there is no objective nonphysical world and that there is no such thing as nonempirical knowledge. On this view, Christianity may be a belief tradition, but Christianity is not a source of knowledge of reality, especially of immaterial reality. Your attempt to integrate a particular problem with your theological views should not contribute to this false stereotype of Christianity.

Integration is hard work, but the rewards are great. Among other things, integration is a way of loving God with all your mind. And remember, when you practice integration, the tools of philosophy are crucial for success. That's one reason why we have tried to sharpen your philosophical tools in this book.

7

WHAT IS BEAUTY? WHAT ABOUT ART?

Aesthetics

"Beauty is truth, truth beauty,"—that is all ye know on earth, and all ye need to know.
JOHN KEATS

Through art we can know another's view of the universe.
MARCEL PROUST

Never lose an opportunity of seeing anything beautiful, for beauty is God's handwriting.
RALPH WALDO EMERSON

If we think deeply about what we value in our lives, surely beauty will appear near the top of the list. We are drawn, almost irresistibly, to beauty: beautiful landscapes and sunsets, beautiful music and paintings, beautiful poetry and films, beautiful people. Indeed, most of us would think that a house or a life devoid of beauty is somehow impoverished. But why do we think that? And who's to judge what beauty is, anyway?

Aesthetics is, broadly, the study of beauty and art (the two are not synonymous; we'll see why in a moment). It is the study of aesthetics that should tell us what we want to know about judgments of beauty and art. But it's not so simple; as with other areas of philosophy, there are many different approaches, theories, and conclusions about what beauty and art are (or should be).

Aesthetics is one of those roads less traveled in philosophy. It is likely that even most philosophy graduate students have never taken a formal course in aesthetics, and—full disclosure—neither has either of us. Yet through our own study, supervision of a number of students' independent studies in aesthetics, and reflections on implications of a Christian worldview, we do have something to say here. We believe that despite the many pathways and detours in the study of aesthetics, we are able to reach some important conclusions, and later we'll argue that beauty—and art—are important in the Christian life.[58]

BEAUTY

John Keats penned a poetic thesis of the Romantic movement in his "Ode on a Grecian Urn." But it's poetry, after all. Beauty is not truth, and of course there's a lot more we need to know. Yet beauty and truth—along with goodness—are related in some hard-to-define sense. The tradition from Plato and Aristotle through Aquinas and the Scholastics regarded truth, goodness, and beauty as "transcendentals," properties of Being as such, transcending time and place—transcending, that is, the limits of particulars. Consequently they also

---

[58] Some of this chapter draws on sections of chapter seven, "What Should I Value? Ethics and Aesthetics," in Garrett J. DeWeese, Doing Philosophy as a Christian (Downers Grove, IL: IVP Academic, 2011).

transcend personal tastes, cultural values, and religious traditions. The transcendentals were proper objects of affection, proper aims of a well-ordered and fulfilled life.

The doctrine of the transcendentals is poorly appreciated today, and we won't pursue the topic here. We mention it simply to note this: in the long tradition of philosophy and medieval philosophical theology, truth, goodness, and beauty were regarded as immutable and objective. The true, the good, and the beautiful were thus believed to be objective properties of parts of reality independent of individual or cultural tastes or beliefs.

Not so today.

"Beauty is in the eye of the beholder" is such a common aphorism that questioning it is right up there with questioning motherhood and the infield fly rule. Yet it should be questioned, and (with proper qualifications) we believe it is false. The "eye of the beholder" aphorism is an example of subjectivism about beauty; the contrary is objectivism.

Subjectivism. Immanuel Kant's "third critique," the *Critique of Judgment* (1790), is still widely influential. In it he speaks of "judgments of taste," arguing that two necessary (but not jointly sufficient) features of such judgments are subjectivity and universality.[59] By *subjectivity,* Kant meant to call attention to the subjective judgment of pleasure, that a work of art is agreeable, beautiful, sublime, or good. By *universality,* however, Kant held that a person's judgment of beauty, based on her subjective experience of pleasure, seems to her that it *should* be universal or normative, such that when she judged something to be beautiful, she was "demanding the same delight from others."

In these more individualistic days, though, the normative aspect of Kant's judgment of taste has been widely abandoned, replaced by a purely subjective concept of beauty. The sense of pleasure Kant referred to, it is

---

[59] Immanuel Kant, Critique of Judgment, trans. Werner S. Pluhar (Indianapolis: Hackett, 1987).

argued, needs explication, and a plethora have been given, so there is no consensus as to what makes a particular experience an aesthetic experience or, more narrowly, how the subjective pleasure of the experience of beauty differs from other pleasurable experiences.

The result of this line of argument is a very liberal pluralism: if something (a painting, a piece of music, a landscape) gives you a certain sort of pleasure, then it's beautiful *to you*. Surely this is by far the most popular "man on the street" view. And it seems to be supported by thought experiments such as this: Suppose we learn that for generations, residents of some remote mountain valley regarded the peaks above with fear, as the source of storms, avalanches, floods, and so on; they never saw beauty, majesty, or sublimity in the mountains. But then one day, a group of Romantic poets came into the valley and were awed by the vistas, declaring the mountains to be beautiful, majestic, sublime. And after a time the residents also came to say the same about their surroundings.

Is it the case that the mountains gained new aesthetic qualities when the Romantics arrived, or had they always been beautiful and the valley residents simply mistaken all along? Or were both groups wrong to ascribe aesthetic qualities to the mountains instead of merely reporting personal feelings? And is there any way to decide?[60]

Similarly, while you may regard the music of Bach as more beautiful than Brubeck, and both more beautiful than Beyoncé, your brother may reverse the order. And both of you may be mystified as to why someone thinks that a "velvet Elvis" painting is beautiful enough to hang in the living room. So isn't it really the case that beauty is, after all, a purely subjective judgment?

But as already indicated, we think this confuses personal taste or

---

[60] See Margaret P. Battin, John Fisher, Ronald Moore, and Anita Slivers, Puzzles About Art: An Aesthetics Casebook (Boston: Bedford/St. Martin's, 1989), 28.

preference with genuine aesthetic judgment.[61]

Objectivism. The objectivist agrees that even though there is a necessary subjective component in aesthetic judgments, those judgments can be evaluated and be deemed correct or incorrect. The mere experience of aesthetic pleasure alone is insufficient to secure the truth or correctness of the judgment.

Objectivism attempts to explain the concept of beauty in an objective way—that is, in a way that is independent of the judgments or feelings of any individual or group. Objectivists differ about issues such as whether beauty is a transcendental, a simple property, or a complex property; whether beauty is a degreed property; whether beauty refers to the same property when used of visual art or music or a landscape or a face; whether beauty must be tied to a perceptual

---

[61] C.S. Lewis insightfully critiques subjectivism (about both aesthetics and ethics) in The Abolition of Man (New York: Macmillan, 1947).

experience (or whether, say, deaf Beethoven could experience the beauty of his Ninth Symphony); whether abstract structures such as mathematical equations can rightly be said to be beautiful; and whether beauty is a self-presenting property or is such that observers need (some degree of) training or education to apprehend it. And that's just for starters.

A Christian should believe that if the supremely authoritative God declares something beautiful, that would seem to be the strongest possible grounds for maintaining that beauty is objective, independent of human judgments. And there are a number of biblical texts in which God, or his authorized spokesmen, do in fact ascribe beauty to things.

Among those things called beautiful in the Bible are the starry sky (Job 38:31), a singing voice (Ezek 33:32), a city in its setting (Ps 48:2), the land of Israel (Jer 3:19), jewelry (Ezek 7:20), clothing (27:24), trees (31:3; Dan 4:12), and of course people, especially women (the word is used sixteen times in the Song of Solomon), in both their physical appearance and their "inner beauty" of character (1 Pet 3:3-4).[62] And perhaps surprisingly, the Bible speaks of the beauty of angelic beings (Ezek 28:12-17). So, then, *pace* Kant, (human) subjective experience is not a necessary condition of beauty.

Finally, in addition to such immaterial entities as personality and angels, which may legitimately be called beautiful, we need to attend to the ultimate: God himself is beautiful![63] The

---

[62] A critic might claim that these biblical texts are instances of accommodation—God using, for the sake of communication, certain culturally relative beliefs about beauty without thereby implying anything about beauty as a universal property. We'd reply that it's quite difficult to articulate a consistent hermeneutic that allows a principled distinction to be drawn between accommodation and assertion when it comes to property ascription as opposed to physical object or event description (e.g., "the sun rose").

[63] See, for example, F. Duane Lindsey, "Essays Toward a Theology of Beauty." Bibliotheca Sacra 131 (1974): 120-36; 209-18; 311-19. See also the sweeping

psalmist proclaims, "One thing I ask of the Lord, this only do I seek: that I may dwell in the house of the Lord all the days of my life, to gaze on the beauty of the Lord and to seek him in his temple" (Ps 27:4). And he exhorts, "Give unto the Lord the glory due to His name; worship the Lord in the beauty of holiness" (Ps 29:2 NKJV). If God is beautiful, then surely he is beautiful regardless of human judgment and was so in the eternity before humans appeared on earth.

Such rich diversity of things called beautiful in the Bible leads us to question the idea that beauty is a simple property. Extrapolating from the biblical examples, we would say that a talented performance of a Puccini aria, a Monet water lily painting, and the view of Mount Rainier from amid the abundance of wildflowers above Paradise Ranger Station are all truly beautiful. But the Puccini is a human creation and

---

and difficult work of David Bentley Hart, The Beauty of the Infinite: The Aesthetics Of Christian Truth (Grand Rapids, MI: Eerdmans, 2004).

a human performance that must be experienced serially. The Monet is also a human creation but can be experienced as a whole or attended to in segments in no particular order. The Rainier vista is (so we believe) a divinely produced landscape using natural geological and botanical processes and is dramatically affected by time of day, season, and weather. To account for the ascription of beauty to such diverse objects, it seems that beauty must be a complex property that supervenes on an appropriate interplay (sorry—we can't be more precise) of such properties as melody and harmony (or color and tone), salience and balance, rhythm and voicing (or texture), and perhaps other discrete properties.[64] Performance arts and plastic arts, poetry buildings and landscapes, if beautiful, all share these properties,

---

[64] While the manner in which ancient and medieval philosophers explicated beauty as a transcendental is attractive, we don't see clearly enough how to square this idea with our understanding of beauty as a complex property.

in some degree, in appropriate interplay.[65]

Clearly, different cultures will produce works that exemplify these properties in quite different styles, but it should take only a bit of work to distinguish a cultural style from the properties constitutive of beauty for a thing of that kind.* And culture, experience, and education contribute to personal taste, so that while someone may judge a particular work to be beautiful, she still may not like it. A person can recognize beauty and not prefer it, and prefer mediocrity and not call it beautiful. And a person can use the terms *beauty* and *ugly* uncritically,

---

[65] St. Thomas Aquinas believed beauty was transcendental; he also claims that "beauty relates to the cognitive faculty; for beautiful things are those which please when seen. Hence beauty consists in due proportion; for the sense delights in things duly proportioned." Summa Theologica, trans. Fathers of the English Dominican Province (New York: Benzinger Bros., 1948), 1.Q5.5. Perhaps "due proportion" captures what we mean by "appropriate interplay."

thereby meaning only that he likes or dislikes something. *De gustibus non est disputandum*—there's no disputing matters of taste.

[* "The latest findings on the cultural basis of singing have ascertained that certain song types—whether lullaby, dance, love or healing melodies—turn up in all cultures. And each kind of song has common cross-cultural acoustic features." Jim Daley, "What Makes a Song? It's the Same Recipe in Every Culture," Scientific American, November 21, 2019, www.scientificamerican.com/article/what-makes-a-song-its-the-same-recipe-in-every-culture/?utm_source=newsletter&utm_medium=email&utm_campaign=weekly-review&utm_content=link&utm_term=2019-11-27_morestories&spMailingID=61644161&spUserID=NTM5ODMwODI5OAS2&spJobID=1764376199&spReportId=MTc2NDM3NjE5OQS2.]

Still, the objectivist will insist that there is an appropriate response to instances of true beauty—something we call the aesthetic experience. We take pleasure in attending to beautiful things and understand that one thing can be more beautiful than another. The experience of beauty, as C.S. Lewis says, awakens our longing for the source of beauty. It draws us in, asks us to contemplate the beautiful.

We do not want merely to *see* beauty, though, God knows, even that is bounty enough. We want something else that can hardly be put into words—to be united with the beauty we see, to pass into it, to receive it into ourselves, to bathe in it, to become part of it.[66]

When we judge a thing to be beautiful, majestic, sublime, and so on, we understand ourselves to be describing the thing itself, not only our inner feelings.

To say this a bit differently, just as we have argued that there are genuinely objective physical properties in the world (see chapter two) and genuinely objective moral properties in the world (see chapter four), so too there are genuinely objective aesthetic

---

[66] C.S. Lewis, The Weight of Glory and Other Essays, rev. and exp. ed. (New York: Macmillan, 1980), 16.

properties in the world, whether perceived accurately or at all. When stepping onto the surface of the moon, Buzz Aldrin exclaimed, "Beautiful, beautiful. Magnificent desolation." The beauty that Aldrin experienced was there the day before Apollo 11 landed, even though no human judgments of that beauty had been made.

ART

If defining beauty seems difficult, defining art is even more fraught. But let's avoid the tall weeds and think about works of art rather than art in the abstract. We can say simply this: works of art are products of *intentional acts* on the part of artists. Artists are trying to *do something* when they produce a work of art. An artist's motive might be to make money, but no serious artist would say that is his *only* motivation. He wants to *say something* with his art.[67] Nicholas

---

[67] And this is true even of the nihilistic Dadaists and Fauves; of artists like Jackson Pollack, whose "drip paintings" convey a sense of a reality that is "rotten"

Wolterstorff calls the action most prevalent in works of art "world projection." The artist, he says, is "presenting to us a world for our consideration, ... a world that is normally incompatible with the actual world."[68] Wolterstorff's account is richly nuanced and in places highly theoretical, but the basic idea is clear. In almost every case, an artist, through her work of art, is asking us to think about something differently than how we normally think about it. Hans Rookmaaker, the Dutch art historian, makes the same point about Renaissance painting:

> Paintings give a philosophy of the world and of life. They are more than decorations or simply

---

or "inappropriate" (H.R. Rookmaaker, Modern Art and the Death of a Culture [Downers Grove, IL: InterVarsity Press, 1973], 168); the randomized musical compositions of John Cage; or the novels, plays, and films of existentialists such as Albert Camus and Ingmar Bergman.

[68] Nicholas Wolterstorff, Art in Action (Grand Rapids, MI: Eerdmans, 1980), 123.

pleasant to look at. They have a message, and, what is vital to notice, a message realized by artistic means. The picture gets across what it wants to say, not just by its title, but by its own built-in qualities of artistry and method.[69]

Three consequences follow from the insight that the artist is projecting a world, saying something about reality. First, although it is often a laugh line, it *does* make sense to look at a painting, hear a piece of serious music, or read a well-crafted work of fiction, and ask, "What is it saying?" To answer that question, we need to listen to the critics and historians of each particular art form. The artist works from a philosophy of life, with an idea of the "world" he wants to put before us, and understanding the work of art requires some effort on our part.

Second, all art need not be beautiful—art may well be ugly if the world being projected is ugly, evil,

---

[69] Rookmaaker, Modern Art, 28.

dehumanizing. An excellent example of this is Alban Berg's opera *Lulu*. Berg used an atonal serialist style of composition (which is not beautiful) to depict the descent of Lulu from a courtesan in Paris to a street walker in London where she is murdered by Jack the Ripper. No, it's not a pretty story! But in portraying the characters as victims of dehumanizing social forces over which they have no control, Berg uses ugliness to project a world to force the audience to react to social ills and dehumanizing sexuality.[70]

Third, we may well prefer art that is beautiful to art that is ugly. But we need to distinguish art from decoration. No one does (or should) deliberately choose ugly decorations, and there is nothing at all wrong with artisans who produce artifacts that merely decorate, make surroundings more pleasant, bring touches of beauty to a location—but in doing so they are not (or generally are not) projecting a world for us to consider.

---

[70] See also Wolterstorff, Art in Action, 160-63.

There's so much more we'd like to address, such as the ontology of a work of art,[71] or the morality of a work of art,[72] or the merits and meaning of particular works of art. But we must stop somewhere.

BEAUTY AND GOD

A Christian worldview recognizes God as the ultimate source of all beauty. Since God declares some things to be good or beautiful, then it is true that there are objective values of goodness and beauty (and the like) in the world. And since God made humanity in his image, it is reasonable to believe both that we are able to recognize truth, goodness, and beauty and to rejoice in the true, the good, and the beautiful.

But, as artists, critics, and philosophers through the millennia have recognized, it might well take education to develop our innate capacity to

---

[71] Battin et al., Puzzles About Art, 9-11.

[72] Roger Scruton, Beauty: A Very Short Introduction (New York: Oxford University Press, 2011), 109-11.

apprehend these values. In our day, when courses such as art appreciation or music appreciation, not to mention art and music themselves, are being cut from school curricula, when the value of a good liberal arts education is being questioned, when exposure to great prose and poetry is rare in public schools, perhaps the church should take on itself the task of educating in aesthetic values.

This begins, of course, with demonstrating those values. God made us to enjoy beauty (among other things), so shouldn't the church be a place of beauty? Those responsible for church architecture, decoration, and landscaping should at least raise the issue of beauty. Church musicians should think about the beauty of music and lyrics—and this is not a criticism of contemporary styles in worship music, for as we said above, beauty can be exemplified in many different styles. And what if a Sunday school class devoted a number of weeks to looking at photographs or reproductions of great religious art of past centuries and asking what—in addition to the subject matter—makes this work great? And what can or should a congregation do to encourage gifted young people to pursue art seriously as a Christian?[73]

Lastly, we'll return briefly to the aesthetic experience itself, so eloquently described by C.S. Lewis above. Why do we humans have such experiences anyway? William Davis puts the matter this way:

> If everything (including humanity) is the result of random, impersonal forces which encouraged only survival, then it seems highly unlikely that the process would yield organisms (humans) which recognized values like these which aren't survival conducive. But values like these are what we would expect if humans (and the human environment) were created by a personal, loving, and beauty-valuing God. God's existence is a much better explanation for the existence

---

[73] See Rookmaaker, Modern Art, 225-52; Wolterstorff, Art in Action, 183-99.

of nonutilitarian values than any explanation without God.[74]

---

[74] William C. Davis, "Theistic Arguments," in Reason for the Hope Within, ed. Michael J. Murray (Grand Rapids, MI: Eerdmans, 1999), 39.

8

WHAT SHOULD WE WORSHIP?

Philosophy of Religion

Well, it may be the devil or it may be the Lord But you're gonna have to serve somebody.
BOB DYLAN

My concern with religion is that it allows us by the millions to believe what only lunatics or idiots could believe on their own.
SAM HARRIS

It may surprise you that religion can be a subject of philosophy. Yet a previous chapter, "Philosophy of Science," demonstrates the fruit of thinking critically (that is, philosophically) about science. Similarly, philosophical thinking about religion may also bear fruit, as we hope to show in this chapter.

DEFINING RELIGION

It should be no surprise that defining something as complex and varied as religion is next to impossible. We want a definition to include all major religions, such as the Abrahamic religions (Judaism, Christianity, and Islam) and major Eastern religions (Hinduism, Buddhism, Taoism, Shintoism, and Sikhism). And we want the definition to rule out such things as the fans of Manchester United Football Club or the Orange County Corvette Club.

But should we include Theravada Buddhism, which is atheistic? Or Confucianism, which is more of a social ethic? Or Marxism? Or secular humanism? If we try to compile a list of all characteristics that the religions have in common, we would find that none of the characteristics are shared by all religions, and many are shared by fans of soccer teams and sports cars. In other words, there is no characteristic or set of characteristics that is both necessary and sufficient to pick out a religion from other phenomena.

Following most philosophers of religion, we take religion to be a "family resemblance concept." The term comes from Wittgenstein and is often applied to phenomena that resemble one another but defy definition in terms of necessary and sufficient conditions.[75] As an approximation, we'll say that the term *religion* refers to any system of beliefs, behaviors, and rituals, centered on some idea of Ultimate Reality, that followers take to be transformative of their lives.[76] That's messy and imprecise, and it leaves questions around the edges where we are not sure whether to regard some system as a religion, but that's the best we can do. And starting with this attempt to define

---

[75] Ludwig Wittgenstein, Philosophical Investigations, trans. G.E.M. Anscombe (Oxford: Blackwell, 1963), 66.

[76] See Michael Peterson, William Hasker, Bruce Reichenbach, and David Basinger, Philosophy of Religion: Selected Readings, 4th ed. (New York: Oxford, 2010), 1.

religion, we are already doing philosophy of religion.

WHAT IS PHILOSOPHY OF RELIGION?

Philosophy of religion, then, is critical, analytical thought about the phenomenon of religion. It is not religious studies, simply describing the beliefs and practices of different religious communities. It is not sociology of religion, which looks at the social structures and interactions of and between religious communities.

Nor is philosophy of religion theology. We note in passing, though, that in the past fifty years or so there has been a remarkable surge of interest among Christian philosophers in analyzing, interpreting, and defending various doctrinal claims of Christian theology, a movement now known as analytic theology.[77] While we believe this

---

[77] For a helpful introduction, see Oliver D. Crisp and Michael C. Rea, eds., Analytic Theology: New Essays in Philosophical Theology (New York: Oxford, 2009).

effort has been quite beneficial to Christianity, it is not the central focus of philosophy of religion.

Philosophers of religion seek to understand and interpret the terms and claims made in religions. They try to discern and explicate critical issues that arise within the system of beliefs, behaviors, and rituals. The epistemology, ontology, and ethics of the religion are of central concern.

Understood in this way, philosophy of religion may well represent the oldest form of philosophy. Xenophanes of Colophon, a Greek philosopher of the sixth century BC, thought hard about the superstitious religion of Homer and Hesiod, and for what clearly are philosophical reasons he rejected it.[78]

Setting aside the historical precedent, philosophy of religion today will be a very wide study, given the many religions that are followed. As we are writing primarily for a Christian audience, we'll confine our discussion

---

[78] Jonathan Barnes, Early Greek Philosophy, 2nd ed. (London: Penguin Books, 2001), 40-47.

to the philosophy of the Christian religion.[79]

What, then, are the central questions that philosophy of religion investigates? William Lane Craig lists six relevant topics for Christian philosophy of religion: (1) religious epistemology, (2) natural theology, (3) coherence of theism, (4) problem of evil, (5) the soul and life everlasting, and (6) Christian theology. We have already touched on (1) in our chapter on epistemology and on (5) in the chapter on philosophical and theological anthropology. And as intimated above, (6) is more central to analytic theology. Further, the coherence of theism (3) largely is an investigation of proposed attributes of God, showing that they are logically consistent and

---

[79] For a very influential attempt to think about all religions, see John Hick, An Interpretation of Religion: Human Responses to the Transcendent, 2nd ed. (New York: Yale University Press, 2004). In our view, Hick's attempt to show that all religions in the end are largely equivalent is gravely mistaken, beginning as it does from a faulty Kantian epistemology.

metaphysically compossible. While a rich and edifying investigation, we'll leave that aside also. In the remainder of this chapter, we'll zero in on natural theology and the problem of evil.

NATURAL THEOLOGY

Natural theology is the investigation of the existence and nature of God, using only reason unaided by special revelation.[80] Christian theology holds that humans could know nothing about God unless he revealed something about himself in some way and that even if he does reveal, since he is an infinite being, there is much that humans can never know about him. But almost all Christian theologians and philosophers have believed that we can know *something* about God using natural reason alone. Thomas Aquinas offers a clear example of this understanding:

> Some truths of God exceed all the ability of the human reason.

---

[80] In Christianity, special revelation refers to what God himself has revealed in Scripture and preeminently in Jesus Christ.

Such is the truth that God is triune. But there are some truths which the natural reason also is able to reach. Such are that God exists, that He is one, and the like. In fact, such truths about God have been proved demonstratively by the philosophers, guided by the light of natural reason.[81]

Now, we do not think that God's existence can be "proved," to use Aquinas's word, in the same sense that a mathematical or logical proof yields certainty. But the arguments for God's existence that have been offered through the centuries are, we think, able to establish the existence of God—and indeed, of a certain kind of God—by a preponderance of the evidence, if not beyond a reasonable doubt. We will present the five "classical" theistic arguments, then briefly mention several of the more

---

[81] St. Thomas Aquinas, Summa Contra Gentiles, book 1, God, trans. Anton C. Pegis (Notre Dame, IN: University of Notre Dame Press, 1955), 1.3.2.

recent arguments that philosophers have offered.

The ontological argument. This venerable argument is probably the only purely a priori argument for God's existence. In the 850 years since its first appearance, it has been regarded as perhaps the most sublime piece of philosophical reasoning in Western philosophy, as a fraudulent attempt to define being into existence, and as everything in between. Yet the fact that it has seemed to every succeeding generation of philosophers and theologians either to need defending or refuting says something about its subtlety and the sophistication of the concepts and logic involved.

In 1078, Anselm, the prior of a Benedictine abbey in Normandy who would later become the archbishop of Canterbury, wrote *Proslogion,* in which he sought to prove the existence and nature of God using only natural reason. The first chapter frames the entire work in the context of the prayer that God would allow him to understand "in some degree" God's truth. At the end of the chapter Anselm penned his famous *credo ut intelligam,* "I believe in order to understand. For this I also believe,—that unless I believed, I should not understand."[82]

Chapter two of *Proslogion* contains the first version of Anselm's ontological argument. He begins by saying that God is "a being than which nothing greater can be conceived." And surely this must be correct, since if anything greater *could* be conceived, then that would be a thing greater than God—which seems contradictory. But then Anselm claims that a being than which nothing greater can be conceived "cannot exist in the understanding alone. For, suppose it exists in the understanding alone: then it can be conceived to exist in reality, which is greater." In other words, if we

---

[82] St. Anselm, Proslogium, Monologium, Cur Deus Homo, Gaunilo's In Behalf of the Fool, trans. S.N. Deane, 2nd ed. (Chicago: Open Court, 1962). Subsequent quotations for the Proslogion are from this translation. For a discussion of Anselm's understanding of faith and reason, see Garrett J. DeWeese, Doing Philosophy as a Christian (Downers Grove, IL: IVP Academic, 2011).

understand what is meant by a being than which nothing greater can be conceived, then we must understand that such a being exists in reality. Here's a reconstruction of this argument in different language:

1. The greatest possible being possesses all possible great-making properties.
2. God is the greatest possible being.
3. Therefore, God possesses all possible great-making properties.
4. Existence is a great-making property.
5. Therefore, God possesses the property of existence (i.e., God exists).

This argument has been subjected to serious objections. In Anselm's lifetime, a monk named Gaunilo argued "in behalf of the fool" that he could conceive of an island than which no greater island could be conceived, so therefore that perfect island must exist. Anselm replied, in essence, that if Gaunilo could show that it was possible that the qualities that make for a great island are conceptually maximal, then he, Anselm, would find the island and guarantee it would never be lost again! For example, say that the great-making properties of your greatest island are white sandy beaches and abundant tropical fruit. Well, I can imagine an island with more of both, which would be even greater than your island. Those qualities have no maximums, so there cannot be a greatest such island. But the qualities of God are not like that. Attributes like knowledge, power, and moral perfection do have maximums (e.g., knowledge of all true propositions) and are the kind of great-making properties predicated in premise (1). So the objection fails.

But the objections continued through history; we'll look at just one more, Immanuel Kant objected not to premise (1) but to premise (4), claiming that existence was not a great-making property. More precisely, existence is not a "real predicate"—to say that something exists adds nothing to the concept beyond the properties already implicated by the concept. As an example, think of the properties that constitute the concept of a unicorn. Now, whether the unicorn exists or not, the content of the concept remains unchanged. What is different is the unicorn's relation to the actual world but not the concept of a unicorn. The argument here is dense, perhaps, but it seems to us that Kant is correct. So we'll agree that the argument fails.

"But wait! There's more!" as the commercials say. There is a different version of the argument in chapter three of *Proslogion.* In Anselm's words,

> And it assuredly exists so truly, that it cannot be conceived not to exist. For, it is possible to conceive of a being which cannot be conceived not to exist, and this is greater than one which can be conceived not to exist. Hence, if that, than which nothing greater can be conceived, can be conceived not to exist, it is not that, than which nothing greater can be conceived. But this is an irreconcilable contradiction. There is, then, so truly a being than which nothing greater can be conceived to exist, that it cannot even be conceived not to exist; and

this being thou art, O Lord, our God.[83]

Here Anselm introduces the notion of *necessary* existence. We can represent the argument this way:
1. The greatest possible being possesses all possible great-making properties.
2. God is the greatest possible being.
3. Therefore, God possesses all possible great-making properties.
4. Necessary existence is a great-making property.
5. Therefore, God possesses the property of necessary existence (i.e., God necessarily exists).

It seems that necessary existence, as opposed to mere existence, is indeed a "real predicate," thus avoiding Kant's criticism. And surely a being than which nothing greater can be conceived cannot *not* exist—assuming, that is, that we can make sense of the notion of necessary existence.

---

[83] St. Anselm, Basic Writings, trans. S.N. Deane (Chicago: Open Court, 1963), 54-55.

The real impact of this second version of Anselm's argument was not appreciated until the mid-1950s. That's because it was only then that philosophers made real progress in understanding what is known as modal logic using *possible world semantics.* (Modal logic deals with the concepts of necessity, possibility, impossibility, and actuality.) The idea is this: Say that a possible world is the way things possibly could be. For example, there is a possible word in which you lost one more hair in the shower this morning than you actually did: that is surely a possible way things could be, but it is a world virtually indistinguishable from the actual world. Or imagine a world in which the United States and the Soviet Union had engaged in a nuclear war: again, that is possible, but it would be quite different from the actual world. Both of these two are indeed *possible worlds.*

Now, could there be a world in which there were square circles and married bachelors, or where 5+7 = green chocolate middle-C? Well, if we hold these terms to mean what they clearly mean in standard English, the answer is no—such things are logically impossible, so there is no possible world in which these things exist or are true; they are *logically impossible worlds.* Or, to put it positively, it is *logically necessary* that in any world, circles are round, bachelors are unmarried, and 5+7=12.

But there is another kind of impossible world, one that is impossible not because of logical impossibilities but because of metaphysical impossibilities. Metaphysical impossibility has to do with the nature of being. For example, and again holding meaning fixed, there cannot be anything that instantiates color properties that is not extended in space; that is metaphysically impossible. So a world in which there are colored non-extended things is a *metaphysically impossible world.* Or, to put it positively, it is *metaphysically necessary* that in any world, colored things are extended.

Notice that logically impossible worlds in our examples are impossible simply because the terms (square circles, married bachelors) are logically contradictory. But the metaphysically impossible worlds are not impossible that way; rather, they are impossible in virtue of what it is *to be* something (colored, in our example). So the question is this: When the ontological argument says that God necessarily exists, is it logical or metaphysical necessity? While some have thought the argument employed the notion of logical necessity, that doesn't seem right. If we take "God" to name or refer to the God of Christianity, then God is the uncreated creator of all that exists. So if there were not such a God, there would be nothing at all, not even an empty universe (for that is something, not nothing). So we think that it's best to take God's necessary existence as metaphysical, not logical. That is, *there is no metaphysically possible world in which God does not exist.*

In 1960 Norman Malcolm formulated a version of Anselm's second argument, which we'll summarize this way:
1. The existence of a necessary being must be
    a. impossible; or
    b. possible; or
    c. necessary.

2. But the existence of a necessary being is not impossible. (The concept of a necessary being is not contradictory or incoherent.)
3. And the existence of a necessary being cannot be merely possible. (A necessary being cannot be merely possibly necessary.)
4. Therefore, the existence of a necessary being must be necessary.[84]

While this is a nice, clear version of the argument, it seems to rely on *logical* modality. More recently, Alvin Plantinga has developed a version of the argument that involves *metaphysical* modality. His argument is densely (and impressively) argued but would take us too far afield in a chapter such as this to go into the details.[85]

---

[84] See Norman Malcolm, "Anselm's Ontological Arguments," Philosophical Review 69, no.1 (1960): 41-62.

[85] If you're interested, you can find his argument in Alvin Plantinga, The Nature of Necessity (Oxford: Clarendon, 1974), 196-221.

What can we say in conclusion about Anselm's argument, and attempts to reformulate it? It is a challenging argument, and especially Plantinga's version seems free from any clear logical errors. But it is not especially easy to understand, and so it is not rationally compelling for most people. Still, the modal version of the argument has this going for it: it clarifies what we mean when we say God is (metaphysically) necessary, and that concept seems to be one that we can understand. "There is, then, so truly a being than which nothing greater can be conceived to exist, that it cannot even be conceived not to exist; and this being thou art, O Lord, our God."

Cosmological arguments. "The" cosmological argument actually comes in several varieties. All trade on the idea that if one kind of thing exists, then some other kind of thing must exist, and this second kind of thing has properties that could belong only to God. In the version of the argument found in Plato, Aristotle, Thomas Aquinas, and John Duns Scotus, the second kind of thing must be the first cause or the prime mover—properties that could belong only to God.[86] In the second version, found in Spinoza, Leibniz, and Samuel Clarke, the second kind of thing has the property (roughly) of being self-explaining, or needing no external explanation.[87] The third version, found in the Islamic philosophers Avicenna and Averroës, the Jewish philosopher Maimonides, and several contemporary philosophers, notably William Lane Craig, argues that the second kind of being has the property of existing eternally.[88] Here we will only

---

[86] For Aquinas's version, see Norman Kretzmann, The Metaphysics of Theism: Aquinas's Natural Theology in Summa Contra Gentiles I (New York: Oxford University Press, 1997).

[87] For Leibniz's version, see Alexander R. Pruss, "The Leibnizian Cosmological Argument," in William Lane Craig and J.P. Moreland, eds., The Blackwell Companion to Natural Theology (Malden, MA: Wiley-Blackwell, 2012), 24-100.

[88] For a history of the argument, see William Lane Craig, The Cosmological Argument from Plato to Leibniz (New York: Harper

look at this third version of the argument, called the Kalām version, and will generally follow Craig's exposition.*

[* Craig presents and defends his version in many places, most fully in *The* Kalām *Cosmological Argument* (New York: Macmillan, 1979; repr., Eugene, OR: Wipf and Stock, 2000).]

The Kalām argument claims that the universe cannot be eternal: it must have had a beginning in time. But it cannot be uncaused, so it must have been caused by a being, God, who did not have a beginning in time (i.e., who has always existed). The argument moves in two parts. Part one argues that the universe could not have existed for an infinitely long time:

1. An actual infinite cannot exist.
2. A beginningless series of events in time is an actual infinite.
3. Therefore, a beginningless series of events in time cannot exist.
4. Therefore, the universe had a beginning.

and Row, 1980; repr., Eugene, OR: Wipf and Stock, 2001).

Notice, premise (1) is not speaking of the mathematical concept of infinity; mathematical entities are abstract. Rather, it claims that an actual infinite collection of concrete objects cannot exist. To motivate this premise, Kalām defenders offer thought experiments such as "Hilbert's Hotel," an example attributable to the German mathematician David Hilbert. Imagine a hotel with an infinite number of rooms (an actual infinite), all of which are occupied. Suppose a tour bus arrives with an infinite number of passengers (another actual infinite), all needing a room for the night. But the desk clerk knows her math. She moves the occupant of room 1 to room 2, the occupant of room 2 to room 4, and so on, moving the occupant of each room *n* to room number 2*n*. She can do that because there are an infinite number of rooms, and now the infinite number of passengers all has a room. Impossible, you say? Precisely! What works in the abstract realm of math doesn't work in the concrete realm of actual rooms and passengers. Other examples can be given, all of which underline the impossibility of an actual infinite.

In addition to the thought experiments, Kalām defenders can point to scientific arguments in support of the conclusion (4). For example, according to Big Bang cosmology, the observed expansion of the universe implies the universe had a beginning.[89]

Given the conclusion of part one that the universe had a beginning, the Kalām argument moves to part two, arguing that the universe has a cause that itself must be uncaused.

5. Whatever has a beginning has a cause.
6. The universe has a beginning.
7. Therefore, the universe has a cause.
8. This cause must itself be uncaused.
9. Therefore, there is an uncaused cause of the universe.

---

[89] See the arguments, pro and con, in William Lane Craig and Quentin Smith, Theism, Atheism, and Big Bang Cosmology (Oxford: Clarendon Press, 1993).

Premise (5) relies on what has been called the "metaphysical intuition" that everything that comes into existence must have a cause of it doing so. While this intuition has been challenged, it seems to us to be more plausible than not.[90]

We won't say that the argument is flawless; there is a vast literature on the Kalām version of the cosmological argument alone. But if it's successful (and we think it is), then it shows that God must exist as the uncaused cause of everything else that exists.[91]

Design arguments. Arguments from design to the conclusion that God exists

---

[90] Wes Morriston, "Doubts About the Kalam Argument," in J.P. Moreland, Chad Meister, and Khaldoun A. Sweis, eds., Debating Christian Theism (New York: Oxford University Press, 2013), 20-32.

[91] An objection is often raised: Who or what caused God? But that is to misunderstand what is meant by saying God is the uncaused cause. As an eternal being, who never came into existence but has always existed, he needs no external cause.

also come in several varieties.[92] One version looks at the number of "cosmological constants" that had to be "fine-tuned" in order for our universe, or any universe that could support intelligent life, to exist.[93] Other versions are arguments from analogy, such as the argument of the English clergyman William Paley in his 1802 book *Natural Theology; or, Evidences of the Existence and Attributes of the Deity.*

The version we'll discuss is an argument to the best explanation—from the information in the genome of living things to the conclusion that the information must be due to an intelligent designer.

1. The genome (DNA) of organisms contains information.

---

[92] Traditionally these are called teleological arguments. We think "design arguments" is a better and more understandable name.

[93] See, for example, Robin Collins, "The Fine-Tuning of the Universe Is Convincing," in Moreland, Meister, and Sweis, Debating Christian Theism, 35-46.

2. Information content is the product of (an) intelligence.
3. Therefore the information-containing genome is the product of (an) intelligence.

Premise (1) is widely accepted; indeed, there are numerous books with titles including "information," "DNA," and the like. This is such a commonplace that it needs almost no defense.[94]

Premise (2), we think, is highly intuitive, if not a conceptual truth. Consider, for a moment, the probability that human DNA was assembled by random processes: the probability of assembling the genome with its high information content through random processes is infinitesimal. To produce even one molecule of cytochrome c, with a probability of 0.95, would require 1.5×10^{44} trials. If one trial were completed each second, this would take

---

[94] See, for example, Hubert Yockey, Information Theory and Molecular Biology (Cambridge: Cambridge University Press, 1992).

10^{23} years. But the universe itself is only about 1.3×10^{10} years old![95]

Given the cogency of this argument, we can say that there must be an Intelligent Agent behind the design of the biological systems of our world, and coupled with the argument from fine-tuning, that Intelligence must be behind the design of the entire universe.

Moral arguments. Many apologists claim that "you can't be good without God." But that's false. Christian theology says you can't be good enough to inherit eternal life—salvation is by grace, not works—but it doesn't follow that you can't be good without God. So if there is a moral argument for God's existence, it must be somewhat different. And there are, in fact, several

---

[95] Much theoretical work in probability theory related to design has been done by William A. Dembski in The Design Inference: Eliminating Chance Through Small Probabilities (New York: Cambridge University Press, 1998); and No Free Lunch: Why Specified Complexity Cannot Be Purchased Without Intelligence (New York: Rowman & Littlefield, 2002).

moral arguments. It's important at the outset to notice that moral arguments do not necessarily presuppose a common morality or a universal moral code (such as the Ten Commandments). Rather, they recognize that there is among humans (aside from sociopaths, of course) a common moral consciousness, a universal tendency to make moral judgments.

C.S. Lewis, in his classic *Mere Christianity*, offers one version of a moral argument. We can present it this way:
- An impersonal source cannot explain universal morality.
- This morality cannot be herd instinct.
- Nor can this morality be mere convention.
- Nor can this morality be a law of nature.
- Nor is this morality mere imagination.
- A finite personal source cannot explain universal morality.

- Therefore, only an infinite personal source can explain universal morality.[96]

(By "universal morality," Lewis means what we have called a common moral consciousness.) We'll let you work through Lewis's premises on your own. Here's another version of a moral argument similar to a more complicated argument from the philosopher Robert Adams:

1. We have great confidence in the truth of certain moral judgments.
2. The truth of those moral judgments is best explained by the existence of a divine moral lawgiver.
3. Therefore, we are justified in believing in the existence of a divine moral lawgiver.

Both of these versions, notice, take the form of an inference to the best explanation. That is, humans invariably make moral, not merely prudential,

---

[96] C.S. Lewis, Mere Christianity (New York: Macmillan, 1943), book 1.

judgments.[97] The question is why we do that, and the best explanation is that there is some universal principle or principles that we all instinctively recognize as binding.[98] And the best explanation for that is that there is indeed a divine universal lawgiver who has written basic morality on our natures.

Arguments from religious experience. The final traditional family of arguments for God's existence moves from religious experience to the

---

[97] A prudential judgment is a judgment about a wise, or helpful, or productive course of action, and making a prudential mistake only leads to an unhelpful or foolish outcome. A moral judgment, however, is a judgment about what is required by ethical obligations, and a person may be held morally blameworthy of praiseworthy for her moral judgments.

[98] For a compelling presentation of this idea, see J. Budziszewski, What We Can't Not Know: A Guide, rev. ed. (San Francisco: Ignatius Press, 2011). See also the last section of chapter four in this book, "Why Be Moral?"

conclusion that God exists. First, though, we need to say something about arguments from experience in general. If a person S experiences some object O, then it is likely that O exists and is very much like what S experienced, provided that the experience meets two conditions: (1) givenness condition: O is given in S's experience in a powerful, persistent, intrusive way; and (2) possibility condition: it is reasonable to believe that it is possible that O exists. In defense of (1), if you have a fleeting glimpse of something that seems to be moving fast and high in the edge of your visual field, you are not justified on that basis alone in concluding that you saw a UFO. But if the object is in the center of your visual field, if it's still there after you rub your eyes and look away briefly, and if it repeatedly appears in your visual field in the same persistent way, then the givenness condition is satisfied. But you are not yet justified in concluding you saw a UFO; the possibility condition must also be satisfied. Suppose that the object, which appears massive, seems to move incredibly rapidly across the sky, stops or changes direction instantly, and so on. Now, the laws of physics as we know them disallow that a massive object could move like that. So at least initially it does not seem reasonable to believe that such an object is possible, and some other explanation, including illusions, would be preferable. However, if the object persisted in your experience, behaving in the same way, and nothing you tried—more sleep, no alcohol or even prescription drugs, new glasses—stopped the experience, then what?

Here we enter a new phase of an argument from experience. The strength of the experience meeting the givenness condition might sufficiently overcome the resistance of the possibility condition so that you would be justified in believing you had seen a UFO. But it does not follow that anyone else, not having had that experience, would be justified in believing that you had in fact seen a UFO, let alone that UFOs exist. So how do we move from a claim that someone has had an experience of God to the conclusion that such an experience justifies belief that God exists?

Here an argument from William Alston helps.[99] Alston begins by discussing "doxastic practices"—ways of forming beliefs—and he argues that it is clearly a valid doxastic practice to form beliefs on the basis of sensory experience (we would add, provided it meets our two conditions stated above). In fact, sensory doxastic practice (call it SP) is common to virtually all people, everywhere, throughout all history. Since SP is so pervasive and widespread, it must be valid. Alston then argues that religious perceptual practice (MP), while not as widespread as SP, is actually quite common and structurally similar to SP. His argument goes like this:

1. Beliefs produced by a commonly accepted doxastic practice are justified.

---

[99] William P. Alston, Perceiving God: The Epistemology of Religious Experience (Ithaca, NY: Cornell University Press, 1991).

2. Sensory perceptual practice (SP) is a commonly accepted doxastic practice.
3. Hence, beliefs produced by sensory experience are justified.
4. Religious perceptual practice (MP) is a commonly accepted doxastic practice.
5. There is no difference between the theoretical structure of SP and MP.
6. Hence, beliefs produced by religious experience are justified.

We think, to go back to our UFO example, that if millions of people in many different cultures, locations, and times had similar experiences, then we would be justified in believing that UFOs exist, even if we ourselves never had such an experience. By analogy, the same goes for belief in God. In fact, we say that belief in God fares better than belief in UFOs would since nothing in an experience of God violates laws of physics.

But there's more to say. Studying world religions, Rudolph Otto described widespread moments reported by religious people where they were experiencing something ineffable, a divine presence, a wonderful presence, something wholly other.[100] Otto called this an experience of the "numinous." Martin Buber adds to Otto's description the idea that what is experienced in a religious experience is not a mere object as we experience in the inanimate world around us. Rather than being "it," the object of religious experience is "Thou," a personal Being.[101] And personal beings can be known as persons. So religious experience, then, is the experience of a personal God who exists and can be known.

A cumulative case? Many theistic philosophers have thought that the five traditional arguments could be combined into a cumulative case; that is, each one adds to the explanatory power of the previous one(s), explaining more and more of the universe around us

---

[100] Rudolph Otto, The Idea of the Holy, trans. John W. Harvey, 2nd ed. (New York: Oxford University Press, 1950).

[101] Martin Buber, I and Thou, trans. R.G. Smith, 2nd ed. (New York: Scribner, 1958).

and our life in it. Here's how it works. The ontological argument gives us a being that exists necessarily. The cosmological argument says that this necessary being is the first cause of everything. The design argument adds that this being is responsible for the design we see in nature, design without which neither the universe nor living things would exist. The moral argument claims this being is a moral lawgiver. And the religious experience argument says this being can be known. While this is not yet the God of the Bible, the cumulative case gives us good reason to think that it's more likely than not—or likely beyond a reasonable doubt—that something like the God of the Bible exists.

    That's about as far as philosophy of religion can go; to go farther, we'd have to look at the specific evidence of the Bible (or other specific religion) and see if that evidence could advance us to religious belief. For our part, we're convinced that the reliability of the Bible, credible reports of miracles, and the historical evidence for the resurrection of Jesus are compelling reasons to believe that the God of the Bible is the one true God.

Other theistic arguments. In addition to the five traditional arguments, many other arguments have been offered by philosophers and apologists. Alvin Plantinga once sketched out "two dozen (or so) theistic arguments," which have been defended in separate essays in a recent book.[102] J.P. Moreland argues that theism is the only explanation for human consciousness.[103] Gregory Ganssle argues that the Christian story best answers human aspirations.[104] And so it goes, with many more books and arguments than we could list here. Suffice it to say that if anyone says there are no

---

[102] Jerry L. Walls and Trent Dougherty, eds., Two Dozen (or so) Arguments for God's Existence (New York: Oxford University Press, 2018).

[103] J.P. Moreland, Consciousness and the Existence of God (New York: Routledge, 2008).

[104] Gregory E. Ganssle, Our Deepest Desires (Downers Grove, IL: IVP Academic, 2017).

good reasons to believe in God, that person simply has not done her homework.

THE PROBLEM(S) OF EVIL

Of course, as is the case with almost every serious philosophical claim, arguments that God exists have been challenged, often powerfully. Here we'll consider perhaps the oldest and most powerful argument that a good God does not exist: the argument from evil.[105] The basic argument is easy to state. Here it is in the words of David Hume, repeating an ancient question of Epicurus: "Is he willing to prevent evil, but not able? Then he is impotent. Is he able, but not willing? Then he is malevolent. Is he both able and willing? Whence then is evil?"[106]

---

[105] For a fine collection of theistic and anti-theistic arguments, see Moreland, Meister, and Sweis, Debating Christian Theism.

[106] David Hume, Dialogues Concerning Natural Religion, in Antony Flew, ed., David Hume: Writings on Religion (La Salle, IL: Open Court, 1992), 261.

We need to begin this discussion with several preliminaries. First, just what counts as evil? A number of philosophers have addressed this question, with unclear results. It often seems that before evil can be defined, good must be defined, and it is alleged that genuine good cannot be distinguished from such notions as survival or reproductive advantage apart from a universal moral standard such as the moral argument for God argues. So theists may be in the right to insist that the atheist first provide a non-question-begging definition of evil.

Be that as it may, for our purposes here we'll simply stipulate that cases of underserved or pointless suffering by sentient creatures count as instances as evil. So we agree that evil exists in our world. But the next question is, For whom is evil a problem? Well, not for atheists, surely; what more could be expected in a mechanistic world where randomly evolved nature is "red in tooth and claw"? And not for many theists or deists for whom God is a distant, unknowable entity beyond categories of good and evil.

But evil is a problem for Christians who believe that God is all-powerful, all-knowing, and all-good. And the problem really comes in three forms: the logical problem, the evidential problem, and the existential problem.

The existential problem of evil. We'll begin with the existential problem. This is the very real problem faced by someone experiencing severe pain, heartbreaking loss, psychological trauma, and so on. In the midst of horrendous evil, a person often questions the goodness of God or even his existence. Both of the authors of this book have experienced evil, and both of us as pastors have counseled and consoled others in suffering. In such circumstances, philosophical discussions and even theological explanations do little. The pastoral response is presence and prayer, not problem-solving. C.S. Lewis surely knew the theological and philosophical responses to the problem of evil; his book *The Problem of Pain* is a classic.[107] But when his wife died

---

[107] C.S. Lewis, The Problem of Pain (New York: Macmillan, 1962).

of cancer, Lewis needed something more. In *A Grief Observed,* he writes,

> Meanwhile, where is God? This is one of the most disquieting symptoms. When you are happy, so happy that you have no sense of needing Him, so happy that you are tempted to feel His claims upon you as an interruption, if you remember yourself and turn to Him with gratitude and praise, you will be—or so it feels—welcomed with open arms. But go to Him when your need is desperate, when all other help is vain, and what do you find? A door slammed in your face, and a sound of bolting and double bolting on the inside.... Why is He so present a commander in our time of prosperity and so very absent a help in our time of trouble?[108]

Lewis came through his time of grief, and any one of us can too. We should recall the lesson Job learned. After his three friends' disastrous

---

[108] C.S. Lewis, A Grief Observed (San Francisco: HarperSanFrancisco, 2001), 5-6.

attempts to console him, and Elihu's marginally better reply, God himself spoke to Job from the whirlwind. But God did not explain, he did not justify himself, he did not intimate that Job had served to demonstrate to Satan that one could remain faithful to God even when the victim of horrific evil. Rather, God gave Job a wonderfully enlarged sense of God's power (Job 38–39) and justice (40–41). And Job repented of his challenges to God. The lesson? If we find ourselves suffering, the question should not be "Why?" but "Who?" A deeper understanding of God awaits the one who remains faithful.

The logical problem of evil. The logical problem of evil purports to prove that the existence of God is logically incompatible with the existence of evil. If successful, it would decisively disprove God's existence. And the logical problem has been around for a long time, as Hume's repetition of Epicurus's argument shows. We can state the argument this way:

1. An *omnipotent* God would be able to eliminate evil.

2. An *omniscient* God would know how to eliminate evil.
3. An *omnibenevolent* God would want to eliminate evil.
4. But evil exists.
5. Therefore, God is not omnipotent, or not omniscient, or not omnibenevolent.
6. Therefore, the God of Christianity does not exist.

Fortunately for theists, the argument is not successful (although it is the standard fare of internet atheists). Alvin Plantinga developed a rebuttal to the logical problem that almost every philosopher believes is successful.[109] Plantinga notes that in responding to the problem of evil, Christians have taken one of two strategies. A *theodicy* seeks to explain what God's reasons for allowing evil

---

[109] Alvin Plantinga, God, Freedom, and Evil (Grand Rapids, MI: Eerdmans, 1974). Daniel Howard-Snyder says that the logical problem "has found its way to the dustbin of philosophical fashion." The Evidential Argument from Evil (Bloomington: Indiana University Press, 1996), xiii.

actually are, while a *defense* is more modest, seeking only to offer a logically possible reason for why God might have allowed evil.[110] Plantinga offers a defense.
1. A world with moral good is better than a world with no moral good.
2. Only free agents can do moral good.
3. Even God cannot create free moral agents who *never* go wrong.
4. Therefore, it is not within God's power to create a world with moral good but no moral evil.

Plantinga's argument in defense of the logical possibility of the premises is elegant and detailed but cannot detain us here. The point is that if it is *even logically possible* that (1) and (3) are true, then the logical problem fails.

The evidential problem of evil. But evil is not so easily disposed of. The evidential problem is rather more difficult. The intuitive idea is that the amount, kinds, and distribution of evil

---

[110] Plantinga, God, Freedom and Evil, 24-26.

that we see in the world count as probabilistic evidence against the claim that a good God exists. This would be a strong argument against God's existence if successful. But again, the theist, especially the Christian, can offer good responses. Here's a general form of the evidential argument:

1. No good we know of justifies God in permitting E (a particular horrific evil).
2. Therefore, it is probable that there *is* no good that justifies God in permitting E.
3. Therefore, it is probable that God does not exist.

Note that the step from (1) to (2) is inferential, going from "There is no good that we know of" to "It is probable that there is no good." How is that inference justified? Michael Tooley responds that it is very unlikely that the universe contains kinds of goods of which we are totally ignorant that could be achieved only via the actual amount and kinds of evil.[111]

But is that indeed "very unlikely"? Stephen Wykstra responds with what he calls CORNEA, his acronym for a Condition Of Reasonable Epistemic Access. Basically, Wykstra's claim is that we could never know enough—comparing our intelligence and imagination to God's—to conclude that there are in fact no goods that would justify God in allowing *E:* that is, the inferential step is not justified.[112]

Another response is open to the theist. It is a principle of logic that no conclusion of an argument can be stronger than the argument's weakest premise. So if a person has better reasons to reject a premise than to accept the conclusion, the person is

---

[111] See Tooley's chapters in Alvin Plantinga and Michael Tooley, Knowledge of God (Malden, MA: Blackwell, 2008).

[112] Stephen John Wykstra, "Rowe's Noseeum Argument from Evil," in Howard-Snyder, ed., Evidential Argument from Evil, 126-50.

justified in doing so. Even if we have no *knockout* rebuttal to the evidential argument, it doesn't follow that it wins the day, as this example shows:

A. (Premise)	probably true
B. (Premise)	questionable
C. (Conclusion)	independent reasons to reject the conclusion

In this situation we are justified in saying that premise (B) is probably false. Thus, if we reject the conclusion (3) of the evidential argument above because we judge we have stronger independent evidence that (3) is false, we can then conclude that (2) must be false. So the question is whether the independent, *positive* evidence *for* the existence of God outweighs the *negative* evidence *against* the existence of God? And we believe that the positive theistic arguments do indeed outweigh the evidence of evil.

Sadly, we need to conclude this chapter, even though there is so much more that awaits exploration in philosophy of religion, especially philosophy of the Christian religion. It should be clear that philosophical thinking about religion in general, and the Christian religion in particular, pays healthy dividends.

9

WHERE DO I GO FROM HERE?

Worldview Struggle and Intellectual Crisis

> For though we live in the world, we do not wage war as the world does. The weapons we fight with are not the weapons of the world. On the contrary, they have divine power to demolish strongholds. We demolish arguments and every pretension that sets itself up against the knowledge of God, and we take captive every thought to make it obedient to Christ.
> **2 CORINTHIANS 10:3-5**

It is time to wrap things up and point to some implications of what we've said that, we believe, are vitally important for your own life and for the future health of the church. In our discussions in the previous eight chapters, we have attempted to explain, illustrate, and show the importance of certain contemporary philosophical arguments and concepts. We will have succeeded at this if you now have a better understanding and appreciation for the contributions philosophy can make to understanding and declaring our faith in our world, even if philosophy sometimes seems arcane and isolated from practical concerns.

WORLDVIEW STRUGGLE AND INTELLECTUAL CRISIS

Beneath the surface news of politics, disasters, and celebrity gossip, our world seethes with the conflict of competing worldviews. The intellectual climate of North America is witnessing the battle among the worldviews of Christian theism, scientific naturalism, and postmodernism. We have pointed out where we believe the Christian worldview must stand opposed to the competition, and we have given arguments why that is so. We have shown, with sorrow, where some Christian thinkers have accommodated to scientific naturalism (e.g., in denying the existence of an immaterial soul) or to postmodernism (e.g., in denying objective truth or the possibility of knowing objective truth). We are firmly convinced that as Christian thinkers, we must follow our Lord Jesus Christ intellectually, seeking to understand, believe, and defend what he—the incarnate God—believed or would believe about these issues.

Still, many in Western culture have a suspicion that Christianity has been weighed in the intellectual balance and found wanting. As Dallas Willard notes,

> The crushing weight of the secular outlook ... permeates or pressures every thought we have today. Sometimes it even forces those who self-identify as Christian teachers to set aside Jesus' plain statements about the reality and total relevance of the kingdom of God and replace them with philosophical speculations whose only recommendation is their consistency with a "modern" [that is, contemporary] mindset. The powerful though vague and

unsubstantiated presumption is that *something has been found out* that renders a spiritual understanding of reality in the manner of Jesus simply foolish to those who are "in the know."[113]

In fact, nothing could be further from the truth. Christianity has not been weighed and found wanting. Sadly, it has often been inadequately defended and proclaimed and thus too frequently ignored.

SAVING THE SOUL AND SAVING THE MIND

On a clear spring day in 1980, twenty-five miles west of Chicago in Wheaton, Illinois, Charles Malik, a distinguished academic and statesman, rose to the podium to deliver the inaugural address at the dedication of the new Billy Graham Center on the campus of Wheaton College. His announced topic was "The Two Tasks

---

[113] Dallas Willard, The Divine Conspiracy (San Francisco: HarperSanFrancisco, 1998), 92.

of Evangelism." What he said must have shocked his audience.[114]

We face two tasks in our evangelism, he told them, "saving the soul and saving the mind"—that is, converting people not only spiritually but intellectually as well. And the church, he warned, is lagging dangerously behind with respect to this second task. We would do well to ponder Malik's words:

> I must be frank with you: the greatest danger confronting American evangelical Christianity is the danger of anti-intellectualism. The mind in its greatest and deepest reaches is not cared for enough. But intellectual nurture cannot take place apart from profound immersion for a period of years in the history of thought and the spirit. People who are in a hurry to get out of the university

---

[114] This section is adapted from J.P. Moreland and William Lane Craig, Philosophical Foundations for a Christian Worldview, 2nd ed. (Downers Grove, IL: IVP Academic, 2017), 4-7.

and start earning money or serving the church or preaching the gospel have no idea of the infinite value of spending years of leisure conversing with the greatest minds and souls of the past, ripening and sharpening and enlarging their powers of thinking. The result is that the arena of creative thinking is vacated and abdicated to the enemy. Who among evangelicals can stand up to the great secular scholars on their own terms of scholarship? Who among evangelical scholars is quoted as a normative source by the greatest secular authorities on history or philosophy or psychology or sociology or politics? Does the evangelical mode of thinking have the slightest chance of becoming the dominant mode in the great universities of Europe and America that stamp our entire civilization with their spirit and ideas? For the sake of greater effectiveness in witnessing to Jesus Christ, as well as for their own sakes, evangelicals cannot afford to keep on living on the periphery of responsible intellectual existence.[115]

These words hit like a hammer, and they are still relevant today, forty years later. The average Christian does not realize that there is an intellectual struggle going on in the universities and scholarly journals and professional societies. Scientific naturalism and postmodernism are arrayed in an unholy alliance against a broadly theistic and specifically Christian worldview.

Christians cannot afford to be indifferent to the outcome of this worldview struggle. For the gospel is never heard in isolation. It is always heard against the background of a worldview. A person raised in a cultural milieu in which Christianity is still seen as an intellectually viable option will display an openness to the gospel that a person with a naturalistic or postmodern worldview will not. One may

---

[115] Charles Malik, "The Other Side of Evangelism," Christianity Today (November 7, 1980): 40. For the original address, see The Two Tasks (Wheaton, IL: Billy Graham Center, 2000).

as well tell her to believe in fairies or leprechauns as in Jesus Christ!

One of the awesome tasks of thoughtful Christians in our day is to help turn the contemporary intellectual tide in such a way as to foster a worldview in which Christian faith can be regarded as an intellectually credible option for thinking men and women.

And that is already happening. The fact that you are reading this book is itself a sign of a growing desire among Christians to engage intellectually with the surrounding culture.

To take another relevant example, in the last sixty years or so there has been a dramatic revolution in Anglo-American philosophy. Since the late 1960s Christian philosophers have openly identified themselves as believing Christians and defended the truth of the Christian worldview with philosophically sophisticated arguments in the finest scholarly journals and professional societies. And the face of Anglo-American philosophy has been transformed as a result. In a recent article lamenting "the desecularization of academia that evolved in philosophy departments since the late 1960s," a prominent atheist philosopher observes that whereas theists in other disciplines tend to compartmentalize their theistic beliefs from their professional work, "in philosophy, it became, almost overnight, 'academically respectable' to argue for theism, making philosophy a favored field of entry for the most intelligent and talented theists entering academia today." He complains that "naturalists passively watched as realist versions of theism ... began to sweep through the philosophical community, until today perhaps one-quarter or one-third of philosophy professors are theists, with most being orthodox Christians." He concludes, "God is not 'dead' in academia; he returned to life in the late 1960s and is now alive and well in his last academic stronghold, philosophy departments."[116]

But it is not just those who plan to enter the academy professionally who need to understand philosophy. Christian philosophy is also an integral part of

---

[116] Quentin Smith, "The Metaphilosophy of Naturalism," Philo 4, no.2 (2001): 4.

training for Christian ministry. We (the authors of this book) can both testify personally to the immense practicality and even indispensability of philosophical training for Christian ministry. We both served as pastors before entering academia, and for many years we have both been involved not just in scholarly work but also in speaking evangelistically on university campuses with groups like InterVarsity Christian Fellowship, Cru, and the Veritas Forum. Again and again we have seen the practical value of philosophical studies in reaching students for Christ. From questions dealing with the meaning of life or the basis of moral values to the problem of suffering and evil and the challenge of religious pluralism, the profound philosophical questions that students are asking are much more difficult to answer than to pose. They deserve a thoughtful response rather than pat answers or appeals to mystery.

The conventional wisdom says that "you can't use arguments to bring people to Christ." This has not been our experience. The fact is that there is tremendous interest among unbelieving students in hearing a rational presentation and defense of the gospel, and some will be ready to respond with trust in Christ.[117] To speak frankly, we do not know how one could minister effectively in a public way on our university campuses without training in philosophy.

Finally, it is not just scholars and ministers who will benefit from a working understanding of philosophy; all Christians must be intellectually

---

[117] Just as we were completing the first edition of this book, the intellectual world in the United States and the United Kingdom was rocked by news that Antony Flew, a distinguished world-renowned philosopher who had staunchly and repeatedly defended atheism, had converted to a form of theism at the age of eighty-one. His conversion was based, in part, on the argument from intelligent design. Although in fairness we must note that Flew's theism is decidedly not Christianity, it is still a highly significant change of belief. See Antony Flew, "My Pilgrimage from Atheism to Theism," Philosophia Christi 6, no.2 (2004): 197-211.

engaged if our culture is to be effectively reformed. Our churches are unfortunately overpopulated with people whose minds, as Christians, are going to waste. As Malik observed, they may be spiritually regenerate, but their minds have not been converted; they still think like nonbelievers. Despite their Christian commitment, they remain largely empty selves.

Imagine now a church filled with such people. What will be the theological understanding, the evangelistic courage, the cultural penetration of such a church? If the interior life does not really matter all that much, why should one spend the time trying to develop an intellectually and spiritually mature life? If someone is basically passive, he will just not make the effort to read, preferring instead to be entertained. If a person is sensate in orientation, then music, magazines filled with pictures, and visual media in general will be more important than mere words on a page or abstract thoughts. If one is hurried and distracted, one will have little patience for theoretical knowledge and too short an attention span to stay with an idea while it is being carefully developed. And if someone is overly individualistic and narcissistic, what *will* that person read, if he reads at all? Books about Christian celebrities; Christian romance novels imitating the worst that the world has to offer; Christian self-help books filled with slogans, simplistic moralizing, lots of stories and pictures, and inadequate diagnoses of the problems facing the reader. What will *not* be read are books that equip people to develop a well-reasoned theological understanding of the Christian faith and to assume their role in the broader work of the kingdom of God. Such a church will become impotent to stand against the powerful forces of secularism that threaten to wash away Christian ideas in a flood of thoughtless pluralism and misguided scientism. Such a church will be tempted to measure its success largely in terms of numbers—numbers achieved by cultural accommodation to empty selves. In this way the church will become its own gravedigger. The church's means of short-term "success" will turn out in the long run to be the very thing that buries it.

If we as the church are to engender a current of reform throughout our culture, then we need laypeople who are intellectually engaged with their faith and take their Christian identity to be definitive for their self-conception.

Philosophical reflection is, indeed, a powerful means of kindling the life of the mind in Christian discipleship and in the church. Again, we both can testify that our worship of God is deeper precisely because of, not in spite of, our philosophical studies. As we reflect philosophically on our various areas of specialization within the field of philosophy, our appreciation of God's truth and awe of his person have become more profound. We look forward to future study because of the deeper appreciation we are sure it will bring of God's person and work. Christian faith is not an apathetic, brain-dead faith, but a living, inquiring faith. As St. Anselm put it, ours is a faith that seeks understanding.

These are very exciting times in which to be alive and working in the field of philosophy, where God is doing a fresh work before our eyes. It is our hope and prayer that he will be pleased to use this book to call even more Christians to think critically about the questions that matter in order to equip the church to serve him and his kingdom even more effectively as we move deeper into the twenty-first century.

FOR FURTHER READING

CHAPTER ONE: WHERE DO I START?

Foreman, Mark W. *Prelude to Philosophy: An Introduction for Christians.* Downers Grove, IL: IVP Academic, 2013. (basic)

Kelley, David. *The Art of Reasoning.* 3rd ed. New York: W.W. Norton, 1998. (intermediate)

Moreland, J.P., and William Lane Craig. *Philosophical Foundations for a Christian Worldview.* Downers Grove, IL: InterVarsity Press, 2017. (intermediate)

Morris, Thomas V. *Philosophy for Dummies.* Foster City, CA: IDG Books, 1999. (basic)

CHAPTER TWO: WHAT IS REAL? METAPHYSICS

Connell, Richard. *Substance and Modern Science.* Notre Dame, IN: University of Notre Dame Press, 1988. (basic)

Hasker, William. *Metaphysics: Constructing a World View.* Contours of Christian Philosophy. Downers Grove, IL: InterVarsity Press, 1983. (basic)

Loux, Michael. *Metaphysics.* London: Routledge, 1998. (intermediate)

Lowe, E.J. *The Possibility of Metaphysics.* Oxford: Clarendon, 1998. (advanced)

Moreland, J.P. *Universals.* Montreal: McGill-Queen's University Press, 2001. (advanced)

van Inwagen, Peter. *Metaphysics.* Boulder, CO: Westview, 1993. (intermediate)

CHAPTER THREE: HOW DO I KNOW? EPISTEMOLOGY

Audi, Robert. *Epistemology.* New York: Routledge, 1998. (intermediate)

Pearcy, Nancy R., and Philip E. Johnson, *Total Truth: Liberating Christianity from Its Cultural Captivity.* Wheaton, IL: Crossway, 2004. (basic)

Plantinga, Alvin. *Warranted Christian Belief.* New York: Oxford University Press, 2000. (intermediate)

Wood, W. Jay. *Epistemology: Becoming Intellectually Virtuous.* Contours of Christian Philosophy. Downers Grove, IL: InterVarsity Press, 1998. (basic)

CHAPTER FOUR: HOW SHOULD I LIVE? ETHICS

Budziszewski, J. *What We Can't Not Know: A Guide.* Dallas: Spence, 2004. (intermediate)

Lewis, C.S. *The Abolition of Man.* San Francisco: HarperSanFrancisco, 2001. (intermediate)

Rae, Scott B. *Moral Choices: An Introduction to Ethics.* 4th ed. Grand Rapids, MI: Zondervan, 2018. (basic)

Wilkens, Steve. *Beyond Bumper Sticker Ethics: An Introduction to Theories of Right and Wrong.* Downers Grove, IL: InterVarsity Press, 1995. (basic)

CHAPTER FIVE: WHAT AM I? PHILOSOPHICAL AND THEOLOGICAL ANTHROPOLOGY

Churchland, Paul. *Matter and Consciousness.* Cambridge, MA: MIT Press, 1984. (intermediate)

Cooper, John W. *Body, Soul and Life Everlasting: Biblical Anthropology and the Monism-Dualism Debate.* Rev. ed. Grand Rapids, MI: Eerdmans, 2000. (intermediate)

Hasker, William. *The Emergent Self.* Ithaca, NY: Cornell University Press, 1999. (advanced)

Kim, Jaegwon. *Philosophy of Mind.* Boulder, CO: Westview, 1996. (intermediate)

Moreland, J.P., and Scott B. Rae. *Body and Soul: Human Nature and the Crisis in Ethics.* Downers Grove, IL: InterVarsity Press, 2000. (intermediate)

O'Connor, Timothy. *Persons and Causes.* New York: Oxford University Press, 2000. (advanced)

CHAPTER SIX: HOW SHOULD CHRISTIANS THINK ABOUT SCIENCE? PHILOSOPHY OF SCIENCE

Dembski, William A. *Intelligent Design.* Downers Grove, IL: InterVarsity Press, 1999. (intermediate)

Moreland, J.P. *Christianity and the Nature of Science: A Philosophical Investigation.* Grand Rapids, MI: Baker Books, 1989. (intermediate)

Pearcey, Nancy, and Charles Thaxton. *The Soul of Science.* Wheaton, IL: Crossway, 1994. (intermediate)

Ratzsch, Del. *The Battle of Beginnings.* Downers Grove, IL: InterVarsity Press, 1996. (basic)

_____. *Science and Its Limits: The Natural Sciences in Christian Perspective.* Contours of Christian Philosophy. Downers Grove, IL: InterVarsity Press, 2000. (intermediate)

CHAPTER SEVEN: WHAT IS BEAUTY? AESTHETICS

Battin, Margaret P., John Fisher, Ronald Moore, and Anita Silvers. *Puzzles About Art: An Aesthetics Casebook.* Boston: Bedford/St. Martin's, 1989. (intermediate)

Lewis, C.S. *The Abolition of Man.* New York: Macmillan, 1955. (basic)

Rookmaaker, H.R. *Modern Art and the Death of a Culture.* 2nd ed. Downers Grove, IL: InterVarsity Press, 1973. (basic)

Scruton, Roger. *Beauty: A Very Short Introduction.* New York: Oxford University Press, 2011. (intermediate)

Wolterstorff, Nicholas. *Art in Action.* Grand Rapids, MI: Eerdmans, 1996. (advanced)

CHAPTER EIGHT: WHAT SHOULD WE WORSHIP? PHILOSOPHY OF RELIGION

Craig, William Lane, and J.P. Moreland. *The Blackwell Companion to Natural Theology.* Malden, MA: Wiley-Blackwell, 2012. (advanced)

Meister, Chad, and James K. Dew. *God and Evil: The Case for God in a World*

Filled with Pain. Downers Grove, IL: InterVarsity Press, 2013. (basic)

Moreland, J.P., Chad Meister, and Khaldoun A. Sweis. *Debating Christian Theism.* New York: Oxford University Press, 2013. (advanced)

Peterson, Mishaal, William Hasker, Bruce Reichenbach, and David Basinger. *Reason and Religious Belief: An Introduction to the Philosophy of Religion.* 5th ed. New York: Oxford University Press, 2020. (intermediate)

CHAPTER NINE: WHERE DO I GO FROM HERE? WORLDVIEW STRUGGLE AND INTELLECTUAL CRISIS

Evans, C. Stephen. *Philosophy of Religion: Thinking About Faith.* Contours of Christian Philosophy. Downers Grove, IL: InterVarsity Press, 1985. (basic)

Morris, Thomas V. *Our Idea of God: An Introduction to Philosophical Theology.*

Contours of Christian Philosophy. Downers Grove, IL: InterVarsity Press; Notre Dame, IN: University of Notre Dame Press, 1991. Reprint, Vancouver, BC: Regent College Publishing, 1997. (basic)

PRAISE FOR PHILOSOPHY MADE SLIGHTLY LESS DIFFICULT

"This book, written by two men who are both high-level philosophers and exemplary Christians, will serve to initiate neophytes into the significance, joys, and challenges of philosophy as well as offer journeymen philosophers (such as myself) a rich banquet of philosophical reflection. I applaud the inclusion of new chapters (on aesthetics and the philosophy of religion) to this edition."

Douglas Groothuis, professor of philosophy at Denver Seminary, author of *Philosophy in Seven Sentences*

"I think the title of this book is misleading. DeWeese and Moreland, who have trained countless students to think clearly and pursue truth, don't make philosophy slightly less difficult, they make it incredibly *more accessible*. It is no easy task to simplify without being simplistic, to explain without short-selling the essentials, but by succeeding they've served us all well."

John Stonestreet, president of the Colson Center for Christian Worldview and host of *BreakPoint*

"Fuzzy thinking leads to careless living. This is true even for Christians. The world cries out for meaning but many believers remain silent, embarrassed by their shallow faith. *Philosophy Made Slightly Less Difficult* is a boot camp for the mind led by two 'drill instructors' who are at the same time highly respected philosophers and committed Jesus followers. DeWeese and Moreland help the reader think more clearly about thinking and also about reality, knowledge, ethics, and the good life. Don't read this book just to have your mind tickled. Read it to sharpen your thinking so you can love God with all of your mind."

Jeff Myers, president of Summit Ministries

"In my opinion, *Philosophy Made Slightly Less Difficult* is unrivaled among introductions to philosophy—Christian or not. DeWeese and Moreland cover all the philosophical terrain with clarity, depth, and insight. More than that, they weave their conclusions into a fully integrated, captivating, biblical world picture. This is a rarity—certainly not something you can do on your own. The result is a Christian and intellectual tour de force. I have assigned this book to students for fifteen years and more. I can tell you this with confidence: it will sharpen your thinking and increase your faith. It is indispensable for prevailing in our spiritually troubled times."

Richard Brian Davis, professor of philosophy at Tyndale University

"Philosophy is never an easy subject to master, but it *can* be made easier! Here two well-known, well-respected, and excellent philosophers, Garrett DeWeese and J.P. Moreland, provide an outstanding roadmap that attempts to do just this—provide an overview with easier explanations and punctuated with many examples and illustrations to help along the way. Highly recommended!"

Gary R. Habermas, distinguished research professor at Liberty University

"Here's your chance to learn the fundamentals of philosophy in an accessible, easy-to-understand format. In the end, you'll wonder how you ever got along without this essential foundation to your faith."

Lee Strobel, author of *The Case for Christ* and *God's Outrageous Claims*

"If you want clear thinking on thinking clearly, this book's for you. DeWeese and Moreland undertake an ambitious project, explaining philosophy to nonphilosophers, with a good sense of subject and audience. Readers receive a working introduction to philosophical vocabulary and concepts in an accessible, applied style. It requires effort (they promised it would be only slightly less difficult!), but the reward is greater clarity on what is real, true, and good—a worthy goal for any Christian."

Robert Drovdahl, Seattle Pacific University

"Few writers in philosophy are as accessible to the novice as Garrett DeWeese and J.P. Moreland. Once again, they have filled a great need for an introduction to philosophy in *Philosophy Made Slightly Less Difficult,* second edition. Two features contribute to making this book an excellent introduction. First is its comprehensiveness. With the addition of two new chapters on aesthetics and philosophy as well as the expansion of a number of other chapters, the book now covers a host of subjects on the traditional topics in philosophy. The metaphysics chapter itself is worth the price of the book. Second, they write in such an accessible style that it makes philosophical discussions not only clear but also enjoyable to read. The book is full of excellent examples and illustrations that clarify many philosophical concepts. I would highly recommend this book to anyone interested in the basics of philosophy and would especially recommend it as a text for an introduction to philosophy. I plan to use it for my future classes."

Mark W. Foreman, professor of philosophy and religion at Liberty University and coauthor of *How Do We Know?*

ABOUT THE AUTHORS

Garrett J. DeWeese (PhD, University of Colorado; ThM, Dallas Theological Seminary) is professor of philosophy and philosophical theology at Talbot School of Theology, Biola University, in La Mirada, California. He is the author of *God and the Nature of Time* and *Doing Philosophy as a Christian.*

J.P. Moreland (PhD, University of Southern California) is Distinguished Professor of Philosophy at Talbot School of Theology, Biola University. His many books include *Consciousness and the Existence of God*, *Philosophical Foundations for a Christian Worldview*, *In Search of a Confident Faith*, *Love Your God With All Your Mind*, and *The God Question*

***

Please visit us at ivpress.com *for more information about Garrett J. DeWeese and J.P. Moreland and a list of other titles they've published with InterVarsity Press.*

Discover more titles from InterVarsity Press

View the newest and trending titles in

Academic Texts & Reference

IVP Academic covers disciplines such as theology, philosophy, history, science, psychology, and biblical studies with books ranging from introductory texts to advanced scholarship and authoritative reference works.

Culture, Mission, and Christian Life

Our books are deeply biblical and profoundly practical, discussing topics like Christian spirituality, prayer, evangelism, apologetics, justice, mission, and cultural engagement.

Bible Studies & Group Resources

IVP provides Bible studies and small group resources for you and your church, helping individuals and groups discover God's Word and grow in discipleship.

Spiritual Formation

Formatio books follow the rich tradition of the church in the journey of spiritual formation. These books are not merely about being informed, but about being transformed by Christ and conformed to his image.

Church Leadership

ivpraxis

IVP Praxis brings together theory and practice for the advancement of your ministry using sound biblical and theological principles to address the daily challenges of contemporary ministry.

View more books in these categories

Apologetics
Biblical Studies
Career & Vocation
Church & Culture
Church History
Commentaries
Discipleship
Family, Children & Youth
Fiction
Justice/Peace
Spiritual Formation
Missions & Missiology
Philosophy

**Psychology
Race & Ethnicity
Science
Theology
Youth Ministry**

For a list of IVP email newsletters please visit ivpress.com/newsletters.

Index

A
absolutism, *221, 224*
academic skepticism, *160*
accidental property, *90*
ad hominem, *28*
aesthetics, *388*
affirming the consequent, *24*
Alston, William, *439, 443*
animalism, *289, 292, 294, 296, 299, 301, 304*
Anselm, *417, 419, 421, 424*
antecedent, *22*
anti-intellectualism, *462, 464*
antirealism, *372, 375, 377*
appeal to pity, *28*
appeal to the people, *28*
applied ethics, *188*
Aquinas, St. Thomas, *44, 81, 153, 156, 208, 231, 318, 388, 417, 426*
arguments, overview of, *14, 16, 19, 22, 24, 26, 28, 30, 33, 35*
Aristotle, *37, 44, 46, 81, 85, 100, 107, 132, 153, 156, 204, 208, 231, 233, 319, 388, 426*
art, *401, 403, 406*
Augustine, St., *44, 160, 271, 322*
awareness, *267*
axioms, *12*

B
Bayes's Theorem, *33*
beauty, *388, 391, 393, 397, 399, 401*
begging the question, *26, 277, 280, 367, 369*
belief, *114, 117, 119, 144, 147, 148*
Bentham, Jeremy, *204, 212*

blind watchmaker thesis, *348, 355*
Boethius, *78*
brain view, *304, 306, 308, 311*

C

Calvin, John, *153, 204, 322*
capacities, *85, 88*
categorical imperative, *224, 226*
certainty, *22*
Churchland, Paul, *277*
classical foundationalism, *142*
cogency, *14, 19, 22, 41*
cognitive ethics, *196*
cognitive theories, *188, 191*
coherentism, *134, 136, 148, 180*
compatibilism, *311, 313, 315, 318, 319*
conceptual analysis, *35, 41*
conciliatory view, *168, 170, 174, 175*
conditional statement, *22*
conformist view, *168, 170, 174, 175, 177, 180*
consciousness, *248, 251, 253, 256, 258, 260*
consequent, *22*
consequentialism, *204, 207, 208, 212, 214, 217, 219, 221*
correspondence theory, *129, 132*
cosmic authority problem, *175*
cosmological argument, *426, 431, 434*
creationism, *345, 348*
    See also intelligent design,
criterion, problem of, *163, 166, 168*
cultural relativism, *196, 197, 200, 202*

D

Davis, William, *407*
deductive arguments, *22, 24, 26*
definitions, *37, 41*

deflationary theories, *125, 127*
demarcation problem, *359, 362, 365*
denying the antecedent, *24*
deontology, *219, 221, 224, 226, 229, 231*
Descartes, René, *44, 142, 166*
descriptive ethics, *188*
disjunctive syllogism, *24*
divine command theory of morality, *226, 229, 231*
dualism,
  See substance dualism,
duty-based ethics, *219, 221, 224, 226, 229, 231*

E

efficient cause, *94, 95*
eliminative materialism, *282, 287, 289*
emotivism, *191*
empirical knowledge, *329*
epistemic probability, *33*
epistemic theories, *125, 129*
epistemology of peer disagreement, *168, 170, 174, 175, 177, 180*
equal-weight view, *168, 170, 174, 175*
equivocation, *26, 28*
essences, *78, 81, 83, 85, 88, 90, 94, 95*
essential property, *88, 90*
ethical naturalism, *204*
ethical nonnaturalism, *207*
ethical relativism, *202, 204*
ethics, *196, 197, 200, 202, 204, 207, 208, 212, 214, 217, 219, 221, 224, 226, 229, 231, 233, 235, 237*
Euthryphro dilemma, *229*
evil, *446, 451, 453, 455*

evolution, *235, 243, 277, 280, 329, 331, 334, 336, 345, 348, 350, 352, 355, 357, 359, 362, 365, 367, 369, 372, 381*
excluded middle, law of, *12, 14*
extensional definition, *37*
externalism, *148, 151, 153*

F

false dilemma, *26*
feminist logic, *12*
final cause, *95*
first-person perspective, *263, 265, 267*
folk psychology, *287*
formal fallacy, *16*
foundationalism, *136, 142, 144, 147, 148, 180*
free will, *42, 243, 272, 313, 315, 318, 319, 322, 324, 380*
functionalism, *258, 260, 282, 285, 287*
fundamental principles, *12*

G

Gandhi, Mahatma, *202*
Gettier problem, *156, 158*
Giberson, Karl, *329, 331, 334*
God,
    argument for, *19*
    beauty and, *393, 397*
    essential properties, *48, 58, 105*
    evil and, *446, 451, 453, 455*
    existence of, *414, 417, 419, 421, 424, 426, 431, 434, 436, 439, 443, 446*
    free will and, *322, 324*
    knowledge of, *114, 153*
    law of identity and, *14*
    logic and, *10, 12, 14*
    love for, *384*
    morality and, *207, 226, 229, 231, 239, 241*

nature of, *42, 414, 417, 419, 421, 424, 426, 431, 434, 436, 439, 443, 446*
necessary existence of, *105*
philosophy and, *469, 470*
scientific explanation and, *326, 329, 348, 350, 352, 355, 357, 359*
sovereignty of, *322, 324*
as a substance, *81*
worldviews and, *2*

H
Hobbes, Thomas, *202*
Hume, David, *343, 446*
hypothetical reasoning, *33, 35*
hypothetical syllogism, *24*

I
identity, *10, 12, 73, 76, 78, 85, 90, 94, 246, 267, 271, 272, 282*
imperativalism, *191, 193*
incorrigible beliefs, *144*
induction, *30, 343*
inductive arguments, *14, 16, 19, 22, 30, 33, 35*
inference to the best explanation, *35*
informal fallacy, *26, 28, 30*
inseparable parts, *83, 85*
intelligent design, *345, 348, 350, 352, 355, 357, 359, 362, 365, 367, 369, 372, 434, 436*
intensional definition, *37*
intentional states, *117*
internalism, *148, 151, 153*

J
justification (epistemic), *132, 134, 136, 142, 144, 147, 148*

justification skepticism, *160, 163*

K
Kant, Immanuel, *208, 224, 226, 391, 421*
Kekes, John, *340*
King, Martin Luther, Jr., *202*
knowledge, *109, 112, 114*
knowledge argument, *253*
Kripke, Saul, *12, 14*

L
law change, *94*
legislation, *193, 196*
Lewis, C.S., *122, 182, 399, 401, 436, 439, 446, 451*
lexical definition, *37*
libertarianism, *313, 315, 318, 319, 322*
logic, *10, 12, 14, 16, 19, 22, 24, 26, 28, 30, 33, 35*
love, as property, *56*

M
macroevolution, *345*
Malcolm, Norman, *426*
Malik, Charles, *460, 462*
materialism, eliminative, *282, 287, 289*
memory beliefs, *147, 148*
mereological aggregate/essentialism, *95, 98, 100*
metaethics, *188, 191, 193, 196, 197, 200, 202, 204, 207*
metaphysical impossibilities, *424, 426*
metaphysical theories, *125*
metaphysics, *44, 46, 48*
methodist, *163, 166*
microevolution, *345, 348*
Mill, John Stuart, *204, 212, 214*
mind-body interaction, *272*
modality, *100, 102, 105, 267, 271, 272, 424, 426*
modest foundationalism, *142*

modus ponens, *24, 144, 280*
modus tollens, *24, 280*
moral realism, *204, 207*
morality, *436, 439*

N

native skepticism, *160*
natural theology, *414, 417, 419, 421, 424, 426, 431, 434, 436, 439, 443, 446*
naturalism,
  ethical, *188, 191, 193, 196, 197, 200, 202, 204, 207*
  methodological, *345, 348, 350, 352, 355, 357, 359, 362, 365, 367, 369, 372*
  philosophical, *289, 350*
  scientific, *384*
natures, *78, 81, 83, 85, 88, 90, 94, 95*
Nazi Germany, *200*
necessary and sufficient conditions, *37, 186, 188, 334, 359*

necessary existence, *421*
noetic structure, *134, 136*
nominalism, *53, 56, 58, 60, 62, 65, 67, 69, 71, 73*
noncognitive theories, *188, 191*
noncontradiction, law of, *10, 12*
normative ethics, *188, 207, 208, 212, 214, 217, 219, 221, 224, 226, 229, 231, 233, 235, 237*
NEW TESTAMENT,
  Matthew,
    10:28, *248*
    22:23-33, *248*
    27:50, *248*
  Luke,
    23:42-43, *248*
  John,
    17:3, *114*
    18:38, *122*
  Acts,
    5:10, *248*
  Romans,
    1:18-20, *153*
    1:26-27, *233*

2:1-16, *231*
2:15, *221*
1 Corinthians, *30, 56*
2 Corinthians,
  5:1-10, *248*
  12:1-4, *248, 272*
Philippians,
  3:15, *180*
2 Timothy,
  3:16, *180*
Hebrews,
  12:23, *248*
1 Peter,
  3:3-4, *397*
Revelation,
  6:9-11, *248*

O

objectivism, *221, 224, 393, 397, 399, 401*
objectivist ethics, *204, 207*
occurent belief, *119*
ontological argument, *19*
Overton, William, *359, 362*
OLD TESTAMENT,
Genesis,
  35:18, *246*
Deuteronomy,
  18:11, *248*
Judges,
  21:25, *202*
1 Samuel,
  28, *248*
1 Kings,
  17:21-23, *246*
Job,
  38-39, *451*
  38:31, *397*
Psalms,
  27:4, *397*
  29:2, *397*
  48:2, *397*
  88:10-12, *248*
  146:04, *246*
Proverbs,
  26:4, *160*
Isaiah,
  14:9-10, *248*
  45:5, *14*
Jeremiah,
  3:19, *397*
Ezekiel,
  7:20, *397*
  28:12-17, *397*

33:32, *397*
37, *246*
Daniel,
4:12, *397*

P

particularist, *166*
particulars, *53, 56, 58, 60, 62, 65, 67, 69, 71, 73, 78, 241, 260*
peer disagreement, *168, 170, 174, 175, 177, 180*
perceptual beliefs, *148*
philosophy, definition of, *4*
physicalism, *246, 265, 277, 280, 282, 285, 287, 289, 304*
Plantinga, Alvin, *19, 151, 451, 453*
Plato, *44, 160, 207, 229, 237, 388, 426*
pluralism, *391*
possible world semantics, *424*
postmodernism, *56, 58, 460, 462*
prescriptivism, *191, 193*
probability, *33, 357, 359*
property dualism, *248, 251, 253, 256, 258, 260*
proposition, *109, 112, 114, 117, 119, 122, 125, 127, 129, 132, 134, 136, 180, 253, 256, 331, 334, 336, 338, 380, 381*
Psychological Individuation Principle (PIP), *304, 306*

R

realism, *60, 62, 65, 67, 69, 71, 73, 204, 207, 338, 372, 375, 377*
Reformed epistemology, *148, 151, 153*
relativism, *129, 196, 197, 200, 202, 204*
religion, *409, 412, 414*

S

scientism, *129, 177, 336, 338, 340, 343, 345, 469*
self, awareness of, *260, 263*
self-evident beliefs, *144*

semantics, *35*
sensation, *248, 253, 256, 304, 306*
sensory doxastic practice (SP), *439, 443*
separable parts, *83*
skepticism, *160, 163, 166, 168, 275, 381*
skill knowledge, *112, 114*
Socrates, *229, 237, 239*
soul, *42, 85, 239, 243, 246, 248, 260, 263, 265, 267, 272, 275, 352, 380, 381, 460, 462, 464, 467, 469, 470*
soundness, *14, 16*
spiritual disciplines, *233*
standing belief, *119*
state-object view, *117*
steadfast view, *175, 177, 180*
stipulative definitions, *37, 41*
straw man, *28, 30*
subjectivism, *391, 393*
subjectivist ethics, *196, 197, 200, 202, 204*

substance dualism, *243, 246, 248, 251, 253, 256, 258, 260, 263, 265, 267, 271, 272, 275, 277, 280, 282, 285, 287, 289, 296*
substances, *78, 81, 83, 85, 88, 90, 94, 95*

T
theistic evolutionists, *348, 350*
theories of truth, *125, 127*
Thinking Subject Maximalism (TSM), *304*
thought, laws of, *12, 14*
tolerance, *197, 200*
transcendentals, *388*
truth, *119, 122, 125, 127, 129, 132*

U
universals, *10, 52, 53, 56, 58, 60, 62, 65, 67, 69, 71, 73, 83, 221, 241*
utilitarianism, See consequentialism,

V

validity, *14, 16, 22, 24, 26, 28, 30*
virtue epistemology, *153, 156*
virtue ethics, *231, 233, 235, 237*

W

Wennberg, Robert, *90*
Wesley, John, *2, 46*
Wilberforce, William, *202*
Willard, Dallas, *460*
William of Sherwood, *100, 102*
Williams, Bernard, *214, 217*
Wolterstorff, Nicholas, *401, 403*
worldview, *2, 4, 41, 42, 180, 239, 241, 326, 329, 380, 381, 384, 460, 462, 464, 467, 469, 470*

www.ingramcontent.com/pod-product-compliance
Lightning Source LLC
Chambersburg PA
CBHW010718300426
44115CB00019B/2951